A CHRISTIAN'S PRAYER BOOK

A Christian's Prayer Book offers a regular pattern of prayer for the beginning and end of the day.

Poetry, prayer, psalms, canticles and bible readings provide a regular pattern of Morning and Evening Prayer, varied to reflect the seasons of the year and the major Christian festivals.

Individuals and groups will find here a pattern in which to feel at home with prayer, a form that provides an easiness and a content from which the mind may move forward to God.

3/14/85

To Mike Grim

To more Red Rivers!!! Enjoyed the weekend very much. Thanks for your "reflective contributions."

s you in

laheha

DAYS OF PRAISE   Robert Broderick
Contains meditations for each day, prayers of great men and women, prayers from scripture. Illustrated by Virginia Broderick. Flexible cover (4" x 6").   **$5.50**

EVENING WITH GOD: Thoughts and Prayers
Paul Haschek, trans. by David Smith, adapted by Dr. L. A. M. Gossens O.F.M. and A. Klamer
As people get older and find more time for prayer, it is sometimes difficult to find the words needed to describe their situation, to express gratitude, or to make longings known. **Evening with God** fills these needs. Paper.   **$5.50**

FRANCISCAN CROWN   Marion Habig O.F.M.
Beautifully illustrated explanation of the Rosary of the Seven Joys of Mary. Also contains a new scriptural method of saying the Crown. Hardbound.   **$3.00**

LIGHT AND TWILIGHT: Thoughts and Prayers for the Sick   F. C. van de Bilt and T. J. Moorman
The booklet presents thoughts and prayers assembled from some of the world's greatest sources, human and divine. Truly uplifting. Paper.   **$5.50**

MY GOD AND MY ALL   Ed. Marion Habig O.F.M.
A prayerbook for private and public use with current liturgies and new rites of penance and anointing of the sick. Hymns, novenas and traditional devotions. Illustrated. Flexible cover (3½" x 5").   **$4.50**

Send for information on our other prayerbooks.

A Christian's Prayer Book

Poems, Psalms and Prayers
for the Church's Year

Edited by
Peter Coughlan,
Ronald C. D. Jasper,
Teresa Rodrigues OSB

FRANCISCAN HERALD PRESS
1434 WEST 51st STREET ● CHICAGO, 60609

© compilation Geoffrey Chapman Publishers, A division
of Crowell Collier and Macmillan Publishers Ltd
Acknowledgements of copyright material, see p. 373.
PUBLISHED IN USA BY
FRANCISCAN HERALD PRESS
1434 WEST 51ST STREET
CHICAGO, ILLINOIS 60609

LIBRARY OF CONGRESS CATALOG NUMBER: 72-9357
ISBN: 8199-0447-3

WITH ECCLESIASTICAL PERMISSION

MADE IN THE UNITED STATES OF AMERICA

Contents

Introduction   vii

Season of Advent   1
Christmastide   61
Epiphanytide   71
Baptism of the Lord   81
Temporal Season   91
Season of Lent   155
Holy Thursday   217
Good Friday   227
Holy Saturday   239
Eastertide   248
Pentecost Sunday   310
Feast of the Holy Trinity   319
Feasts of Our Lady   328
Feasts of Saints   335
Prayer for the Departed   345
Midday Prayer   353
Night Prayer   356
Prayers for Special Occasions   360
Index of Poems   370
Index of Psalms and Songs   372
Acknowledgements   373

Introduction

The purpose of this book is to offer Christians, to whatever Church or community they belong, a book which helps them to pray, either corporately or individually.

Provision is made for Morning and Evening Prayer for each day of the week. Poetry and prayer, psalms, canticles, and bible readings combine to offer a variety of content with a consistent pattern. The reader will soon find himself at home with the book, since the structure is simple and straightforward, while the variety helps to avoid monotony and tedium. Special provision is made for the seasons of Advent, Lent and Easter and for the major festivals such as Christmas and Pentecost.

The book is limited in scope. It is primarily intended for those who do not use the official Daily Offices of the various Christian traditions, but we hope that it will eventually encourage them to make use of the richer resources of those Offices and thereby share more fully in the corporate prayer of the whole body of Christ.

That we should pray regularly, the New Testament leaves us in no doubt. Our Lord taught us by word and example 'always to pray and not lose heart'. This finds an echo in the continuous refrain of Paul and the other writers in the New Testament: 'be constant in prayer'. Every Christian spirituality worthy of the name mirrors the teaching and practice of Christ on this point.

This is only one prayer book among many: people must choose that form of prayer best suited to themselves. However, the value of a book like this, which takes as its pattern the traditional daily Office of the Christian Church, is that, quite apart from containing all the essential elements of prayer, it also offers a form of prayer for regular use, irrespective of our mood. This regularity in prayer at the beginning and end of the day is important. The daily Office and breviaries used by many Christians have their origin in the desire to devote certain periods of the day to prayer, and thus help to sanctify the day and consecrate its activities to God.

Here we might take note of a deep-seated objection to producing a book of this nature. Stephen Winward, a Baptist minister, has written: 'It must be accepted that within certain traditions, especially where great stress has been laid on spontaneity in prayer, a certain suspicion of, and even hostility against, prescribed Offices is still to be found. They are associated with the formal and the mechanical, and may even be regarded as the initial stages of a process which, if carried through to its logical conclusion, would end up with something like the Tibetan prayer-wheel! For some, the word 'Office' has an ancient or a medieval connotation; it conjures up pictures of monks or clerics, of the 'churchy' or the other-worldly.' [1]

Suspicion and misunderstanding of this sort serve to remind us of the danger of formalism. If prayer is to qualify as Christian prayer, it must always be prayer 'in spirit and truth'. Our heart must be in it. However, this suspicion should not blind us to the potential value of prayer in the form of a daily Office. The same writer goes on to say: 'There is a widespread tendency to identify the heart with the feelings, and thus mistake the part for the whole. This may lead to an overstress on spontaneity, and to the assumption that a man cannot pray acceptably unless his feelings are stirred, his affections kindled. Yet the responsible citizen discharges the duties of his office and the trustworthy worker goes to the office whether he feels like it or not. To worship God is an obligation to be discharged irrespective of the presence or absence of feeling. The Office is the embodiment of this intention, this determination to praise and pray with disciplined regularity.' [2]

Furthermore, through this form of prayer, whether it be corporate or individual, one shares in the prayer which the whole Church offers to the Father through Jesus Christ and in the power of the Holy Spirit. This common prayer of the Body of Christ never ceases; it is something in which we

1. Joint Liturgical Group, *The Daily Office* (ed, Ronald C. D. Jasper), London 1968 p.14.
2. *Ibid*, p.18.

are called to share by reason of our baptism in the one Lord Jesus Christ. We hope that those who use *A Christian's Prayer Book* will do so with the intention of joining in this unceasing prayer and so become increasingly aware of our common Christian heritage.

The layout of *A Christian's Prayer Book*

The pattern of Morning and Evening Prayer is straight-forward.

A brief introductory sentence intended to stimulate an awareness of God's presence, is followed by some poetry offered as a pause for reflection and a springboard for personal prayer. Those who find it helpful will use it; those who do not, may move straight on to the psalms. When the book is being used by a group, a hymn or song may be used instead of the poem. Since the book is primarily intended for those not accustomed to saying the daily Office, a relatively small number of psalms suitable for the time or season is provided and many psalms are given in part, not in full.

The Scripture readings are intended to direct attention to particular themes, but the reader is obviously free to follow any other pattern of systematic Bible reading. A canticle, either from the Old or New Testament, follows the reading. Since some users may prefer the Song of Zechariah in the morning or the Song of the Virgin Mary in the evening every day, these texts are printed on a separate card which may be useful as a book mark.

Prayers of intercession follow the Canticle; these prayers have the quality of praise in the morning and thanks-giving in the evening. Morning and Evening Prayer close with a final collect. Many readers probably know from their own experience that where prayers of intercession are concerned, their expression will vary according to the tem-perament and needs of the individual or group at prayer. The texts here provided are therefore merely examples or aids to prayer. Spontaneous prayer, therefore, is strongly encouraged at this point, and the reader should not allow himself to be tied too closely to the texts.

At the back of the book there is a short selection of prayers that have been used over the centuries by successive generations of Christians. We have included them because we feel that as they have provided spiritual nourishment for so many Christian men and women in the past, there is a good chance that they may still prove helpful. But the selection is by no means exhaustive.

While the format is that of a daily Office, the reader must feel free to use the book in the way best suited to his devotional needs, even if this means departing from the pattern provided. The purpose of the pattern is simply to help the reader to feel at home with prayer, to provide a certain restfulness from which prayer may spring forward. If other patterns prove to be more beneficial to the individual, no one should hesitate to use them.

We should like to thank the many people who have encouraged and aided us in the preparation of this book. But for their insistence that something was needed on the lines of *A Christian's Prayer Book*, we should never have finished it. Particular thanks are due to David Jasper and Philip O'Dowd for their suggestions about the poetry, and to Philip Holroyd and Kevin McGinnell for assistance in composing the prayers of intercession at Morning and Evening Prayer.

Time will show which aspects of the book require readjustment. Compilers and publishers welcome any suggestions for making it better suited to the needs of the present day.

Season of Advent

SUNDAY

MORNING PRAYER

Lord, open my lips, and my mouth shall proclaim your praise.
To you be glory in the Church and in Christ Jesus
from generation to generation evermore. Amen.

To Christ our Lord
Hail, heavenly beam, brightest of angels thou,
sent unto men upon this middle-earth!
Thou art the true refulgence of the sun,
radiant above the stars, and from thyself
illuminest for ever all the tides of time.
And as thou, God indeed begotten of God,
thou Son of the true Father, wast from aye,
without beginning, in the heaven's glory,
so now thy handiwork in its sore need
prayeth thee boldly that thou send to us
the radiant sun, and that thou comest thyself
to enlighten those who for so long a time
were wrapt around with darkness, and here in gloom
have sat the livelong night, shrouded in sin.

Cynewulf

Ps 23(24)I
The ruler of the universe enters his chosen dwelling-place.

Are you the One who is to come, or are we to expect some other? (Mt 11:3).
Ant. On that day living waters shall issue from Jerusalem:
then the Lord shall become king over all the earth.

The Lord's is the earth and its fullness,
the world and all its peoples.
It is he who set it on the seas;
on the waters he made it firm.

1

Who shall climb the mountain of the Lord?
Who shall stand in his holy place?
The man with clean hands and pure heart,
who desires not worthless things,
who has not sworn so as to deceive his neighbour.

He shall receive blessings from the Lord
and reward from the God who saves him.
Such are the men who seek him,
seek the face of the God of Jacob.

Glory to the Father, and to the Son, and to the Holy Spirit:
as in the beginning, so now, and for ever. Amen.
The Glory to the Father *is said at the end of each psalm or song.*

Ps 23(24)II

O gates, lift high your heads;
grow higher, ancient doors.
Let him enter, the king of glory!

Who is the king of glory?
The Lord, the mighty, the valiant,
the Lord, the valiant in war.

O gates, lift high your heads;
grow higher, ancient doors.
Let him enter the king of glory!

Who is he, the king of glory?
He, the Lord of armies,
he is the king of glory.

Ant. On that day living water shall issue from Jerusalem:
then the Lord shall become king over all the earth.

Word of God   Rom 13:11–14

It is time for you to wake out of sleep, for deliverance is
nearer to us now than it was when first we believed. It is
far on in the night; day is near. Let us therefore throw off
the deeds of darkness and put on our armour as soldiers
of the light. Let us behave with decency as befits the day:
no revelling or drunkenness, no debauchery or vice, no
quarrels or jealousies! Let Christ Jesus himself be the armour
that you wear; give no more thought to satisfying the
bodily appetites.

2

Song of Zechariah

Ant. Are you the One who is to come,
   or are we to expect some other?

Song of Zechariah, p. 94.

The following Old Testament Song *may be said in place of the* Song of Zechariah.

Old Testament Song   Is 35:1–6

*He will wipe away every tear from their eyes; there shall
be an end to death and to mourning and crying and pain;
for the old order has passed away* (Rev 21:4).

Ant. You shall see the glory of the Lord,
   the splendour of our God.

Let the wilderness and the thirsty land be glad,
let the desert rejoice and burst into flower.
Let it flower with fields of asphodel,
let it rejoice and shout for joy.

The glory of Lebanon is given to it,
the splendour too of Carmel and Sharon;
these shall see the glory of the Lord, the splendour of our
   God.

Strengthen the feeble arms,
steady the tottering knees;
say to the anxious, Be strong and fear not.
See, your God comes with vengeance,
with dread retribution he comes to save you.

Then shall blind men's eyes be opened,
and the ears of the deaf be unstopped.
Then shall the lame man leap like a deer,
and the tongue of the dumb shout aloud;
for water springs up in the wilderness,
and torrents flow in dry land.

Ant. You shall see the glory of the Lord,
   the splendour of our God.

Prayers

Lord God, our need of you is greater than we can know or
express: do not wait, do not delay, but come quickly to
our aid.

As you come to us, Lord, bring us forgiveness:
we are ungrateful to those who love us;
we are indifferent to the needs of others;
where we see injustice we do not protest;
help us to love others with the love you have shown to us.

Bring us peace, that we may meet difficulties and disappointments with calm and courage.

Bring us joy, because God has become man
so that all men may be again the family of God.

Further prayers. . . Our Father. . .

Almighty God, give us grace to cast away the works of darkness and put on the armour of light, now in the time of this mortal life in which your Son Jesus Christ came to us in great humility, so that on the last day when he shall come again in his glorious majesty to judge the living and the dead, we may rise to the life immortal, through him who is alive and reigns with you and the Holy Spirit now and forever. Amen.

The Conclusion is always as follows:

May the Lord bless us,
may he keep us from all evil
and lead us to life everlasting. Amen.

Evening Prayer

Lord, open my lips, and my mouth shall proclaim your praise.
Glory to the Father, and to the Son, and to the Holy Spirit:
as in the beginning, so now, and for ever. Amen, alleluia!

The Call

Come, my Way, my Truth, my Life:
Such a Way, as gives us breath:
Such a Truth, as ends all strife:
Such a Life, as killeth death.

Come, my Light, my Feast, my Strength:
Such a Light, as shows a feast:
Such a Feast, as mends in length:
Such a Strength, as makes his guest.

Come, my Joy, my Love, my Heart:
Such a Joy, as none can move:
Such a Love, as none can part:
Such a Heart, as joyes in Love.

George Herbert

Thanksgiving and further plea for help.   Ps 39(40)

*Sacrifice and offering you did not desire,
but you prepared a body for me* (Heb 10:5).

Ant. When that day comes,
the mountains shall run with fresh wine
and the hills flow with milk, alleluia!

I waited, I waited for the Lord
and he stooped down to me;
he heard my cry.

He drew me from the deadly pit,
from the miry clay.
He set my feet upon a rock
and made my footsteps firm.

He put a new song into my mouth,
praise of our God.
Many shall see and fear
and shall trust in the Lord.

How many, O Lord my God,
are the wonders and designs
that you have worked for us;
you have no equal.
Should I proclaim and speak of them,
they are more than I can tell!

You do not ask for sacrifice and offerings,
but an open ear.
You do not ask for holocaust and victim.
Instead, here am I.

In the scroll of the book it stands written
that I should do your will.
My God, I delight in your law
in the depth of my heart.

Ant. When that day comes,
　the mountains shall run with fresh wine
　and the hills flow with milk, alleluia!

The annointed one of God. Ps 44(45)

Bend your necks to my yoke, and learn from me,
for my yoke is good to bear, my load is light (Mt 11:29, 30).

Ant. Rejoice, rejoice, daughter of Zion,
　shout aloud, daughter of Jerusalem:
　See, your king is coming to you, alleluia!

My heart overflows with noble words.
To the king I must speak the song I have made;
my tongue as nimble as the pen of a scribe.

You are the fairest of the children of men
and graciousness is poured upon your lips:
because God has blessed you for evermore.

O mighty one, gird your sword upon your thigh;
in splendour and state, ride on in triumph
for the cause of truth and goodness and right.

Take aim with your bow in your dread right hand.
Your arrows are sharp: peoples fall beneath you.
The foes of the king fall down and lose heart.

Your throne, O God, shall endure for ever.
A sceptre of justice is the sceptre of your kingdom.
Your love is for justice; your hatred for evil.

Therefore God, your God, has anointed you
with the oil of gladness above other kings:
your robes are fragrant with aloes and myrrh.

Ant. Rejoice, rejoice, daughter of Zion,
　shout aloud, daughter of Jerusalem:
　see, your king is coming to you, alleluia!

Word of God Heb 1:1-3

When in former times God spoke to our forefathers, he
spoke in fragmentary and varied fashion through the
prophets. But in this the final age he has spoken to us in the

Son whom he has made heir to the whole universe, and through whom he created all orders of existence: the Son who is the effulgence of God's splendour and the stamp of God's very being, and sustains the universe by his word of power.

Song of the Virgin Mary

Ant. Wisdom of the Most High,
from whose mouth you came forth,
who order all things with strength and gentleness:
Come and teach us the way of truth.

Song of the Virgin Mary, p. 99.

The following Old Testament Song *may be said in place of the* Song of the Virgin Mary.

Old Testament Song   Wis 7:22–8:1

*Christ is the power of God and the wisdom of God
(*1 Cor 1:24).

Ant. The image of the invisible God,
he exists before everything, and all things are held
together in him.

In wisdom there is a spirit intelligent and holy,
unique in its kind yet made up of many parts,
subtle, free-moving, lucid, spotless, clear,
invulnerable, loving what is good, eager, unhindered,
beneficent, kindly towards men, steadfast, unerring,
untouched by care, all-powerful, all-surveying,
and permeating all intelligent, pure, and delicate spirits.

For wisdom moves more easily than motion itself,
she pervades and permeates all things because she is so pure.
Like a fine mist she rises from the power of God,
a pure effluence from the glory of the Almighty;
she is the brightness that streams from everlasting light,
the flawless mirror of the active power of God
and the image of his goodness.

She is but one, yet can do everything;
herself unchanging, she makes all things new;
age after age she enteres into holy souls,
and makes them God's friends and prophets.

7

She is more radiant than the sun,
and surpasses every constellation;
compared with the light of day, she is found to excel;
for day gives place to night,
but against wisdom no evil can prevail.
She spans the world in power from end to end,
and orders all things benignly.

Ant. The image of the invisible God,
   he exists before everything, and all things are held
      together in him.

Prayers

Father, during Advent, help us to become aware of our
need for you, to be full of thankfulness and joy,
and to repay love with love.

> We thank you that in your love for us you have taken our
> part, and shared our human life. Grant us a share in your
> divine life.

> We pray for those who find life a great burden.

> We pray for those who destroy their life and dignity with
> alcohol or drugs.

> Show us, Lord, that the story of Bethlehem is a message
> of joy and power for the society in which we live.

Further prayers . . . Our Father . . .

Almighty God, you have given us grace at this time to make
our prayers to you with one accord and you have promised
that when two or three are gathered together in your name
you will grant their requests. Fulfil now the desires of your
servants, if it is fitting; and give us knowledge of your truth
in this world and eternal life in the world to come, through
Jesus Christ our Lord. Amen.

May the Lord bless us,
may he keep us from all evil
and lead us to life everlasting. Amen.

MONDAY

Lord, open my lips ...
To you be glory ...

God's Grandeur

The world is charged with the grandeur of God.
    It will flame out, like shining from shook foil;
    It gathers to a greatness, like the ooze of oil
Crushed. Why do men then now not reck his rod?
Generations have trod, have trod, have trod;
    And all is seared with trade; bleared, smeared with toil;
    And wears man's smudge and shares man's smell: the soil
Is bare now, nor can foot feel, being shod.

And for all this, nature is never spent;
    There lives the dearest freshness deep down things;
And though the last lights off the black West went
    Oh, morning, at the brown brink eastward, springs –
Because the Holy Ghost over the bent
    World broods with warm breast and with ah! bright wings.
                               Gerard Manley Hopkins

Appeal for victory and peace   Ps 143 (144)I
    Blessings on the coming kingdom of our father David
    (Mk 11:10).
Ant. Lower your heavens and come down;
    reach down from heaven and save us.

Blessed be the Lord, my rock
who trains my arms for battle,
who prepares my hands for war.

He is my love, my fortress;
he is my stronghold, my saviour,
my shield, my place of refuge.
He brings peoples under my rule.

Lord, what is man that you care for him,
mortal man, that you keep him in mind;

man, who is merely a breath
whose life fades like a passing shadow?

Lower your heavens and come down;
touch the mountains; wreathe them in smoke.
Flash your lightnings; rout the foe,
shoot your arrows and put them to flight.

Reach down from heaven and save me;
draw me out from the mighty waters,
from the hands of alien foes
whose mouths are filled with lies,
whose hands are raised in perjury.

Ps 143(144)II

To you, O God, will I sing a new song;
I will play on the ten-stringed lute
to you who give kings their victory,
who set David your servant free.

You set him free from the evil sword;
you rescued him from alien foes
whose mouths were filled with lies,
whose hands were raised in perjury.

Let our sons then flourish like saplings
grown tall and strong from their youth:
our daughters graceful as columns,
adorned as though for a palace.

Let our barns be filled to overflowing
with crops of every kind;
our sheep increasing by thousands,
myriads of sheep in our fields,
our cattle heavy with young,

no ruined wall, no exile,
no sound of weeping in our streets.
Happy the people with such blessings;
happy the people whose God is the Lord.

Ant. Lower your heavens and come down;
reach down from heaven and save us.

Word of God   Rom 15: 8–13

Christ became a servant of the Jewish people to maintain the truth of God by making good his promises to the patriarchs, and at the same time to give the Gentiles cause to glorify God for his mercy. As Scripture says, 'Therefore I will praise thee among the Gentiles and sing hymns to thy name'; and again, 'Gentiles, make merry together with his own people'; and yet again, 'All Gentiles, praise the Lord; let all peoples praise him.' Once again, Isaiah says, 'There shall be the Scion of Jesse, the one raised up to govern the Gentiles; on him the Gentiles shall set their hope.' And may the God of hope fill you with all joy and peace by your faith in him, until, by the power of the Holy Spirit, you overflow with hope.

Song of Zechariah

Ant. A shoot shall grow from the stock of Jesse:
 thus shall the glory of the Lord be revealed,
 and all mankind together shall see it.

Or as follows:

Old Testament Song   Is 61:10–62:2

 Christ gave himself up . . . so that he might present the church to himself all glorious, with no stain or wrinkle (Eph 5:25, 27).

Ant. I will not keep silence until the nations see your glory.

Let me rejoice in the Lord with all my heart,
let me exult in my God;
for he has robed me in salvation as a garment
and clothed me in integrity as a cloak,
like a bridegroom with his priestly garland,
or a bride decked in her jewels.

For, as the earth puts forth her blossom
or bushes in the garden burst into flower,
so shall the Lord God make righteousness
blossom before all the nations.

For Zion's sake I will not keep silence,
for Jerusalem's sake I will speak out,
until her right shines forth like the sunrise,

her deliverance like a blazing torch,
until the nations see the triumph of your right
and all kings see your glory.

Ant. I will not keep silence until the nations see your glory.

Prayers

Lord, as we begin this day, enlighten our understanding and
fill our hearts with your love, so that everything we do may
be offered to you.

> Lord Jesus, you stand unknown in our midst: teach us to
> seek you out in the poor and the oppressed, in the hungry
> and the needy.

> Lord, we praise you for the presence of the Spirit in our
> lives, making men and women the bearers of your
> message and your purpose.

> Come to us, Lord, in our family life: may your presence
> be the deep love in which we grow together, and the
> peace that overcomes all conflict.

Further prayers ... Our Father ...

Lord, in your loving-kindness listen to our prayers. Dispel
the darkness of our hearts by the gracious light of the
coming of your Son, who lives and reigns with you for ever.
Amen.

May the Lord bless us,
may he keep us from all evil
and lead us to life everlasting. Amen.

EVENING PRAYER

Lord, open my lips ...
Glory to the Father ...

The World

I saw Eternity the other night
Like a great Ring of pure and endless light,
All calm, as it was bright,
And round beneath it, Time in hours, days, years,
Driv'n by the spheres

Like a vast shadow moved, in which the world
And all her train were hurl'd;

Yet some, who all this while did weep and sing,
And sing, and weep, soar'd up into the Ring,
But most would use no wing.
O fools – said I – thus to prefer dark night
Before true light,
To live in grots, and caves, and hate the day
Because it shews the way –
The way which from the dead and dark abode
Leads up to God,
A way where you might tread the Sun, and be
More bright than he.
But as I did their madness so discuss,
One whisper'd thus,
This Ring the Bridegroom did for none provide
But for his Bride.

Henry Vaughan

Praise of God's grandeur   Ps 144(145)I
The Kingdom of God is justice, peace and joy,
inspired by the Holy Spirit (Rom 14:17).

Ant. Great shall the dominion be, and boundless the peace
  bestowed on David's throne and on his kingdom.

I will give you glory, O God my King,
I will bless your name for ever.

I will bless you day after day
and praise your name for ever.
The Lord is great, highly to be praised,
his greatness cannot be measured.

Age to age shall proclaim your works,
shall declare your mighty deeds,
shall speak of your splendour and glory,
tell the tale of your wonderful works.

They will speak of your terrible deeds,
recount your greatness and might.
They will recall your abundant goodness;
age to age shall ring out your justice.

The Lord is kind and full of compassion,
slow to anger, abounding in love.
How good is the Lord to all,
compassionate to all his creatures.

All your creatures shall thank you, O Lord,
and your friends shall repeat their blessing.
They shall speak of the glory of your reign
and declare your might O God,
to make known to men your mighty deeds
and the glorious splendour of your reign.
Yours is an everlasting kingdom;
your rule lasts from age to age.

Ps 144(145)II

The Lord is faithful in all his words
and loving in all his deeds.
The Lord supports all who fall
and raises all who are bowed down.

The eyes of all creatures look to you
and you give them their food in due time.
You open wide your hand,
grant the desires of all who live.

The Lord is just in all his ways
and loving in all his deeds.
He is close to all who call him,
who call on him from their hearts.

He grants the desires of those who fear him,
he hears their cry and he saves them.
The Lord protects all who love him;
but the wicked he will utterly destroy.

Let me speak the praise of the Lord,
let all mankind bless his holy name
for ever, for ages unending.

Ant. Great shall the dominion be, and boundless the peace
bestowed on David's throne and on his kingdom.

Word of God   Phil 4:4–7
I wish you all joy in the Lord. I will say it again: all joy be
yours. Let your magnanimity be manifest to all. The Lord
14

is near; have no anxiety, but in everything make your requests known to God in prayer and petition with thanksgiving. Then the peace of God, which is beyond our utmost understanding, will keep guard over your hearts and your thoughts, in Christ Jesus.

Song of the Virgin Mary

Ant. Adonai, Ruler of the house of Israel,
who appeared to Moses in the burning bush
and gave the law to him on Sinai:
come and save us with outstretched arm.

Or as follows:

Old Testament Song   Based on Is 64 and 40

Hold your heads high, because your liberation is near (Lk 21:28).

Ant. Come down on us, O heavenly dew,
O clouds, rain down the Just One!

Lord, do not be angry,
do not remember our iniquity for ever.
Behold, the holy cities have become a wilderness,
Zion has become a wilderness, Jerusalem is desolate;
our holy and beautiful house has been burnt to the ground,
the place where our fathers praised you.

Behold, despite your anger, we have sinned,
have all become like one who is unclean,
have faded like a leaf.
Like wind, all our iniquities bear us away.
Your face you have concealed from us,
and unto our iniquities delivered us.

Behold the affliction of your people,
and send the One who is to come:
the Lamb, the Ruler of the earth,
by desert ways, from Sela
to Zion's holy mountain,
that he may take away the yoke of our captivity.

Be comforted, be comforted, my people,
for your salvation now is very near.

Why are you consumed with grief,
and why has sorrow changed you?
Fear not, for I am with you.
I am the Lord your God;
your Saviour is the Holy One of Israel.

Ant. Come down on us, O heavenly dew,
O clouds, rain down the Just One!

Prayers

Lord Jesus Christ, as at your first coming you sent your messenger to prepare a way for you, help us now to respond eagerly to the message of repentance, and to await your coming with hearts prepared.

We thank you for our health and well-being: move us to welcome into our homes those who are bereaved or orphaned, those who have no home of their own.

We thank you for our health and well-being: move us to share our strength and joy with those who are ill or lonely.

We thank you, Father, for all that we have: move those of us who have received much to give of our plenty to those who have little

Further prayers . . . Our Father . . .

Lord, may we diligently await the coming of your Son. When he knocks, may he find us watching in prayer and rejoicing in his praise who lives and reigns with you for ever. Amen.

May the Lord bless us,
may he keep us from all evil
and lead us to life everlasting. Amen.

TUESDAY

Lord, open my lips . . .
To you be glory . . .

Grace
My stock lies dead, and no increase
Doth my dull husbandrie improve:
O let thy graces without cease
                Drop from above!

If still the sunne should hide his face,
Thy house would but a dungeon prove,
Thy works nights captives: O let grace
                Drop from above!

The dew doth ev'ry morning fall;
And shall the dew out-strip thy Dove?
The dew, for which grasse cannot call,
                Drop from above.

Death is still working like a mole,
And digs my grave at each remove:
Let grace work too, and on my soul
                Drop from above.

Sinne is still hammering my heart
Unto a hardnesse, void of love:
Let suppling grace, to crosse his art,
                Drop from above.

O come! for thou dost know the way:
Or if to me thou wilt not move,
Remove me, where I need not say,
                Drop from above.

George Herbert

God's wisdom and providence

Ps 91(92)

O depth of wealth, wisdom and knowledge in God! How unsearchable his judgments, how untraceable his ways (Rom 11:33).

Ant. While the law was given through Moses,
grace and truth came through Jesus Christ, alleluia!

It is good to give thanks to the Lord
to make music to your name, O Most High,
to proclaim your love in the morning
and your truth in the watches of the night,
on the ten-stringed lyre and the lute,
with the murmuring sound of the harp.

Your deeds, O Lord, have made me glad;
for the work of your hands I shout with joy.
O Lord, how great are your works!
How deep are your designs!
The foolish man cannot know this
and the fool cannot understand.

Though the wicked spring up like grass
and all who do evil thrive:
they are doomed to be eternally destroyed.
But you, Lord, are eternally on high.

Ant. While the law was given through Moses,
grace and truth came through Jesus Christ, alleluia!

God's majesty, man's dignity

Ps 8

In Jesus we see one who for a short while was made lower than the angels (Heb 2:9).

Ant. Our eyes shall see his glorious majesty,
our ears shall hear the glory of his voice, alleluia!

How great is your name, O Lord our God,
through all the earth!

18

Your majesty is praised above the heavens;
on the lips of children and of babes
you have found praise to foil your enemy,
to silence the foe and the rebel.

When I see the heavens, the work of your hands,
the moon and the stars which you arranged,
what is man that you should keep him in mind,
mortal man that you care for him?

Yet you have made him little less than a god;
with glory and honour you crowned him,
gave him power over the works of your hand,
put all things under his feet.

All of them, sheep and cattle,
yes, even the savage beasts,
birds of the air, and fish
that make their way through the waters.

How great is your name, O Lord our God,
through all the earth!

Ant. Our eyes shall see his glorious majesty,
   our ears shall hear the glory of his voice, alleluia!

Word of God   1 Cor 1:4–9

Grace and peace to you from God our Father and the Lord
Jesus Christ.
I am always thanking God for you. I thank him for his
grace given to you in Christ Jesus. I thank him for all the
enrichment that has come to you in Christ. You possess
full knowledge and you can give full expression to it,
because in you the evidence for the truth of Christ has found
confirmation. There is indeed no single gift you lack,
while you wait expectantly for our Lord Jesus Christ to
reveal himself. He will keep you firm to the end, without
reproach on the Day of our Lord Jesus. It is God himself
who called you to share in the life of his Son Jesus Christ
our Lord; and God keeps faith.

Song of Zechariah

Ant. On that great Day
the Lord Jesus will come to be glorified among his own,
and to be adored among all believers, alleluia!

Or as follows:

Old Testament Song   Is 54:4–8, 10

The gracious gifts of God and his calling are irrevocable
(Rom 11:29).

Ant. Your ransomer is the Holy One of Israel.

Fear not; you shall not be put to shame,
you shall suffer no insult, have no cause to blush.
It is time to forget the shame of your younger days
and remember no more the reproach of your widowhood;
for your husband is your maker, whose name is the Lord of
     Hosts;
your ransomer is the Holy One of Israel
who is called God of all the earth.

The Lord has acknowledged you a wife again,
once deserted and heart-broken,
your God has called you a bride still young
though once rejected.
On the impulse of a moment I forsook you,
but with tender affection I will bring you home again.
In sudden anger I hid my face from you for a moment;
but now I have pitied you with a love which never fails,
says the Lord who ransoms you.

Though the mountains move and the hills shake,
my love shall be immovable and never fail,
and my covenant of peace shall not be shaken.
So says the Lord who takes pity on you.

Ant. Your ransomer is the Holy One of Israel.

Prayers

Loving Father, we praise you and thank you because you
have come to us in your son Jesus.

We praise you as you come to us through those who love
us and care for us: may we love them in return.

We praise you for the example of Mary: as she brought your son Jesus into the world, so may all Christians continue to bring him to men.

We praise you when you come to us in your Church as we worship together: may our worship be in spirit and in truth.

Further prayers . . . Our Father . . .

Eternal God, you have made known your salvation to the ends of the earth; give us grace to prepare ourselves with joy for the glorious birth of our Saviour, Jesus Christ, who lives and reigns with you for ever. Amen.

May the Lord bless us,
may he keep us from all evil
and lead us to life everlasting. Amen.

EVENING PRAYER

Lord, open my lips . . .
Glory to the Father . . .

From La Corona
Deigne at my hands this crown of prayer and praise,
Weav'd in my low devout melancholie,
Thou which of good, hast, yea art treasury,
All changing unchang'd Antient of dayes,
But doe not, with a vile crowne of fraile bayes,
Reward my muses white sincerity,
But what thy thorny crowne gain'd, that give mee,
A crowne of Glory, which doth flower alwayes;
The ends crowne our workes, but thou crown'st our ends,
For, at our end begins our endlesse rest,
The first last end, now zealously possest,
With a strong sober thirst, my soule attends.
'Tis time that heart and voice be lifted high,
Salvation to all that will is nigh.

John Donne

21

Homesickness in exile Ps 136(137)

> *You are no longer aliens in a foreign land, but fellow-citizens with God's people* (Eph 2:19).

Ant. Look, I am laying a stone in Zion, a block of granite,
a precious corner-stone for a firm foundation, alleluia!

By the rivers of Babylon
there we sat and wept,
remembering Zion;
on the poplars that grew there
we hung up our harps.

For it was there that they asked us,
our captors, for songs,
our oppressors, for joy.
'Sing to us,' they said,
'one of Zion's songs.'

O how could we sing
the song of the Lord
on alien soil?
If I forget you, Jerusalem,
let my right hand wither!

O let my tongue
cleave to my mouth
if I remember you not,
if I prize not Jerusalem
above all my joys!

Ant. Look, I am laying a stone in Zion, a block of granite,
a precious corner-stone for a firm foundation, alleluia!

Thanksgiving to a faithful God Ps 137(138)

> *The arrogant of heart and mind he has put to rout,
> but the humble have been lifted high* (Lk 1:51, 52).

Ant. Behold the Lord: he comes from afar.
The whole earth is full of his glory, alleluia!

I thank you, Lord, with all my heart,
you have heard the words of my mouth.
Before the angels I will bless you.
I will adore before your holy temple.

I thank you for your faithfulness and love
which excel all we ever knew of you.
On the day I called, you answered;
you increased the strength of my soul.

All earth's kings shall thank you
when they hear the words of your mouth.
They shall sing of the Lord's ways:
'How great is the glory of the Lord!'

The Lord is high yet he looks on the lowly
and the haughty he knows from afar.
Though I walk in the midst of affliction
you give me life and frustrate my foes.

You stretch out your hand and save me,
your hand will do all things for me.
Your love, O Lord, is eternal,
discard not the work of your hands.

Ant. Behold the Lord: he comes from afar.
The whole earth is full of his glory.

Word of God   Jn 1: 6–8, 19–23
There appeared a man named John, sent from God; he
came as a witness to testify to the light, that all might
become believers through him. He was not himself the
light; he came to bear witness to the light.
This is the testimony which John gave when the Jews of
Jerusalem sent a deputation of priests and Levites to ask
him who he was. He confessed without reserve and avowed,
'I am not the Messiah.' 'What then? Are you Elijah?'
'No,' he replied. 'Are you the prophet we await?' He
answered 'No.' 'Then who are you?' they asked. 'We must
give an answer to those who sent us. What account do you
give of yourself?' He answered in the words of the prophet
Isaiah: 'I am a voice crying aloud in the wilderness, "Make
the Lord's highway straight."'

Song of the Virgin Mary
Ant. Root of Jesse, given to the peoples as a sign,
before whom kings shall be silent,
whom the nations shall seek:
Come to save us and delay no longer.

Or as follows:
Old Testament Song   Bar 4:21–29

*Awake, sleeper, rise from the dead, and Christ will shine
upon you* (Eph 5:14).

Ant. He will bring you everlasting joy when he delivers you,
alleluia!

Take heart, my children! Cry out to God,
and he will rescue you from tyranny and from the power of
your enemies.
For I have set my hope of your deliverance on the
Everlasting;
the Holy One, your everlasting saviour, has filled me with joy
over the mercy soon to be granted you.

I saw you go with mourning and tears,
but God will give you back to me with joy and gladness for
ever.
For as the neighbours of Zion have now seen your captivity,
so they will soon see your deliverance coming upon you from
your God
with the great glory and splendour of the Everlasting.

My children, endure in patience the wrath God has brought
upon you;
your enemy has hunted you down, but soon you will see him
destroyed,
and will put your foot upon his neck.
My pampered children have trodden rough paths;
they have been carried off like a flock seized by raiders.

Take heart, my children! Cry out to God,
for he who afflicted you will not forget you.
You once resolved to go astray from God;
now with tenfold zeal you must turn about and seek him.
He who brought these calamities upon you
will bring you everlasting joy when he delivers you.

Ant. He will bring you everlasting joy when he delivers you,
alleluia!

Prayers

Almighty God, you have given us in Jesus Christ the fulfilment of all your promises: hasten the coming of the day when all things will be united in him.

We thank you for this day now drawing to a close: forgive us if we have hurt anyone today.

God our Father, you are very near to us; we have only to turn, and we shall know your love.

We pray that this time of coming hope and joy may be a time when men will renew their efforts to rid the world of poverty and want.

Further prayers . . . Our Father . . .

Almighty God, who wonderfully created us in your image, and yet more wonderfully restored us through your son Jesus Christ: grant us to share in his divine life as he shared our humanity, who now is alive and reigns with you in the unity of the Holy Spirit, one God, for ever and ever. Amen.

May the Lord bless us, may he keep us from all evil and lead us to life everlasting. Amen.

WEDNESDAY

Morning Prayer

Lord, open my lips . . .
To you be glory . . .

How many Heavens . . .

The emeralds are singing on the grasses
And in the trees the bells of the long cold are ringing, –
My blood seems changed to emeralds like the spears
Of grass beneath the earth piercing and singing.

The flame of the first blade
Is an angel piercing through the earth to sing
'God is everything!
The grass within the grass, the angel in the angel, flame
Within the flame, and He is the green shade that came
To be the heart of shade.'

25

The grey-beard angel of the stone,
Who has grown wise with age, cried 'Not alone
Am I within my silence, – God is the stone in the still stone,
    the silence laid
In the heart of silence' . . . then, above the glade
The yellow straws of light
Whereof the sun has built his nest, cry, 'Bright
Is the world, the yellow straw
My brother, – God is the straw within the straw:–
    All things are Light.'

He is the sea of ripeness and the sweet apple's emerald lore.
So you, my flame of grass, my root of the world from which
    all Spring shall grow,
O you, my hawthorn bough of the stars, now leaning low
Through the day, for your flowers to kiss my lips, shall know
He is the core of the heart of love, and He, beyond labouring
    seas, our ultimate shore.

                                 Edith Sitwell

Plea for the return of God's favour   Ps 79(80)I
    Come, Lord Jesus! (Rev 22:20).
Ant. Let your face shine on us, O God,
    and we shall be saved.

O shepherd of Israel, hear us,
you who lead Joseph's flock,
shine forth from your cherubim throne
upon Ephraim, Benjamin, Manasseh.
O Lord, rouse up your might,
O Lord, come to our help.

God of hosts, bring us back;
let your face shine on us and we shall be saved.

Lord God of hosts, how long
will you frown on your people's plea?
You have fed them with tears for their bread,
an abundance of tears for their drink.
You have made us the taunt of our neighbours,
our enemies laugh us to scorn.

God of hosts, bring us back;
let your face shine on us and we shall be saved.

Ps 79(80)II

You brought a vine out of Egypt;
to plant it you drove out the nations.
Before it you cleared the ground;
it took root and spread through the land.

The mountains were covered with its shadow,
the cedars of God with its boughs.
It stretched out its branches to the sea,
to the Great River it stretched out its shoots.

Then why have you broken down its walls?
It is plucked by all who pass by.
It is ravaged by the boar of the forest,
devoured by the beasts of the field.

God of hosts, turn again, we implore,
look down from heaven and see.
Visit this vine and protect it,
the vine your right hand has planted.
Men have burnt it with fire and destroyed it.
May they perish at the frown of your face.

May your hand be on the man you have chosen,
the man you have given your strength.
And we shall never forsake you again:
give us life that we may call upon your name.

God of hosts, bring us back;
let your face shine on us and we shall be saved.

Ant. Let your face shine on us, O God,
and we shall be saved.

Word of God   Lk 7: 19–23
Summoning two of his disciples, John sent them to the Lord
with this message: 'Are you the one who is to come, or are
we to expect some other?' The messengers made their way
to Jesus and said, 'John the Baptist has sent us to you:
he asks, "Are you the one who is to come, or are we to
expect some other?"' There and then he cured many

27

sufferers from diseases, plagues, and evil spirits; and on many blind people he bestowed sight. Then he gave them his answer: 'Go,' he said, 'and tell John what you have seen and heard: how the blind recover their sight, the lame walk, the lepers are made clean, the deaf hear, the dead are raised to life, the poor are hearing the good news – and happy is the man who does not find me a stumbling-block.'

Song of Zechariah

Ant. Among you, though you do not know it,
   stands the one who is to come after me.

Or as follows:

Old Testament Song   Is 12: 1–6

The water that I shall give will be an inner spring always welling up for eternal life (Jn 4:14).

Ant. You shall draw water with joy, alleluia,
   from the springs of deliverance.

I will praise you, O Lord,
though you have been angry with me;
your anger has turned back,
and you have comforted me.

God is indeed my deliverer.
I am confident and unafraid;
for the Lord is my refuge and defence
and has shown himself my deliverer.
And so you shall draw water with joy
from the springs of deliverance.

Give thanks to the Lord and invoke him by name,
make his deeds known in the world around;
declare that his name is supreme.

Sing psalms to the Lord, for he has triumphed,
and this must be made known in all the world.
Cry out, shout aloud, you that dwell in Zion,
for the Holy One of Israel is among you in majesty.

Ant. You shall draw water with joy, alleluia,
   from the springs of deliverance.

28

Prayers

Come, Lord, come among us. Save us from our sinfulness by your protection and make us free for new life by your love.

Let us praise and bless God our Father with all our hearts:

We praise you, Lord God, for all the beauty of earth and sky.

We praise you for the love you have shown to men
in the coming of Jesus the Messiah.

We bless you, Lord, for the presence of the Spirit in men's hearts.

Fill our hearts with wakefulness as we wait to welcome Christ your Son
into every moment of our lives.

Further prayers . . . Our Father . . .

Lord Jesus Christ, we know you are coming and will not delay. Bring to light the things now hidden in darkness and reveal to all men your glory, who live and reign forever. Amen.

May the Lord bless us
may he keep us from all evil
and lead us to life everlasting. Amen.

EVENING PRAYER

Lord open my lips . . .
Glory to the Father . . .

This world is not Conclusion
This world is not Conclusion.
A Species stands beyond –
Invisible, as Music –
But positive, as Sound –
It beckons, and it baffles –
Philosophy – don't know –
And through a Riddle, at the last –
Sagacity, must go –
To guess it, puzzles scholars –

To gain it, Men have borne
Contempt of Generations
And Crucifixion, shown –
Faith slips – and laughs, and rallies –
Blushes, if any see –
Plucks at a twig of Evidence –
And asks a Vane, the way –
Much Gesture, from the Pulpit –
Strong Hallelujahs roll –
Narcotics cannot still the Tooth
That nibbles at the soul –

Emily Dickinson

The kingdom of peace

Ps 71(72)I

He has sent me to announce good news to the poor (Lk 4:18).

Ant. He will have pity on the weak
  and save the lives of the poor, alleluia!

O God, give your judgment to the king,
to a king's son your justice,
that he may judge your people in justice
and your poor in right judgment.

May the mountains bring forth peace for the people
and the hills, justice.
May he defend the poor of the people
and save the children of the needy
and crush the oppressor.

He shall endure like the sun and the moon
from age to age.
He shall descend like rain on the meadow
like raindrops on the earth

In his days justice shall flourish
and peace till the moon fails.
He shall rule from sea to sea,
from the Great River to earth's bounds.

The kings of Sheba and Seba
shall bring him gifts.
Before him all kings shall fall prostrate,
all nations shall serve him.

For he shall save the poor when they cry
and the needy who are helpless.
He will have pity on the weak
and save the lives of the poor.

From oppression he will rescue their lives,
to him their blood is dear.
Long may he live,
may the gold of Sheba be given him.
They shall pray for him without ceasing
and bless him all the day.

May his name be blessed for ever
and endure like the sun.
Every tribe shall be blessed in him,
all nations bless his name.

Blessed be the Lord, God of Israel,
who alone works wonders,
ever blessed his glorious name.
Let his glory fill the earth.

Amen! Amen!

Ant. He will have pity on the weak
and save the lives of the poor, alleluia!

Word of God   Rev 20: 11–21:4

I saw a great white throne, and the One who sat upon it;
from his presence earth and heaven vanished away, and no
place was left for them. I could see the dead, great and small,
standing before the throne; and books were opened. Then
another book was opened, the roll of the living. From what
was written in these books the dead were judged upon the
record of their deeds. The sea gave up its dead, and Death
and Hades gave up the dead in their keeping; they were

31

judged, each man on the record of his deeds. Then Death and Hades were flung into the lake of fire. This lake of fire is the second death; and into it were flung any whose names were not to be found in the roll of the living.

Then I saw a new heaven and a new earth, for the first heaven and the first earth had vanished, and there was no longer any sea. I saw the holy city, new Jerusalem, coming down out of heaven from God, made ready like a bride adorned for her husband. I heard a loud voice proclaiming from the throne: 'Now at last God has his dwelling among men! He will dwell among them and they shall be his people, and God himself will be with them. He will wipe every tear from their eyes; there shall be an end to death, and to mourning and crying and pain; for the old order has passed away!'

Song of the Virgin Mary

Ant. Key of David and sceptre of the house of Israel,
　　who open the gates which none may shut,
　　who shut the gates which none may open:
　　Come to liberate from prison
　　the captive who dwells in darkness and in the shadow of
　　　death.

Or as follows:

Old Testament Song　　　　　　　　　　　　Is 25: 6–9

　　*There shall be an end to death, and to mourning and crying
　　and pain* (Rev 21:4).

Ant. I am coming soon, and bringing my recompense with
　　me.

On this mountain the Lord of Hosts will prepare
a banquet of rich fare for all the peoples,
a banquet of wines well matured and richest fare,
well-matured wines strained clear.

On this mountain the Lord will swallow up
that veil that shrouds all the peoples,
the pall thrown over all the nations;
he will swallow up death for ever.

Then the Lord God will wipe away the tears
    from every face
and remove the reproach of his people from the whole earth.
The Lord has spoken.

On that day men will say,
See, this is our God
for whom we have waited to deliver us;
this is the Lord for whom we have waited;
let us rejoice and exult in his deliverance.

Ant. I am coming soon and bringing my recompense with
    me.

Prayers

Father, God of light and peace, we look for the coming of
your Son with joy: may our lives be transformed by his
presence.

    Lord Jesus, bring warmth and comfort
    to the lonely, the sick, the bereaved:
    may we accept your love by sharing our love with them.

    Give what they most need to those far from home tonight:
    to those ill in hospital and to those who care for them,
    to those in prison and those anxious or disturbed.

    Lord, we thank you for this day of life,
    for the capacity to work and to rest,
    for the companionship of others;
    help us to be truly grateful and to show our gratitude
    in the way we use and share your wonderful gifts.

Further prayers . . . Our Father . . .

Heavenly Father, we pray you to pour your grace into our
hearts, that we to whom the incarnation of Christ your Son
was made known by the message of an angel, may by his
passion and cross be brought to the glory of his resurrection, through Christ our Lord. Amen.

May the Lord bless us,
may he keep us from all evil
and lead us to life everlasting. Amen.

33

THURSDAY

Lord, open my lips ...
To you be glory ...
I am coming soon
Let me love thee, O Christ,
    in thy first coming,
      when thou wast made man, for love of men,
        and for love of me.

Let me love thee, O Christ,
    in thy second coming,
  when with an inconceivable love
  thou standest and knockest at the door,
  and wouldest enter into the souls of men,
      and into mine.

Plant in my soul, O Christ, thy likeness of love;
    that when by death thou callest,
  it may be ready,
    and burning
      to come unto thee.

Eric Milner-White

God the protector   Ps 120(121)

*They shall never again feel hunger or thirst,
the sun shall not beat on them nor any scorching heat*
(Rev 7:16).

Ant. I will look for the Lord,
I will wait for God my Saviour; my God will hear me,
alleluia!

I lift up my eyes to the mountains:
from where shall come my help?
My help shall come from the Lord
who made heaven and earth.

May he never allow you to stumble!
Let him sleep not, your guard.
No, he sleeps not nor slumbers,
Israel's guard.

The Lord is your guard and your shade;
at your right side he stands.
By day the sun shall not smite you
nor the moon in the night.

The Lord will guard you from evil,
he will guard your soul.
The Lord will guard your going and coming
both now and for ever.

Ant. I will look for the Lord,
I will wait for God my Saviour; my God will hear me,
alleluia!

Trust in God Ps 122(123)

*Happy are those servants whom the master finds on the
alert when he comes . . . He will seat them at table, and
come and wait on them* (Lk 12:37).

Ant. Behold, the Lord shall come, the Prince of the kings
of the earth. Blessed are they who are ready to meet him.

To you have I lifted up my eyes,
you who dwell in the heavens:
my eyes, like the eyes of slaves
on the hand of their lords.

Like the eyes of a servant
on the hand of her mistress,
so our eyes are on the Lord our God
till he show us his mercy.

Have mercy on us, Lord, have mercy.
We are filled with contempt.
Indeed all too full is our soul
with the scorn of the rich,
with the proud man's disdain.

Ant. Behold, the Lord shall come, the Prince of the kings
of the earth. Blessed are they who are ready to meet him.

Word of God Is 40: 9–11

You who bring Zion good news, up with you to the
mountain-top;

lift up your voice and shout,
you who bring good news to Jerusalem,
lift it up fearlessly;
cry to the cities of Judah, 'Your God is here.'
Here is the Lord God coming in might,
coming to rule with his right arm.
His recompense comes with him,
he carries his reward before him.
He will tend his flock like a shepherd
and gather them together with his arm;
he will carry the lambs in his bosom
and lead the ewes to water.

Song of Zechariah

Ant. Lord, you are the One who is to come, the one whom
we await. Come, Lord Jesus!

Or as follows:

New Testament Song   Rev 22: 12–13, 16–17, 20

Ant. Amen, alleluia! Come, Lord Jesus!

I am coming soon,
and bringing my recompense with me,
to requite everyone according to his deeds!

I am the Alpha and the Omega,
the first and the last,
the beginning and the end.
I am the scion and offspring of David,
the bright star of dawn.

'Come!' say the Spirit and the bride.
'Come!' let each hearer reply.
Come forward, you who are thirsty;
accept the water of life,
a free gift to all who desire it.

He who gives this testimony speaks:
'Yes, I am coming soon!'
Amen. Come, Lord Jesus!

Ant. Amen, alleluia! Come, Lord Jesus!

Prayers

Lord God, we thank you for the peace and refreshment of
the night.
Enter our hearts and minds anew, preparing us for this day.

Loving Father, look after all the members of our family,
and watch over them in everything they do today.

We praise you, Lord God, and lift up our hearts in
gratitude for your love.
Take our lives, our work and our rest,
the small things of the day and the special things,
the sadness and the joy.

All nations have the same Creator and Father.
May they look upon each other as brothers,
regardless of race or nationality,
and seek God's kingdom of peace and joy.

Further prayers ... Our Father ...

Eternal God and Father, by whose power we are created
and by whose love we are redeemed: guide and strengthen
us by your Spirit, that we may give ourselves to your service,
and live this day in love for one another and for you,
through Jesus Christ our Lord. Amen.

May the Lord bless us,
may he keep us from all evil
and lead us to life everlasting. Amen.

EVENING PRAYER

Lord, open my lips ...
Glory to the Father ...

Northumbrian Sequence IV
Let in the wind
Let in the rain
Let in the moors tonight,

The storm beats on my window-pane,
Night stands at my bed-foot,
Let in the fear,

SEASON OF ADVENT: THURSDAY

Let in the pain,
Let in the trees that toss and groan,
Let in the north tonight.

Let in the nameless formless power
That beats upon my door,
Let in the ice, let in the snow,
The banshee howling on the moor,
The bracken-bush on the bleak hillside,
Let in the dead tonight

The whistling ghost behind the dyke,
The dead that rot in mire,
Let in the thronging ancestors
The unfulfilled desire,
Let in the wraith of the dead earl,
Let in the dead tonight.

Let in the cold,
Let in the wet,
Let in the loneliness,
Let in the quick,
Let in the dead,
Let in the unpeopled skies.

Oh how can virgin fingers weave
A covering for the void,
How can my fearful heart conceive
Gigantic solitude?
How can a house so small contain
A company so great?
Let in the dark,
Let in the dead,
Let in your love tonight.

Let in the snow that numbs the grave,
Let in the acorn-tree,
The mountain stream and mountain stone,
Let in the bitter sea.

Fearful is my virgin heart
And frail my virgin form,

And must I then take pity on
The raging of the storm
That rose up from the great abyss
Before the earth was made,
That pours the stars in cataracts
And shakes this violent world?

Let in the fire,
Let in the power,
Let in the invading might.

Gentle must my fingers be
And pitiful my heart
Since I must bind in human form
A living power so great,
A living impulse great and wild
That cries about my house
With all the violence of desire
Desiring this my peace.

Pitiful my heart must hold
The lonely stars at rest,
Have pity on the raven's cry
The torrent and the eagle's wing,
The icy water of the tarn
And on the biting blast.

Let in the wound,
Let in the pain,
Let in your child tonight.

Kathleen Raine

God is faithful to the promise made to David   Ps 88(89)I

David is the man from whose posterity God, as he promised,
has brought Israel a saviour (Acts 13:23).

Ant. Behold, he who is both God and man
  shall come forth from the house of David
  and sit upon his throne.

I will sing for ever of your love, O Lord;
through all ages my mouth will proclaim your truth.

39

Of this I am sure, that your love lasts for ever,
that your truth is firmly established as the heavens.

'I have made a covenant with my chosen one;
I have sworn to David my servant:
I will establish your dynasty for ever
and set up your throne through all ages.

The heavens proclaim your wonders, O Lord;
the assembly of your holy ones proclaims your truth.
For who in the skies can compare with the Lord
or who is like the Lord among the sons of God?

A God to be feared in the council of the holy ones,
great and dreadful to all around him.
O Lord God of hosts, who is your equal?
You are mighty, O Lord, and truth is your garment.

Ps 88(89)II

It is you who rule the sea in its pride;
it is you who still the surging of its waves
It is you who trod Rahab underfoot like a corpse,
scattering your foes with your mighty arm.

The heavens are yours, the world is yours.
It is you who founded the earth and all it holds;
it is you who created the North and the South.
Tabor and Hermon shout with joy at your name.

Yours is a mighty arm, O Lord;
your hand is strong, your right hand ready.
Justice and right are the pillars of your throne,
love and truth walk in your presence.

Happy the people who acclaim such a king,
who walk, O Lord, in the light of your face,
who find their joy every day in your name,
who make your justice the source of their bliss.

For it is you, O Lord, who are the glory of their strength;
it is by your favour that our might is exalted:
for our ruler is in the keeping of the Lord;
our king in the keeping of the Holy One of Israel.

Ant. Behold, he who is both God and man
    shall come forth from the house of David
    and sit upon his throne.

Word of God   1 Thess 5: 1–8

About dates and times, my friends, we need not write to you,
for you know perfectly well that the Day of the Lord comes
like a thief in the night. While they are talking of peace and
security, all at once calamity is upon them, sudden as the
pangs that come upon a woman with child; and there will
be no escape. But you, my friends, are not in the dark,
that the day should overtake you like a thief. You are all
children of light, children of day. We do not belong to night
or darkness, and we must not sleep like the rest, but keep
awake and sober. Sleepers sleep at night, and drunkards
are drunk at night, but we, who belong to daylight, must
keep sober, armed with faith and love for coat of mail,
and the hope of salvation for helmet.

Song of the Virgin Mary

Ant. Morning Star, Radiance of eternal light, Sun of justice:
    Come and enlighten those who dwell in darkness and the
    shadow of death.

Or as follows:

Old Testament Song   Is 24:16–21, 23
And the elders fell down and worshipped (Rev 4:14).

Ant. Holy, holy, holy is God the sovereign Lord of all.

From the ends of the earth we have heard them sing,
How lovely is righteousness!
But I thought: Villainy, villainy!
Woe to the traitors and their treachery!
Traitors double-dyed they are indeed!

The hunter's scare, the pit, and the trap
threaten all who dwell in the land;
if a man runs from the rattle of the scare
he will fall into the pit;
if he climbs out of the pit
he will be caught in the trap.

When the windows of heaven above are opened
and earth's foundations shake,
the earth is utterly shattered,
it is convulsed and reels wildly.
The earth reels to and fro like a drunken man
and sways like a watchman's shelter.
The sins of men weigh heavy upon it,
and it falls to rise no more.

On that day the Lord will punish
the host of heaven in heaven, and on earth the kings of the
    earth;
the moon shall grow pale and the sun hide its face in shame;
for the Lord of hosts has become king
on Mount Zion and in Jerusalem,
and shows his glory before their elders.

Ant. Holy, holy, holy is God the sovereign Lord of all.

Prayers

Let us rejoice and be glad for the Lord God is near: he is
coming in power to save his people.

> Lord Jesus, we pray that your coming may transform our
>   work:
> help us to work eagerly and honestly,
> to know that everything we do has a place in your purpose.

> We pray that your coming may transform our family life:
> may we learn in our homes the peace, love and generosity
> we should show to all men.

> We pray that your coming may transform society:
> inspire us to hunger and thirst for what is right,
> to work against injustice wherever we find it.

> We pray that your coming may transform the world,
> bringing peace and justice to all nations,
> and turning the forces of science and technology to good
>   ends.

Further prayers ... Our Father ...

We ask you, Lord, to fulfil your promise to be with us at all times. Come, Lord Jesus.

May the Lord bless us,
may he keep us from all evil
and lead us to life everlasting. Amen.

FRIDAY

MORNING PRAYER

Lord, open my lips . . .
To you be glory . . .

To Heaven
Good and great God, can I not think of Thee,
But it must, straight, my melancholy be?
Is it interpreted in me disease,
That, laden with my sins I seek for ease?
O, be Thou witness, that the reins dost know
And hearts of all, if I be sad for show,
And judge me after: if I dare pretend
To aught but grace, or aim at other end.
As Thou art all, so be Thou all to me,
First, midst, and last, converted One, and Three;
My Faith, my Hope, my Love: and in this state,
My Judge, my Witness, and my Advocate.
Where have I been this while exiled from Thee?
And whither rapt, now Thou but stoop'st to me?
Dwell, dwell here still: O, being everywhere,
How can I doubt to find Thee ever, here?
I know my state, both full of shame, and scorn,
Conceived in sin, and unto labour born,
Standing with fear, and must with horror fall,
And destined unto judgment, after all.
I feel my griefs too, and there scarce is ground
Upon my flesh to inflict another wound.
Yet dare I not complain, or wish for death
With holy Paul, lest it be thought the breath
Of discontent; or that these prayers be
For weariness of life, not love of Thee.   Ben Jonson

The coming age of peace and justice   Ps 84(85)

Through our Saviour who came down on earth,
God has blessed the earth (Origen).

Ant. He will come to dwell among us,
    and we shall see his glory.

O Lord, you once favoured your land
and revived the fortunes of Jacob,
you forgave the guilt of your people
and covered all their sins.
You averted all your rage,
you calmed the heat of your anger.

Revive us now, God, our helper!
Put an end to your grievance against us.
Will you be angry with us for ever,
will your anger never cease?

Will you not restore again our life
that your people may rejoice in you?
Let us see, O Lord, your mercy
and give us your saving help.

I will hear what the Lord God has to say,
a voice that speaks of peace,
peace for his people and his friends
and those who turn to him in their hearts.
His help is near for those who fear him
and his glory will dwell in our land.

Mercy and faithfulness have met;
justice and peace have embraced.
Faithfulness shall spring from the earth
and justice look down from heaven.

The Lord will make us prosper
and our earth shall yield its fruit.
Justice shall march before him
and peace shall follow his steps.

Ant. He will come to dwell among us,
and we shall see his glory.

Praise to the God of victories   Ps 149

*He will appear a second time to bring salvation to those
who are watching for him* (Heb 9:28).

Ant. See, this is our God.
Let us rejoice and exult in his deliverance.

Sing a new song to the Lord,
his praise in the assembly of the faithful.
Let Israel rejoice in its Maker,
let Zion's sons exult in their king.
Let them praise his name with dancing
and make music with timbrel and harp.

For the Lord takes delight in his people.
He crowns the poor with salvation.
Let the faithful rejoice in their glory,
shout for joy and take their rest.

Ant. See, this is our God.
Let us rejoice and exult in his deliverance.

Word of God   Mk 1: 2–8

In the prophet Isaiah it stands written: 'Here is my herald
whom I send on ahead of you, and he will prepare your way.
A voice crying aloud in the wilderness, "Prepare a way for
the Lord; clear a straight path for him." ' And so it was that
John the Baptist appeared in the wilderness proclaiming a
baptism in token of repentance, for the forgiveness of sins;
and they flocked to him from the whole Judaean country-
side and the city of Jerusalem, and were baptized by him in
the River Jordan, confessing their sins.
John was dressed in a rough coat of camel's hair, with a
leather belt round his waist, and he fed on locusts and wild
honey. His proclamation ran: 'After me comes one who is
mightier than I. I am not fit to unfasten his shoes. I have
baptized you with water; he will baptize you with the Holy
Spirit.'

45

Song of Zechariah

Ant. For you who fear my name,
the sun of righteousness will rise with healing in his wings.
Or as follows:

New Testament Song   Jn 3: 29–36

Ant. As he grows greater, I must grow less.

It is the bridegroom to whom the bride belongs.
The bridegroom's friend, who stands by and listens to him,
is overjoyed at hearing the bridegroom's voice.
This joy, this perfect joy, is now mine.

He who comes from above is above all others;
he who is from the earth belongs to the earth
and uses earthly speech.
He who comes from heaven bears witness to what he has
    seen and heard,
yet no one accepts his witness.
To accept his witness is to attest that God speaks the truth;
for he whom God sent utters the words of God,
so measureless is God's gift of the Spirit.

The Father loves the Son
and has entrusted him with all authority.
He who puts his faith in the Son
has hold of eternal life.

Ant. As he grows greater, I must grow less.

Prayers

Father, turn our hearts and our minds back to you, that we
may listen to the message of John the Baptist, to prepare a
way for the coming of the Saviour.

We praise you with wonder and awe,
because in your Son Jesus Christ
the Eternal God comes to share our human life.

Help us never to despise any man:
to fight against every hurt or degradation of a human
    being;

to give our love and respect to the poor, the suffering,
the oppressed,
for every one of us is brother or sister to Jesus Christ.

Lord Jesus, every home, every family, every human life
has new meaning and dignity because you have come
among us:
make us worthy of your gift to us.

Further prayers . . . Our Father . . .

Almighty God, who sent John the Baptist to herald the
coming of your Son: grant that the ministers and stewards
of your truth may prepare for his coming again by turning
our disobedient hearts to the holy wisdom of your law,
through Christ our Lord. Amen.

May the Lord bless us,
may he keep us from all evil
and lead us to life everlasting. Amen.

EVENING PRAYER

Lord, open my lips . . .
Glory to the Father . . .

We demand a miracle
Alone, alone, about a dreadful wood
Of conscious evil runs a lost mankind,
Dreading to find its Father lest it find
The Goodness it has dreaded is not good:
Alone, alone, about our dreadful wood.

Where is that Law for which we broke our own,
Where now that Justice for which Flesh resigned
Her hereditary right to passion, Mind
His will to absolute power? Gone. Gone.
Where is that Law for which we broke our own?

The Pilgrim Way has led to the Abyss.
Was it to meet such grinning evidence
We left our richly odoured ignorance?
Was the triumphant answer to be this?
The Pilgrim Way has led to the Abyss.

We who must die demand a miracle.
How could the Eternal do a temporal act,
The Infinite become a finite fact?
Nothing can save us that is possible:
We who must die demand a miracle.

W. H. Auden

Hope in God for every need   Ps 24(25)I

*Let us be firm and unswerving in the confession of our
hope* (Heb 10:23).

Ant. On that day, you shall know that I am the Lord
and that none who look to me will be disappointed.

To you, O Lord, I lift up my soul.
I trust you, let me not be disappointed;
do not let my enemies triumph.
Those who hope in you shall not be disappointed,
but only those who wantonly break faith.

Lord, make me know your ways.
Lord, teach me your paths.
Make me walk in your truth, and teach me:
for you are God my saviour.

In you I hope all the day long
because of your goodness, O Lord.
Remember your mercy, Lord,
and the love you have shown from of old.
Do not remember the sins of my youth.
In your love remember me.

The Lord is good and upright.
He shows the path to those who stray,
He guides the humble in the right path;
he teaches his way to the poor.

His ways are faithfulness and love
for those who keep his covenant and will.
Lord, for the sake of your name
forgive my guilt; for it is great.

If anyone fears the Lord
he will show him the path he should choose.
His soul shall live in happiness
and his children shall possess the land.
The Lord's friendship is for those who revere him;
to them he reveals his covenant.

My eyes are always on the Lord;
for he rescues my feet from the snare.
Turn to me and have mercy
for I am lonely and poor.

Relieve the anguish of my heart
and set me free from my distress.
See my affliction and my toil
and take all my sins away.

See how many are my foes;
how violent their hatred for me.
Preserve my life and rescue me.
Do not disappoint me, you are my refuge.
May innocence and uprightness protect me:
for my hope is in you, O Lord.

Redeem Israel, O God, from all its distress.

Ant. On that day, you shall know that I am the Lord
and that none who look to me will be disappointed.

Word of God Eph 2:14–22

Christ is himself our peace. Gentiles and Jews, he has
made the two one, and in his own body of flesh and blood
has broken down the enmity which stood like a dividing
wall between them; for he annulled the law with its rules
and regulations, so as to create out of the two a single new
humanity in himself, thereby making peace. This was his
purpose, to reconcile the two in a single body to God through
the cross, on which he killed the enmity.
So he came and proclaimed the good news: peace to

you who were far off, and peace to those who were near by, for through him we both alike have access to the Father in the one Spirit. Thus you are no longer aliens in a foreign land, but fellow-citizens with God's people, members of God's household. You are built upon the foundation laid by the apostles and prophets, and Christ Jesus himself is the foundation-stone. In him the whole building is bonded together and grows into a holy temple in the Lord. In him you too are being built with all the rest into a spiritual dwelling for God.

Song of the Virgin Mary

Ant. King of the peoples and goal of their desire,
   corner-stone uniting Jew and Gentile:
   Come and save man whom you made from the dust of
      the earth.

Or as follows:

Old Testament Song   Mic 5:2–5

Does not Scripture say that the Messiah is to be of the family of David, from David's village of Bethlehem? (Jn 7:42).

Ant. His greatness shall reach to the ends of the earth.

You, Bethlehem in Ephrathah,
small as you are to be among Judah's clans,
out of you shall come forth a governor for Israel,
one whose roots are far back in the past, in days gone by.

Therefore only so long as a woman is in labour
shall he give up Israel;
and then those that survive of his race
shall rejoin their brethren.

He shall appear and be their shepherd
in the strength of the Lord,
in the majesty of the name of the Lord his God.
And they shall continue, for now his greatness shall reach
to the ends of the earth;
and he shall be a man of peace.

Ant. His greatness shall reach to the ends of the earth.

Prayers

Eternal God, we thank you for showing yourself to us in
Jesus Christ: help us now to prepare to celebrate his birth
with joy.

> We thank you for the birth, childhood and manhood
>   of Jesus:
> may we find in each moment of his life the revelation
>   of your love for us.

> We pray that Christ may become man in each
>   one of us,
> so that through us his love may be visible to all men.

> We pray at this time for the world,
> where love and justice struggle against war and
>   oppression,
> wastefulness and extravagance.

Further prayers . . . Our Father . . .

May the love of the Lord Jesus draw us to himself;
may the power of the Lord Jesus strengthen us in his
    service;
may the joy of the Lord Jesus fill our hearts.

And may the blessing of almighty God, the Father, the
Son and the Holy Spirit, be among us and remain with us
always.

May the Lord bless us,
may he keep us from all evil
and lead us to life everlasting. Amen.

SATURDAY

Morning Prayer

Lord, open my lips . . .
To you be glory . . .

Your Word is near

You wait for us
until we are open to you.
We wait for your word
to make us receptive.

Attune us to your voice,
to your silence,
speak and bring your Son to us –
Jesus, the word of your peace.
Your word is near,
O Lord our God,
your grace is near.

Come to us, then,
with mildness and power.
Do not let us be deaf to you,
but make us receptive and open
to Jesus Christ your Son,
who will come to look for us and save us
today and every day
for ever and ever.

You, God, arouse faith in our hearts,
whoever we are.
You know and accept all your people,
whatever their thoughts are of you.
Speak to the world, then, your word,
come with your heaven among us,
give to good and to bad men your sun,
for ever and ever.

Huub Oosterhuis

God's promise to David
Ps 131(132)

*I am the scion and offspring of David, the bright star
of dawn* (Rev 22:16).

Ant. The days are now coming, says the Lord,
   when I will make a righteous Branch spring from David's
      line.

The Lord swore an oath to David;
he will not go back on his word:
A son, the fruit of your body,
will I set upon your throne.

If they keep my covenant in truth
and my laws that I have taught them,

their sons also shall rule
on your throne from age to age.

For the Lord has chosen Zion;
he has desired it for his dwelling:
This is my resting-place for ever,
here have I chosen to live.

I will greatly bless her produce,
I will fill her poor with bread.
I will clothe her priests with salvation
and her faithful shall ring out their joy.

There the stock of David will flower:
I will prepare a lamp for my anointed.
I will cover his enemies with shame
but on him my crown shall shine.

Ant. The days are now coming, says the Lord,
when I will make a righteous Branch spring from David's
line.

God, the hope of his people   Ps 107(108)

*The Son of God was raised above the heavens, and his
glory has been preached through all the earth* (Arnobius).

Ant. I will grant my deliverance in Zion
and give my glory to Israel.

My heart is ready, O God;
I will sing, sing your praise.
Awake, my soul;
awake, lyre and harp.
I will awake the dawn.

I will thank you, Lord, among the peoples,
praise you among the nations;
for your love reaches to the heavens
and your truth to the skies.
O God, arise above the heavens;
may your glory shine on earth!

O come and deliver your friends;
help with your right hand and reply.

Will you utterly reject us, O God,
and no longer march with your armies?

Give us help against the foe:
for the help of man is vain.
With God we shall do bravely
and he will trample down our foes.

Ant. I will grant my deliverance in Zion
and give my glory to Israel.

Word of God   Lk 1:26-33, 38

In the sixth month the angel Gabriel was sent from God
to a town in Galilee called Nazareth, with a message for
a girl betrothed to a man named Joseph, a descendant
of David; the girl's name was Mary. The angel went in and
said to her, 'Greetings, most favoured one! The Lord is
with you.' But she was deeply troubled by what he said and
wondered what this greeting might mean. Then the angel
said to her, 'Do not be afraid, Mary, for God has been
gracious to you; you shall conceive and bear a son, and you
shall give him the name Jesus. He will be great; he will bear
the title "Son of the Most High"; the Lord God will give
him the throne of his ancestor David, and he will be king
over Israel for ever; his reign shall never end.' 'Here am I,'
said Mary; 'I am the Lord's servant; as you have spoken, so
be it.'

Song of Zechariah

Ant. The Holy Spirit will come upon you,
and the power of the Host High will overshadow you,
alleluia!

Or as follows:

Old Testament Song   Zeph 3:14-18

Greetings, most favoured one! The Lord is with you
(Lk 1:28).

Ant. The Lord is among you as king, O Israel.

Zion, cry out for joy;
raise the shout of triumph, Israel;
be glad, rejoice with all your heart,
daughter of Jerusalem.

The Lord has rid you of your adversaries,
he has swept away your foes;
the Lord is among you as king, O Israel;
never again shall you fear disaster.

On that day this shall be the message to Jerusalem:
Fear not, O Zion; let not your hands fall slack.
The Lord your God is in your midst,
like a warrior to keep you safe;
he will rejoice over you and be glad;
he will show you his love once more;
he will exult over you with a shout of joy
as in days long ago.

Ant. The Lord is among you as king, O Israel.

Prayers

Father, as the virgin Mary accepted the Word of God
into her heart, may our prayer too be that everything
should come to us according to your will.

We praise you, Lord God, for the dignity you have
    given to man,
renewed in the Incarnation of your Son;
we thank you for all who struggle for the rights of men.

Lord Jesus, we thank you that our past mistakes need
    never be the last word,
for you bring us new life to overcome our faults
and turn us back to your love

Lord Jesus, as we see the world divided between the
    overfed and the hungry,
between the comfortable and the homeless,
between the privileged and the oppressed,
teach us to look to Bethlehem and find a message of
    hope for mankind.

Further prayers . . . Our Father . . .

Lord, stir up our hearts, to prepare a way for your Son, that
through his coming we may serve you with pure minds,
through the same Christ our Lord. Amen.

55

SEASON OF ADVENT: SATURDAY

May the Lord bless us,
may he keep us from all evil
and lead us to life everlasting. Amen.

EVENING PRAYER

Lord, open my lips . . .
Glory to the Father . . .

The Annunciation
Nothing will ease the pain to come
Though now she sits in ecstasy
And lets it have its way with her.
The angel's shadow in the room
Is lightly lifted as if he
Had never terrified her there.

The furniture again returns
To its old simple state. She can
Take comfort from the things she knows
Though in her heart new loving burns,
Something she never gave to man
Or god before, and this god grows

Most like a man. She wonders how
To pray at all, what thanks to give
And whom to give them to. 'Alone
To all men's eyes I now must go,'
She thinks 'And by myself must live
With a strange child that is my own.'

So from her ecstasy she moves
And turns to human things at last
(Announcing angels set aside).
It is a human child she loves
Though a god stirs beneath her breast
And great salvations grip her side.

Elizabeth Jennings

Hymn to God's providence and power Ps 32(33) I

*The secret hidden for long ages, but now disclosed to
God's people: Christ in you, the hope of a glory to come
(Col. 1:27).*

Ant. My purpose shall take effect, says the Lord, I will
accomplish all that I please.

Ring out your joy to the Lord, O you just;
for praise is fitting for loyal hearts.

Give thanks to the Lord upon the harp,
with a ten-stringed lute sing him songs.
O sing him a song that is new,
play loudly, with all your skill.

For the word of the Lord is faithful
and all his works to be trusted.
The Lord loves justice and right
and fills the earth with his love.

By his word the heavens were made,
by the breath of his mouth all the stars.
He collects the waves of the ocean;
he stores up the depths of the sea.

Let all the earth fear the Lord,
all who live in the world revere him.
He spoke; and it came to be.
He commanded; it sprang into being.

He frustrates the designs of the nations,
he defeats the plans of the peoples.
His own designs shall stand for ever,
the plans of his heart from age to age.

Ps 32(33)II

They are happy, whose God is the Lord,
the people he has chosen as his own.
From the heavens the Lord looks forth,
he sees all the children of men.

From the place where he dwells he gazes
on all the dwellers on the earth,

57

he who shapes the hearts of them all
and considers all their deeds.

A king is not saved by his army,
nor a warrior preserved by his strength.
A vain hope for safety is the horse;
despite its power it cannot save.

The Lord looks on those who revere him,
on those who hope in his love,
to rescue their souls from death,
to keep them alive in famine.

Our soul is waiting for the Lord.
The Lord is our help and our shield.
In him do our hearts find joy.
We trust in his holy name.

May your love be upon us, O Lord,
as we place all our hope in you.

Ant. My purpose shall take effect, says the Lord,
   I will accomplish all that I please.

Word of God   Mt 1:18–23

This is the story of the birth of the Messiah. Mary his
mother was betrothed to Joseph; before their marriage
she found that she was with child by the Holy Spirit.
Being a man of principle, and at the same time wanting to
save her from exposure, Joseph desired to have the marriage
contract set aside quietly. He had resolved on this, when an
angel of the Lord appeared to him in a dream. 'Joseph son
of David,' said the angel, 'do not be afraid to take Mary
home with you as your wife. It is by the Holy Spirit
that she has conceived this child. She will bear a son;
and you shall give him the name Jesus (Saviour), for
he will save his people from their sins.' All this happened
in order to fulfil what the Lord declared through the
prophet: 'The virgin will conceive and bear a son, and he
shall be called Emmanuel', a name which means 'God
is with us'.

Song of the Virgin Mary

Ant. Emmanuel, our king and lawgiver,
   long-awaited Saviour of the nations:
   Come and save us, O Lord our God.

Or as follows:

Old Testament Song   Is 55:3–5, 10–11

To those who have yielded him their allegiance
he gave the right to become children of God (Jn 1:12).

Ant. My word shall not return to me fruitless, alleluia!

Come to me and listen to my words,
hear me, and you shall have life:
I will make a covenant with you, this time for ever,
to love you faithfully as I loved David.

I made him a witness to all races,
a prince and instructor of peoples,
and you in turn shall summon nations you do not know,
and nations that do not know you shall come running
to you, because the Lord your God,
the Holy One of Israel, has glorified you.

For as the heavens are higher than the earth,
so are my ways higher than your ways
and my thoughts than your thoughts;
and as the rain and snow come down from heaven
and do not return until they have watered the earth,
making it blossom and bear fruit,
and give seed for sowing and bread to eat,
so shall the word which comes from my mouth prevail;

it shall not return to me fruitless
without accomplishing my purpose
or succeeding in the task I gave it.

Ant. My word shall not return to me fruitless, alleluia!

Prayers

Lord, you showed your glory to the world through the
child-bearing of Mary. May we respond to your Word
as she did and be filled with the Holy Spirit.

We pray for all Christians, who in their celebration of the eucharist proclaim the death of the Lord and look forward to his second coming.

We pray for those who have died and for their families; may the peace of Jesus be with them.

We thank you for everything we have received:
for life itself,
for those who love and care for us,
for the world and its beauty,
but always and above all for your Son Jesus
whom you sent to share our life
and so bring your life to us.

Further prayers . . . Our Father . . .

O Wisdom, proceeding from the mouth of the Most High, announced by the prophets, come to teach us the way of salvation. Come, Lord, come to save us.

May the Lord bless us,
may he keep us from all evil
and lead us to life everlasting. Amen.

Christmastide

Lord, open my lips . . .
To you be glory . . .

Sussex Carol

On Christmas night all Christians sing,
To hear the news the angels bring –
News of great joy, news of great mirth,
News of our merciful King's birth.

Then why should men on earth be so sad,
Since our Redeemer made us glad,
When from our sin he set us free,
All for to gain our liberty?

When sin departs before his grace,
Then life and health come in its place;
Angels and men with joy may sing,
All for to see the new-born King.

All out of darkness we have light,
Which made the angels sing this night:
'Glory to God and peace to men,
Now and for evermore. Amen.'

Traditional

The Messianic kingship Ps 2

She gave birth to a male child, who is destined to rule all nations with an iron rod (Rev 12:5).

Ant. You are my Son.
It is I who have begotten you this day.

Why this tumult among nations,
among peoples this useless murmuring?
They arise, the kings of the earth,
princes plot against the Lord and his Anointed.

61

'Come, let us break their fetters,
come, let us cast off their yoke.'

He who sits in the heavens laughs;
the Lord is laughing them to scorn.
Then he will speak in his anger,
his rage will strike them with terror.
'It is I who have set up my king
on Zion, my holy mountain.'

I will announce the decree of the Lord:
The Lord said to me: 'You are my Son.
It is I who have begotten you this day.
Ask and I shall bequeath you the nations,
put the ends of the earth in your possession.
With a rod of iron you will break them,
shatter them like a potter's jar.'

Now, O kings, understand,
take warning, rulers of the earth;
serve the Lord with awe
and trembling, pay him your homage
lest he be angry and you perish;
for suddenly his anger will blaze.
Blessed are they who put their trust in God.

Ant. You are my Son.
It is I who have begotten you this day.

The universal reign of the true God   Ps 95(96)

Today in the city of David a deliverer has been born to you
(Lk 1:11).

Ant. Shepherds, whom have you seen?
Speak, tell us, who has appeared on earth?
We saw a child, and choirs of angels singing the praises of
God, alleluia!

O sing a new song to the Lord,
sing to the Lord all the earth.
O sing to the Lord, bless his name.

Proclaim his help day by day,

tell among the nations his glory
and his wonders among all the peoples.

The Lord is great and worthy of praise,
to be feared above all gods;
the gods of the heathens are naught.

It was the Lord who made the heavens,
his are majesty and state and power
and splendour in his holy place.

Give the Lord, you families of peoples,
give the Lord glory and power,
give the Lord the glory of his name.

Bring an offering and enter his courts,
worship the Lord in his temple.
O earth, tremble before him.

Proclaim to the nations: 'God is king.'
The world he made firm in its place;
he will judge the peoples in fairness.

Let the heavens rejoice and earth be glad,
let the sea and all within it thunder praise,
let the land and all it bears rejoice,
all the trees of the wood shout for joy

at the presence of the Lord for he comes,
he comes to rule the earth.
With justice he will rule the world,
he will judge the peoples with his truth.

Ant. Shepherds, whom have you seen?
Speak, tell us, who has appeared on earth?
We saw a child, and choirs of angels singing the praises of
God, alleluia!

Word of God   Heb 1:1–9
When in former times God spoke to our forefathers,
he spoke in fragmentary and varied fashion through the
prophets. But in this the final age he has spoken to us in the
Son whom he has made heir to the whole universe, and
through whom he created all orders of existence: the Son

63

who is the effulgence of God's splendour and the stamp of God's very being, and sustains the universe by his word of power. When he had brought about the purgation of sins, he took his seat at the right hand of Majesty on high, raised as far above the angels, as the title he has inherited is superior to theirs.

For God never said to any angel, 'Thou art my Son; today I have begotten thee,' or again, 'I will be father to him, and he shall be my son.' Again, when he presents the first-born to the world, he says, 'Let all the angels of God pay him homage.' Of the angels he says,

'He who makes his angels winds,
and his ministers a fiery flame';

but of the Son,

'Thy throne, O God, is for ever and ever,
and the sceptre of justice is the sceptre of his kingdom.
Thou hast loved right and hated wrong;
therefore, God, thy God has set thee above thy fellows,
by anointing with the oil of exultation.'

Song of Zechariah

Ant. I have good news for you:
   there is great joy coming to the whole people.
   Today in the city of David a deliverer has been born to you –
   the Messiah, the Lord.

Or as follows:

Lk 2:14, John 1, passim

Christmas Song

Ant. Glory to God in the highest,
   And on earth peace among men!

In the beginning of the world's creation,
From chaos, God brought all things into being.
In the beginning was the Word with God:
Without him was made nothing that was made.
The Word was God.

Glory to God in the highest,
And on earth peace among men!

The Word is Christ, eternal, uncreated,
Untarnished mirror of God's active power.
For him the earth was made, and all the living,
The boundless universe, the things we see,
And things unseen.

Glory to God in the highest,
And on earth peace among men!

God said: Let there be light, and there was light:
The Word is life, true light of every man
Created in the image of his God.
The Word came down to men and was made flesh,
To dwell with them.

Glory to God in the highest,
And on earth peace among men!

He is the shoot sprung up from Jesse's root,
The Son of God and Mary's virgin womb.
Redeemed by him, we too are sons of God,
Whose glory he has destined us to share
In endless life.

Ant. Glory to God in the highest,
    And on earth peace among men!

Prayers

God our Father, this morning we eagerly greet the birth of
Jesus, our brother and saviour. He is the daystar from on
high, the lightbearer who brings the dawn to us who watch
patiently for his coming.

Father, bless on this holy day the Church all over the
world. May she light afresh in men's hearts the lamps of
hope and peace.

Lord Jesus, you have brought daylight and freedom to our
imprisoned hearts: and you are with us today in the
stranger, the hungry, the unwanted.

Spirit of truth, lighten our dark hearts: kindle our cold
love: that we may echo wholeheartedly the Divine Word's
message, which rings out today through the world.

Further prayers . . . Our Father . . .

All praise to you, Almighty God, heavenly King, who sent your Son into the world, when he took our nature upon him and was born in a stable at Bethlehem. Grant, that as we have been born again in him, so he may evermore live in us, and reign on earth as in heaven with you and the Holy Spirit, God, now and for ever. Amen.

May the Lord bless us,
may he keep us from all evil
and lead us to life everlasting. Amen.

EVENING PRAYER

Lord, open my lips . . .
Glory to the Father . . .

A Child my Choice
Let folly praise that fancy loves, I praise and love that
    Child,
Whose heart no thought, whose tongue no word, whose
    hand no deed defiled.
I praise him most, I love him best, all praise and love is his;
While him I love, in him I live, and cannot live amiss.

Love's sweetest mark, laud's highest theme, man's most
    desired light,
To love him life, to leave him death, to live in him delight.
He mine by gift, I his by debt, thus each to other due,
First friend he was, best friend he is, all times will try him
    true.

Though young, yet wise, though small, yet strong; though
    man, yet God he is;
As wise he knows, as strong he can, as God he loves to bless.
His knowledge rules, his strength defends, his love doth
    cherish all;
His birth our joy, his life our light, his death our end of
    thrall.

Alas! He weeps, he sighs, he pants, yet do his angels sing;
Out of his tears, his sighs and throbs, doth bud a joyful
    spring.

Almighty Babe, whose tender arms can force all foes to fly,
Correct my faults, protect my life, direct me when I die.

Robert Southwell

The Messiah, king, priest and judge   Ps 109(110)

*He is destined to reign until God has put all enemies under
his feet (1 Cor 15:25).*

Ant. A prince from the day of your birth;
from the womb before the daybreak I begot you.

The Lord's revelation to my Master:
'Sit on my right:
I will put your foes beneath your feet.'

The Lord will send from Zion
your sceptre of power:
rule in the midst of all your foes.

A prince from the day of your birth
on the holy mountains;
from the womb before the daybreak I begot you.

The Lord has sworn an oath he will not change.
'You are a priest for ever,
a priest like Melchizedek of old.'

The Master standing at your right hand
will shatter kings in the day of his great wrath.

He shall drink from the stream by the wayside
and therefore he shall lift up his head.

Ant. A prince from the day of your birth;
from the womb before the daybreak I begot you.

Prayer of repentance and trust   Ps 129(130)

He will save his people from their sins (Mt 1:21).

Ant. With the Lord there is mercy and fullness of
redemption.

Out of the depths I cry to you, O Lord.
Lord, hear my voice!
O let your ears be attentive
to the voice of my pleading.

If you, O Lord, should mark our guilt,
Lord, who would survive?
But with you is found forgiveness:
for this we revere you.

My soul is waiting for the Lord,
I count on his word.
My soul is longing for the Lord
more than watchman for daybreak.
Let the watchman count on daybreak
and Israel on the Lord.

Because with the Lord there is mercy
and fullness of redemption,
Israel indeed he will redeem
from all its iniquity.

Ant. With the Lord there is mercy and fullness of
redemption.

Word of God   1 John 1:1–4

It was there from the beginning; we have heard it; we have
seen it with our own eyes; we looked upon it, and felt it
with our own hands; and it is of this we tell. Our theme
is the word of life. This life was made visible; we have
seen it and bear our testimony; we here declare to you the
eternal life which dwelt with the Father and was made
visible to us. What we have seen and heard we declare to
you, so that you and we together may share in a common
life, that life which we share with the Father and his Son
Jesus Christ. And we write this in order that the joy of us all
may be complete.

Song of the Virgin Mary

Ant. Today Christ is born: our Saviour has appeared.
On earth angels, archangels, the just, all sing for joy:
'Glory to God in the highest!'

Or as follows:

68

New Testament Song

Ant. He is the image of the invisible God;
  his is the primacy over all created things.

Give thanks to the Father
who has made you fit to share the heritage of God's people
in the realm of light.

He rescued us from the domain of darkness
and brought us away into the kingdom of his dear Son,
in whom our release is secured and our sins forgiven.

He is the image of the invisible God;
his is the primacy over all created things.
In him everything in heaven and on earth was created,
not only things visible but also the invisible orders
of thrones, sovereignties, authorities, and powers:
the whole universe has been created through him and for
  him.

He exists before everything,
and all things are held together in him.
He is the head of the body, the church.
He is its origin, the first to return from the dead,
to be in all things alone supreme.
For in him the complete being of God came to dwell.

Through him God chose to reconcile the whole universe to
  himself,
making peace through the shedding of his blood upon the
  cross –
to reconcile all things, whether on earth or in heaven,
through him alone.

Ant. He is the image of the invisible God;
  his is the primacy over all created things.

Prayers
Lord God, you are the Father of mankind. Today you have
gathered into one, things earthly and things heavenly
through the gift of your beloved Son, our new-born brother.

69

Help us to live through the dark places of our lives with cheerful hearts: may we comfort others with the comfort of your love.

As we travel on this earthly pilgrimage, may your light shine in our hearts, and may we see the glory of Christ, born in our midst.

May the whole world, transfigured with thankful joy, receive its greatest gift: may we humbly offer back to God what he constantly makes over to us in love.

Further prayers . . . Our Father . . .

Lord, you are with us tonight as our guest, our child, our neighbour. We can be filled with joyful calm. We are never to be alone again: nothing can separate us from your care. We accept anew our lives in your service: for a Child is born to us, a Son is given to us: he rules over all that will befall us, in a peace that has no end. Amen.

May the Lord bless us,
may he keep us from all evil
and lead us to life everlasting. Amen.

Epiphanytide

Lord, open my lips . . .
To you be glory . . .

Royal Presents

The off'rings of the Eastern kings of old
Unto our Lord were incense, myrrh and gold;
Incense because a God; gold as a king;
And myrrh as to a dying man they bring.
Instead of incense (Blessed Lord) if we
Can send a sigh or fervent prayer to thee,
Instead of myrrh if we can but provide
Tears that from penitential eyes do slide,
And though we have no gold; if for our part
We can present thee with a broken heart
Thou wilt accept: and say those Eastern kings
Did not present thee with more precious things.

Nathaniel Wanley

The kingdom of peace　　　　　　　　　Ps 71(72)I
  We have come to pay him homage (Mt 2:2).

Ant. Before him all kings shall fall prostrate.

O God, give your judgment to the king,
to a king's son your justice,
that he may judge your people in justice
and your poor in right judgment.

May the mountains bring forth peace for the people
and the hills, justice.
May he defend the poor of the people
and save the children of the needy
and crush the oppressor.

He shall endure like the sun and the moon
from age to age.

EPIPHANYTIDE MORNING

He shall descend like rain on the meadow,
like raindrops on the earth.

In his days justice shall flourish
and peace till the moon fails.
He shall rule from sea to sea,
from the Great River to earth's bounds.

Before him his enemies shall fall,
his foes lick the dust.
The kings of Tarshish and the sea coasts
shall pay him tribute.

Ps 71(72)II

The kings of Sheba and Seba
shall bring him gifts.
Before him all kings shall fall prostrate,
all nations shall serve him.

For he shall save the poor when they cry
and the needy who are helpless.
He will have pity on the weak
and save the lives of the poor.

From oppression he will rescue their lives,
to him their blood is dear.
Long may he live,
may the gold of Sheba be given him.
They shall pray for him without ceasing
and bless him all the day.

May corn be abundant in the land
to the peaks of the mountains.
May its fruit rustle like Lebanon;
may men flourish in the cities
like grass on the earth.

May his name be blessed for ever
and endure like the sun.
Every tribe shall be blessed in him,
all nations bless his name.

Blessed be the Lord, God of Israel,
who alone works wonders,

ever blessed his glorious name.
Let his glory fill the earth.

Amen! Amen!

Ant. Before him all kings shall fall prostrate.

Word of God   Mt 2:1–11

Jesus was born at Bethlehem in Judaea during the reign of
Herod. After his birth astrologers from the east arrived in
Jerusalem, asking, 'Where is the child who is born to be
king of the Jews? We observed the rising of his star, and we
have come to pay him homage.' King Herod was greatly
perturbed when he heard this; and so was the whole of
Jerusalem. He called a meeting of the chief priests and
lawyers of the Jewish people, and put before them the
question: 'Where is it that the Messiah is to be born?'
'At Bethlehem in Judaea,' they replied; and they referred
him to the prophecy which reads: 'Bethlehem in the land
of Judah, you are far from least in the eyes of the rulers
of Judah; for out of you shall come a leader to be the shepherd of my people Israel.'

Herod next called the astrologers to meet him in private,
and ascertained from them the time when the star had
appeared. He then sent them on to Bethlehem, and said,
'Go and make a careful inquiry for the child. When you have
found him, report to me, so that I may go myself and pay
him homage.'

They set out at the king's bidding, and the star which they
had seen at its rising went ahead of them until it stopped
above the place where the child lay. At the sight of the star
they were overjoyed. Entering the house, they saw the child
with Mary his mother, and bowed to the ground in homage
to him; then they opened their treasures and offered him
gifts: gold, frankincense, and myrrh.

Song of Zechariah

Ant. Entering the house, they saw the child with Mary his
    mother, and bowed to the ground in homage to him.
Or as follows:

73

Old Testament Song   Is 60:1–3, 19–22

The city has no need of sun or moon to shine upon it;
for the glory of God gave it light, and its lamp is the Lamb
(Rev 21:23).

Ant. The Lord shall shine upon you,
and over you shall his glory appear, alleluia!

Arise, Jerusalem,
rise clothed in light; your light has come
and the glory of the Lord shines over you.
For, though darkness covers the earth
and dark night the nations,
the Lord shall shine upon you
and over you shall his glory appear;
and the nations shall march towards your light
and their kings to your sunrise.

The sun shall no longer be your light by day,
nor the moon shine on you when evening falls;
the Lord shall be your everlasting light,
your God shall be your glory.
Never again shall your sun set
nor your moon withdraw her light;
but the Lord shall be your everlasting light
and the days of your mourning shall be ended.

Ant. The Lord shall shine upon you,
and over you shall his glory appear, alleluia!

Prayers

Father, today we celebrate the revelation of Jesus Christ as
your only Son, and we join the Magi in adoring him.

Christ, manifest in the flesh, sanctify us
by the word of God and constant prayer.

Christ, preached among the nations,
open the hearts of men by the power of the Holy Spirit.

Christ, believed in by the world,
revive the faith of all Christians.
Further prayers... Our Father...

Christ our Lord is revealed to the world,
let us adore him, alleluia!

Almighty God, by whose Word and Wisdom the brilliant
constellations declare your glory, and who led the wise men
by the light of a star to your infant Son to worship in him the
glory of the Word made flesh: guide by your truth the
nations of the earth that the whole world may be filled with
your glory, through Jesus Christ our Lord. Amen.

May the Lord bless us,
may he keep us from all evil
and lead us to life everlasting. Amen.

EVENING PRAYER

Lord, open my lips . . .
Glory to the Father . . .

Journey of the Magi

'A cold coming we had of it,
Just the worst time of the year
For a journey, and such a long journey:
The ways deep and the weather sharp,
The very dead of winter.'
And the camels galled, sore-footed, refractory,
Lying down in the melting snow.
There were times we regretted
The summer palaces on slopes, the terraces,
And the silken girls bringing sherbet.
Then the camel men cursing and grumbling
And running away, and wanting their liquor and women,
And the night-fires going out, and the lack of shelters,
And the cities hostile and the towns unfriendly
And the villages dirty and charging high prices:
A hard time we had of it.
At the end we preferred to travel all night,
Sleeping in snatches,
With the voices singing in our ears, saying
That this was all folly.

75

Then at dawn we came down to a temperate valley,
Wet, below the snow line, smelling of vegetation,
With a running stream and a water-mill beating the darkness,
And three trees on the low sky.
And an old white horse galloped away in the meadow.
Then we came to a tavern with vine-leaves over the lintel,
Six hands at an open door dicing for pieces of silver,
And feet kicking the empty wine-skins.
But there was no information, so we continued
And arrived at evening, not a moment too soon
Finding the place; it was (you may say) satisfactory.

All this was a long time ago, I remember,
And I would do it again, but set down
This set down
This: were we led all that way for
Birth or Death? There was a Birth, certainly,
We had evidence and no doubt. I had seen birth and death,
But had thought they were different; this Birth was
Hard and bitter agony for us, like Death, our death.
We returned to our places, these Kingdoms,
But no longer at ease here, in the old dispensation,
With an alien people clutching their gods.
I should be glad of another death.'

T. S. Eliot

The universal reign of the true God　　　　　Ps 95(96)

There is one Lord, Jesus Christ (1 Cor 8:6).
Ant. Give the Lord, you families of peoples,
　　give the Lord glory and power.

O sing a new song to the Lord,
sing to the Lord all the earth.
O sing to the Lord, bless his name.

Proclaim his help day by day,
tell among the nations his glory
and his wonders among all the peoples.

The Lord is great and worthy of praise,
to be feared above all gods;
the gods of the heathens are naught.

It was the Lord who made the heavens,
his are majesty and state and power
and splendour in his holy place.

Give the Lord, you families of peoples,
give the Lord glory and power,
give the Lord the glory of his name.

Bring an offering and enter his courts,
worship the Lord in his temple.
O earth, tremble before him.

Proclaim to the nations: 'God is king.'
The world he made firm in its place;
he will judge the peoples in fairness.

Let the heavens rejoice and earth be glad,
let the sea and all within it thunder praise,
let the land and all it bears rejoice,
all the trees of the wood shout for joy

at the presence of the Lord for he comes,
he comes to rule the earth.
With justice he will rule the world,
he will judge the peoples with his truth.

Ant. Give the Lord, you families of peoples,
give the Lord glory and power.

Earth rejoices in its king

Ps 96(97)

We saw his glory (Jn 1:14).

Ant. The skies proclaim his justice;
all peoples see his glory.

The Lord is king, let earth rejoice,
the many coastlands be glad.
Cloud and darkness are his raiment;
his throne, justice and right.

A fire prepares his path;
it burns up his foes on every side.
His lightnings light up the world,
the earth trembles at the sight.

The mountains melt like wax
before the Lord of all the earth.
The skies proclaim his justice;
all peoples see his glory.

Let those who serve idols be ashamed,
those who boast of their worthless gods.
All you spirits, worship him.

Zion hears and is glad;
the people of Judah rejoice
because of your judgments O Lord.

For you indeed are the Lord
most high above all the earth
exalted far above all spirits.

Light shines forth for the just
and joy for the upright of heart.
Rejoice, you just, in the Lord;
give glory to his holy name.

Ant. The skies proclaim his justice;
all peoples see his glory.

Word of God   Jn 2:1–11

On the third day there was a wedding at Cana-in-Galilee.
The mother of Jesus was there, and Jesus and his disciples
were guests also. The wine gave out, so Jesus's mother said
to him, 'They have no wine left.' He answered, 'Your
concern, mother, is not mine. My hour has not yet come.'
His mother said to the servants, 'Do whatever he tells you.'
There were six stone water-jars standing near, of the kind
used for Jewish rites of purification; each held from twenty
to thirty gallons. Jesus said to the servants, 'Fill the jars with
water,' and they filled them to the brim. 'Now draw some
off,' he ordered, 'and take it to the steward of the feast';
and they did so. The steward tasted the water now turned
into wine, not knowing its source; though the servants who
had drawn the water knew. He hailed the bridegroom and
said, 'Everyone serves the best wine first, and waits until

the guests have drunk freely before serving the poorer sort;
but you have kept the best wine till now.'
This deed at Cana-in-Galilee is the first of the signs by which
Jesus revealed his glory and led his disciples to believe in
him.

Song of the Virgin Mary

Ant. Today the Church is united to Christ, her heavenly
    bridegroom,
  for he has washed away her sins in the Jordan;
  the Magi hasten with their gifts to this royal wedding
  where the guests are gladdened with water made wine,
    alleluia!

Or as follows:

Old Testament Song   Is 60:4–9

They opened their treasures and offered him gifts:
gold, frankincense and myrrh (Mt 2:11).

Ant. Camels in droves shall cover the land, all coming from
    Sheba,
  laden with golden spice and frankincense, alleluia!

Lift up your eyes and look all around:
they flock together, all of them, and come to you;
your sons also shall come from afar,
your daughters walking beside them leading the way.
Then shall you see and shine with joy,
then your heart shall thrill with pride:
the riches of the sea shall be lavished upon you
and you shall possess the wealth of the nations.

Camels in droves shall cover the land,
dromedaries of Midian and Ephah,
all coming from Sheba
laden with golden spice and frankincense,
heralds of the Lord's praise.
All Kedar's flocks shall be gathered for you,
rams of Nebaioth shall serve your need,
acceptable offerings on my altar,
and glory shall be added to glory in my temple.

Who are these that sail along like clouds,
that fly like doves to their dovecotes?
They are vessels assembling from the coasts and islands,
ships from Tarshish leading the convoy;
they bring your sons from afar,
their gold and silver with them,
to the honour of the Lord your God,
the Holy One of Israel;
for he has made you glorious.

Ant. Camels in droves shall cover the land, all coming from
    Sheba,
    laden with golden spice and frankincense, alleluia!

Prayers

Blessed be Christ our Lord who has come to bring light to
those who live in darkness and in the shadow of death.

Christ, who came as God among men,
grant us a share in your divine life.

Christ, adored by both shepherds and wise men,
bring all men to one faith in you.

Christ, who came to bring help to all who suffer,
give your peace to the sick, and to those in trouble of any
    kind.

Further prayers... Our Father...

Christ, the rising sun, show us your light.

Almighty God, by whose Word and Wisdom the brilliant
constellations declare your glory, and who led the wise men
by the light of a star to your infant Son to worship in him
the glory of the Word made flesh: guide by your truth the
nations of the earth that the whole world may be filled with
your glory, through Jesus Christ our Lord. Amen.

May the Lord bless us,
may he keep us from all evil
and lead us to life everlasting. Amen.

Baptism of the Lord
or Third Sunday After Christmas

MORNING PRAYER

Lord, open my lips . . .
To you be glory . . .

Servant of the Lord
When Jesus comes to be baptised,
He leaves the hidden years behind,
The years of safety and of peace,
To bear the sins of all mankind.

The Spirit of the Lord comes down,
Anoints the Christ to suffering,
To preach the word, to free the bound,
And to the mourner, comfort bring.

He will not quench the dying flame,
And what is bruised he will not break,
But heal the wound injustice dealt,
And out of death his triumph make.

Our everlasting Father, praise,
With Christ, his well-beloved Son,
Who with the Spirit reigns serene,
Untroubled Trinity in One.

The Stanbrook Abbey Hymnal

Prayer for guidance   Ps 142(143)

*Then Jesus, armed with the power of the Spirit, returned to
Galilee (Lk 4:14).*

Ant. Let your good spirit guide me,
   for I am your servant, O Lord.

Lord, listen to my prayer:
turn your ear to my appeal.
You are faithful, you are just; give answer.

I remember the days that are past:
I ponder all your works.

I muse on what your hand has wrought
and to you I stretch out my hands.
Like a parched land my soul thirsts for you.

In the morning let me know your love
for I put my trust in you.
Make me know the way I should walk:
to you I lift up my soul.

Rescue me, Lord, from my enemies;
I have fled to you for refuge.
Teach me to do your will
for you, O Lord, are my God.
Let your good spirit guide me
in ways that are level and smooth.

Ant. Let your good spirit guide me,
   for I am your servant, O Lord.

Thanksgiving and plea for help   Ps 39(40)

*It is by the will of God that we have been consecrated
through the offering of the body of Jesus Christ* (Heb 10:10).

Ant. It is meat and drink for me to do the will of him who
   sent me until I have finished his work.

I waited, I waited for the Lord
and he stooped down to me;
he heard my cry.

He drew me from the deadly pit,
from the miry clay.
He set my feet upon a rock
and made my footsteps firm.

He put a new song into my mouth,
praise of our God.
Many shall see and fear
and shall trust in the Lord.

Happy the man who has placed
his trust in the Lord
and has not gone over to the rebels
who follow false gods.

How many, O Lord my God,
are the wonders and designs
that you have worked for us;
you have no equal.
Should I proclaim and speak of them,
they are more than I can tell!

You do not ask for sacrifice and offerings,
but an open ear.
You do not ask for holocaust and victim.
Instead, here am I.

In the scroll of the book it stands written
that I should do your will.
My God, I delight in your law
in the depth of my heart.

Ant. It is meat and drink for me to do the will of him who
sent me until I have finished his work.

Word of God   Mk 1:2–5, 9–12

In the prophet Isaiah it stands written: 'Here is my herald
whom I send on ahead of you, and he will prepare your way.
A voice crying aloud in the wilderness, "Prepare a way for
the Lord; clear a straight path for him."' And so it was that
John the Baptist appeared in the wilderness proclaiming a
baptism in token of repentance, for the forgiveness of sins;
and they flocked to him from the whole Judaean country-
side and the city of Jerusalem, and were baptized by him in
the river Jordan, confessing their sins.

It happened at this time that Jesus came from Nazareth in
Galilee and was baptized in the Jordan by John. At the
moment when he came up out of the water, he saw the
heavens torn open and the Spirit, like a dove, descending
upon him. And a voice spoke from heaven: 'Thou art my
Son, my Beloved; on thee my favour rests.'

Song of Zechariah

Ant. I saw it myself, and I have borne witness:
    This is God's chosen One.

Or as follows:

Old Testament Song Is 11:1–5

Jesus saw the Spirit of God descending like a dove to alight upon him (Mt 3:16).

Ant. The Spirit of the Lord shall rest upon him.

A shoot shall grow from the stock of Jesse,
and a branch shall spring from his roots.
The spirit of the Lord shall rest upon him,
a spirit of wisdom and understanding,
a spirit of counsel and power,
a spirit of knowledge and the fear of the Lord.

He shall not judge by what he sees
nor decide by what he hears;
he shall judge the poor with justice
and defend the humble in the land with equity;
his mouth shall be a rod to strike down the ruthless,
and with a word he shall slay the wicked.
Round his waist he shall wear the belt of justice,
and good faith shall be the girdle round his body.

Ant. The Spirit of the Lord shall rest upon him.

Prayers

Father, when Jesus was baptised in the Jordan, you proclaimed him as your well-beloved Son, and the Holy Spirit came upon him. Come now into our hearts.

Christ, Saviour of the world,
anointed with the Holy Spirit by the Father,
lead all men to see and believe in you.

Lord, your baptism is the beginning of your ministry.
May your Spirit guide and help us
to share in your ministry to men.

Christ, you have filled the world with your light.
May we show that light to all whom we meet today and
every day.

Further prayers . . . Our Father . . .

Almighty God, who proclaimed Jesus to be your beloved
Son when the Holy Spirit came down upon him at his
baptism in the Jordan, grant that we who have been baptised
in his name may rejoice in being your sons and the servants
of all, through Jesus Christ our Lord. Amen.

May the Lord bless us,
may he keep us from all evil
and lead us to life everlasting. Amen.

EVENING PRAYER

Lord, open my lips . . .
Glory to the Father . . .

From Choruses from *The Rock*, *IX*

Son of Man, behold with thine eyes, and hear with thine ears
And set thine heart upon all that I show thee.
Who is this that has said: the House of GOD is a House of
    Sorrow;
We must walk in black and go sadly, with longdrawn faces,
We must go between empty walls, quavering lowly,
    whispering faintly,
Among a few flickering scattered lights?
They would put upon GOD their own sorrow, the grief they
    should feel
For their sins and faults as they go about their daily
    occasions.
Yet they walk in the street proudnecked, like thoroughbreds
    ready for races,
Adorning themselves, and busy in the market, the forum,
And all other secular meetings.
Thinking good of themselves, ready for any festivity,
Doing themselves very well.
Let us mourn in a private chamber, learning the way of
    penitence,
And then let us learn the joyful communion of saints.

85

The soul of Man must quicken to creation.
Out of the formless stone, when the artist unites himself with
 stone,
Spring always new forms of life, from the soul of man that is
 joined to the soul of stone;
Out of the meaningless practical shapes of all that is living or
 lifeless
Joined with the artist's eye, new life, new form, new colour.
Out of the sea of sound the life of music,
Out of the slimy mud of words, out of the sleet and hail of
 verbal imprecisions,
Approximate thoughts and feelings, words that have taken
 the place of thoughts and feelings,
There spring the perfect order of speech, and the beauty of
 incantation.

LORD, shall we not bring these gifts to Your service?
Shall we not bring to Your service all our powers
For life, for dignity, grace and order,
And intellectual pleasures of the senses?
The LORD who created must wish us to create
And employ our creation again in his service
Which is already his service in creating.
For Man is joined spirit and body,
And therefore must serve as spirit and body.
Visible and invisible, two worlds meet in Man;
Visible and invisible must meet in his Temple;
You must not deny the body.

Now you shall see the Temple completed:
After much striving, after many obstacles;
For the work of creation is never without travail;
The formed stone, the visible crucifix,
The dressed altar, the lifting light,
Light
Light
The visible reminder of Invisible Light.

                                        T. S. Eliot

Praise of God's fidelity   Ps 145(146)

God anointed him with the Holy Spirit and with power
(Acts 10:38).

Ant. The Spirit of the Lord has anointed me; he has sent me
to proclaim release for prisoners and recovery of sight
for the blind.

My soul, give praise to the Lord;
I will praise the Lord all my days,
make music to my God while I live.

Put no trust in princes,
in mortal men in whom there is no help.
Take their breath, they return to clay
and their plans that day come to nothing.

He is happy who is helped by Jacob's God,
whose hope is in the Lord his God,
who alone made heaven and earth,
the seas and all they contain.

It is he who keeps faith for ever,
who is just to those who are oppressed.
It is he who gives bread to the hungry,
the Lord, who sets prisoners free,

the Lord who gives sight to the blind,
who raises up those who are bowed down,
the Lord, who protects the stranger
and upholds the widow and orphan.

It is the Lord who loves the just
but thwarts the path of the wicked.
The Lord will reign for ever,
Zion's God, from age to age.

Ant. The Spirit of the Lord has anointed me; he has sent me
to proclaim release for prisoners and recovery of sight
for the blind.

Praise to God the giver of life Ps 146(147)

Jesus went about doing good and healing all who were oppressed by the devil, for God was with him (Acts 10:38).

Ant. He has sent me to let the broken victims go free,
to proclaim the year of the Lord's favour.

Praise the Lord for he is good;
sing to our God for he is loving:
to him our praise is due.

The Lord builds up Jerusalem
and brings back Israel's exiles,
he heals the broken-hearted,
he binds up all their wounds.
He fixes the number of the stars;
he calls each one by its name.

Our Lord is great and almighty;
his wisdom can never be measured.
The Lord raises the lowly;
he humbles the wicked to the dust.
Sing to the Lord, giving thanks;
sing psalms to our God with the harp.

He covers the heavens with clouds;
he prepares the rain for the earth,
making mountains sprout with grass
and with plants to serve man's needs.
He provides the beasts with their food
and young ravens that call upon him.

His delight is not in horses
nor his pleasure in warriors' strength.
The Lord delights in those who revere him,
in those who wait for his love.

Ant. He has sent me to let the broken victims go free,
to proclaim the year of the Lord's favour.

Word of God Jn 3:31–36

He who comes from above is above all others; he who is
from the earth belongs to the earth and uses earthly speech.

He who comes from heaven bears witness to what he has seen and heard, yet no one accepts his witness. To accept his witness is to attest that God speaks the truth; for he whom God sent utters the words of God, so measureless is God's gift of the Spirit. The Father loves the Son and has entrusted him with all authority. He who puts his faith in the Son has hold of eternal life, but he who disobeys the Son shall not see that life; God's wrath rests upon him.

Song of the Virgin Mary

Ant. The bridegroom's friend,
who stands by and listens to him,
is overjoyed at hearing the bridegroom's voice.
This joy, this perfect joy, is now mine.

Or as follows:

Old Testament Song   Is 42:1–8

There is one to come who is mightier than I (Lk 3:16).

Ant. This is my Son, my Beloved, my Chosen One,
on whom my favour rests.

Here is my servant, whom I uphold,
my chosen one in whom I delight,
I have bestowed my spirit upon him,
and he will make justice shine on the nations.

This is my Son, my Beloved, my Chosen One,
on whom my favour rests.

He will not call out or lift his voice high,
or make himself heard in the open street.
He will not break a bruised reed,
or snuff out a smouldering wick.

This is my Son, my Beloved, my Chosen One,
on whom my favour rests.

He will make justice shine on every race,
never faltering, never breaking down,
he will plant justice on earth,
while coasts and islands wait for his teaching.

This is my Son, my Beloved, my Chosen One,
on whom my favour rests.

I, the Lord, have called you with righteous purpose
and taken you by the hand;
I have formed you and appointed you
to be a light to all peoples, a beacon for the nations.

This is my Son, my Beloved, my Chosen One,
on whom my favour rests.

I have appointed you to open eyes that are blind,
to bring captives out of prison,
out of the dungeons where they lie in darkness.
I am the Lord; the Lord is my name.

Ant. This is my Son, my Beloved, my Chosen One,
on whom my favour rests.

Prayers

Father, you sent your Holy Spirit upon your Son at his baptism. Send your Spirit now to us, your sons, so that we may follow the example of Jesus, our brother.

Christ Jesus, you allowed John to baptise you;
show us how we, too, may humbly serve all men.

Through your baptism you made us sons of the Father;
grant that all who seek you may become true sons of God.

Lord, you sanctified all creation through your baptism
and offered salvation to all men.
Make us worthy ministers of your gospel to the world.

Further prayers ... Our Father ...

Most gracious God, through our Saviour Christ you have assured mankind of eternal life, and in our baptism you have made us one with him: grant that, being made free from sin, we may be raised up to new life in him who reigns with you and the Holy Spirit, one God, now and for ever. Amen.

May the Lord bless us,
may he keep us from all evil
and lead us to life everlasting. Amen.

Temporal Season

SUNDAY

MORNING PRAYER

Lord, open my lips, and my mouth shall proclaim your praise.
To you be glory in the Church and in Christ Jesus
from generation to generation evermore.
Amen, alleluia!

From *Murder in the Cathedral*

We praise Thee, O God, for Thy glory displayed in all the
    creatures of the earth,
In the snow, in the rain, in the wind, in the storm; in all of
    Thy creatures, both the hunters and the hunted.
For all things exist only as seen by Thee, only as known by
    Thee, all things exist
Only in Thy light, and Thy glory is declared even in that
    which denies Thee; the darkness declares the glory of light.
Those who deny Thee could not deny, if Thou didst not
    exist; and their denial is never complete, for if it were so,
    they would not exist.
They affirm Thee in living; all things affirm Thee in living;
    the bird in the air, both the hawk and the finch; the beast
    on the earth, both the wolf and the lamb; the worm in the
    soil and the worm in the belly.
Therefore man, whom Thou hast made to be conscious of
    thee, must consciously praise Thee, in thought and in
    word and in deed.
Even with the hand to the broom, the back bent in laying the
    fire, the knee bent in cleaning the hearth, we, the scrubbers
    and sweepers of Canterbury,
The back bent under toil, the knee bent under sin, the hands
    to the face under fear, the head bent under grief,
Even in us the voices of seasons, the snuffle of winter, the

song of spring, the drone of summer, the voices of beasts
and of birds, praise Thee.
We thank Thee for Thy mercies of blood, for Thy
redemption by blood. For the blood of Thy martyrs and
saints
Shall enrich the earth, shall create the holy places.
For wherever a saint has dwelt, wherever a martyr has given
his blood for the blood of Christ,
There is holy ground, and the sanctity shall not depart from
it
Though armies trample over it, though sightseers come with
guide-books looking over it;
From where the western seas gnaw at the coast of Iona,
To the death in the desert, the prayer in forgotten places by
the broken imperial column,
From such ground springs that which forever renews the
earth
Though it is forever denied. Therefore, O God, we thank
Thee
Who hast given such blessing to Canterbury.

T. S. Eliot

Longing for God   Ps 62(63)

*The water that I shall give will be an inner spring
always welling up for eternal life (Jn 4:14).*

Ant. God is spirit, and those who worship him
must worship in spirit and in truth.

O God, you are my God, for you I long;
for you my soul is thirsting.
My body pines for you
like a dry, weary land without water.
So I gaze on you in the sanctuary
to see your strength and your glory.

For your love is better than life,
my lips will speak your praise.
So I will bless you all my life,
in your name I will lift up my hands.

My soul shall be filled as with a banquet,
my mouth shall praise you with joy.

On my bed I remember you.
On you I muse through the night
for you have been my help;
in the shadow of your wings I rejoice.
My soul clings to you;
your right hand holds me fast.

Symphony of praise to God   Ps 150

Praise and honour, glory and might, to him who sits on the throne and to the Lamb for ever and ever (Rev 5:13).

Praise God in his holy place,
praise him in his mighty heavens.
Praise him for his powerful deeds,
praise his surpassing greatness.

O praise him with sound of trumpet,
praise him with lute and harp.
Praise him with timbrel and dance,
praise him with strings and pipes.

O praise him with resounding cymbals,
praise him with clashing of cymbals.
Let everything that lives and that breathes
give praise to the Lord. Alleluia!

Ant. God is spirit, and those who worship him
must worship in spirit and in truth.

Word of God   Eph 3:14–19

I kneel in prayer to the Father, from whom every family in heaven and on earth takes its name, that out of the treasures of his glory he may grant you strength and power through his Spirit in your inner being, that through faith Christ may dwell in your hearts in love. With deep roots and firm foundations, may you be strong to grasp, with all God's people, what is the breadth and length and height and depth of the love of Christ, and to know it, though it is beyond knowledge. So may you attain to fullness of being, the fullness of God himself.

Song of Zechariah

Ant. You are worthy, O Lord our God,
   to receive glory and honour and power,
   because you created all things;
   by your will they were created, and have their being.

Blessed be the Lord, the God of Israel;
he has come to his people and set them free.
He has raised up for us a mighty saviour,
born of the house of his servant David.

Through his holy prophets he promised of old
      that he would save us from our enemies,
      from the hands of all who hate us.
He promised to show mercy to our fathers
and to remember his holy covenant.

This was the oath he swore to our father Abraham:
to set us free from the hand of our enemies,
free to worship him without fear,
holy and righteous in his sight
      all the days of our life.

You, my child, shall be called the prophet of the Most
      High
for you will go before the Lord to prepare his way,
to give his people knowledge of salvation
by forgiving them their sins.

In the tender compassion of our God
the dawn from on high shall break upon us,
to shine on those who dwell in darkness and the
      shadow of death,
and to guide our feet on the road of peace.

Ant. You are worthy, O Lord our God,
   to receive glory and honour and power,
   because you created all things;
   by your will they were created, and have their being.

Or as follows:

Old Testament Song

The Creator, who is blessed for ever (Rom 1:25).

Ant. Let us sing a hymn, let us bless God for ever.

You are blest, Lord God of our fathers.
To you glory and praise for evermore.

Blest your glorious holy name.
To you glory and praise for evermore.

You are blest, in the temple of your glory.
To you glory and praise for evermore.

You are blest who gaze into the depths.
To you glory and praise for evermore.

You are blest in the firmament of heaven.
To you glory and praise for evermore.

You who walk on the wings of the wind,
To you glory and praise for evermore.

May they bless you, the saints and the angels.
To you glory and praise for evermore.

From the heavens, the earth and the sea,
To you glory and praise for evermore.

You are blest, Lord God of our fathers.
To you glory and praise for evermore.

Ant. Let us sing a hymn, let us bless God for ever.

Prayers
Father in heaven, you have given us a mind to know you, a will to serve you, and a heart to love you. Be with us today in all that we do, so that your light may shine out in our lives.

We pray that we may be today what you created us to be, and may praise your name in all that we do.

95

We pray for your Church:
may it be a true light to all nations;
may the Spirit of your Son Jesus
guide the words and actions of all Christians today.

We pray for all who are searching for truth:
bring them your light and your love.

Further prayers... Our Father...

Father, you created all that is;
We praise your name in love and joy.
Blessed be God for ever!

We praise you, Almighty God, for creating all things.
Blessed be God for ever!

We praise you, Almighty God, for creating all things in
time and space, and for making man in your own image:
lead us to recognise your hand in all that you have
created and always to praise you for your wisdom and love;
through Jesus Christ our Lord, who with you and the Holy
Spirit, reigns supreme over all things, now and for ever.
Amen.

May the Lord bless us,
may he keep us from all evil
and lead us to life everlasting. Amen.

EVENING PRAYER

Lord, open my lips, and my mouth shall proclaim your praise.
Glory to the Father, and to the Son, and to the Holy Spirit:
as in the beginning, so now, and for ever. Amen, alleluia!

At a Solemn Music
Blest pair of Sirens, pledges of Heav'n's joy,
Sphere-born harmonious sisters, Voice and Verse,
Wed your divine sounds, and mixed power employ
Dead things with inbreath'd sense able to pierce,
And to our high-rais'd phantasy present,
That undisturbed song of pure concent,
Ay sung before the sapphire-colour'd throne
To him that sits thereon

With saintly shout, and solemn jubilee,
Where the bright seraphim in burning row
Their loud up-lifted angel-trumpets blow,
And the cherubic host in thousand choirs
Touch their immortal harps of golden wires,
With those just spirits that wear victorious palms,
Hymns devout and holy psalms
Singing everlastingly;
That we on earth with undiscording voice
May rightly answer that melodious noise;
As once we did, till disproportion'd sin
Jarr'd against Nature's chime, and with harsh din
Broke the fair music that all creatures made
To their great Lord, whose love their motion sway'd
In perfect diapason, whilst they stood
In first obedience, and their state of good.

John Milton

The Messiah, King, Priest and Judge   Ps 109(110)

*God has made this Jesus, whom you crucified, both Lord
and Messiah* (Acts 2:36).

Ant. If you ask the Father for anything in my name,
he will give it you.

The Lord's revelation to my Master:
'Sit on my right:
I will put your foes beneath your feet.'

The Lord will send from Zion
your sceptre of power:
rule in the midst of all your foes.

A prince from the day of your birth
on the holy mountains;
from the womb before the daybreak I begot you.

The Lord has sworn an oath he will not change.
'You are a priest for ever,
a priest like Melchizedek of old.'

The Master standing at your right hand
will shatter kings in the day of his great wrath.

He shall drink from the stream by the wayside
and therefore he shall lift up his head.

The wonders of the Exodus   Ps 113A(114)

*All of us who have been baptized into Christ Jesus were
baptized into his death* (Rom 6:3).

When Israel came forth from Egypt,
Jacob's sons from an alien people,
Judah became the Lord's temple,
Israel became his kingdom.

The sea fled at the sight:
the Jordan turned back on its course,
the mountains leapt like rams
and the hills like yearling sheep.

Why was it, sea, that you fled,
that you turned back, Jordan, on your course?
Mountains, that you leapt like rams,
hills, like yearling sheep?

Tremble, O earth, before the Lord,
in the presence of the God of Jacob,
who turns the rock into a pool
and flint into a spring of water.

Ant. If you ask the Father for anything in my name,
he will give it you.

Word of God   Eph 1:15–23

Now that I have heard of the faith you have in the Lord
Jesus and of the love you bear towards all God's people,
I never cease to give thanks for you when I mention you
in my prayers. I pray that the God of our Lord Jesus
Christ, the all-glorious Father, may give you the spiritual
powers of wisdom and vision, by which there comes the
knowledge of him. I pray that your inward eyes may be
illumined, so that you may know what is the hope to
which he calls you, what the wealth and glory of the
share he offers you among his people in their heritage, and
how vast the resources of his power open to us who trust

in him. They are measured by his strength and the might
which he exerted in Christ when he raised him from the
dead, when he enthroned him at his right hand in the
heavenly realms, far above all government and authority,
all power and dominion, and any title of sovereignty
that can be named, not only in this age but in the age
to come. He put everything in subjection beneath his feet,
and appointed him as supreme head to the church, which
is his body and as such holds within it the fullness of
him who himself receives the entire fullness of God.

Song of the Virgin Mary

Ant. God has been gracious to you;
　　you shall conceive and bear a son,
　　and you shall give him the name Jesus.

My soul proclaims the greatness of the Lord,
my spirit rejoices in God my Saviour;
for he has looked with favour on his lowly servant,
and from this day all generations will call me blessed.

The Almighty has done great things for me:
holy is his Name.
He has mercy on those who fear him
in every generation.

He has shown the strength of his arm,
he has scattered the proud in their conceit.
He has cast down the mighty from their thrones,
and has lifted up the lowly.
He has filled the hungry with good things,
and has sent the rich away empty.

He has come to the help of his servant Israel
for he has remembered his promise of mercy,
the promise he made to our fathers,
to Abraham and his children for ever.

Ant. God has been gracious to you;
　　you shall conceive and bear a son,
　　and you shall give him the name Jesus.

Or as follows:

New Testament Song Rev 19:2, 5–8

Ant. The Lord is king, let earth rejoice, alleluia!

Alleluia, alleluia!
Victory and glory and power
belong to our God, alleluia!
for true and just are his judgments.
Alleluia, alleluia!

Praise our God,
all you his servants, alleluia!
you that fear him,
both great and small.
Alleluia, alleluia!

The Lord our God,
sovereign over all, alleluia!
has entered on his reign.
Exult and shout for joy and do him homage.
Alleluia, alleluia!

For the wedding day of the Lamb
has come, alleluia!
His bride
has made herself ready.
Alleluia, alleluia!

For her dress
she has been given, alleluia!
fine linen,
clean and shining.
Alleluia, alleluia!

Ant. The Lord is king, let earth rejoice, alleluia!

Prayers

O God of silence and peace, as we stand in your presence,
help us to be still and know that you are God.

We thank you, Father, for showing yourself to us
in the life, death and resurrection of your Son Jesus.

We thank you for all that you have offered us today;
help us to understand your will more fully,
and give us patience and comfort when we fail.

Lord, give us your peace:
the world is tormented by war and hatred, by suffering
    and injustice;
give us the peace that we should give to others,
the peace we should treasure in our hearts,
the peace the world cannot give.

Further prayers . . . Our Father . . .

May the Lord support us all the day long, till the shades
lengthen and the evening comes, and the busy world is
hushed, and the fever of life is over, and our work is done.
Then in his mercy, may he give us a safe lodging and a
holy rest, and peace at the last. Father, we ask this through
Jesus Christ our Lord. Amen.

May the Lord bless us,
may he keep us from all evil
and lead us to life everlasting. Amen.

MONDAY

Morning Prayer

Lord, open my lips, and my mouth shall proclaim your praise.
To you be glory in the Church and in Christ Jesus
from generation to generation evermore.
Amen, alleluia!

St Patrick's Breastplate

I bind unto myself today
The power of God to hold and lead,
His eye to watch, his might to stay,
His ear to hearken to my need.
The wisdom of my God to teach,
His hand to guide, his shield to ward;
The word of God to give me speech,
His heavenly host to be my guard.

Christ be with me, Christ within me,
Christ behind me, Christ before me,
Christ beside me, Christ to win me,

Christ to comfort and restore me,
Christ beneath me, Christ above me,
Christ in quiet, Christ in danger,
Christ in hearts of all that love me,
Christ in mouth of friend or stranger.

I bind unto myself the name,
The strong name of the Trinity;
By invocation of the same,
The Three in One, the One in Three,
Of whom all nature hath creation;
Eternal Father, Spirit, Word,
Praise to the Lord of my salvation;
Salvation is of Christ the Lord. Amen.

Love and longing for God's temple   Ps 83(84)

*I saw no temple in the city, for its temple was the sovereign
Lord God and the Lamb* (Rev 21:22).

Ant. Inquire of the Lord while he is present,
   call upon the Lord when he is close at hand.

How lovely is your dwelling place,
Lord, God of hosts.

My soul is longing and yearning,
is yearning for the courts of the Lord.
My heart and my soul ring out their joy
to God, the living God.

The sparrow herself finds a home
and the swallow a nest for her brood;
she lays her young by your altars,
Lord of hosts, my king and my God,

They are happy, who dwell in your house,
for ever singing your praise.
They are happy, whose strength is in you,
in whose hearts are the roads to Zion.

As they go through the Bitter Valley
they make it a place of springs,

the autumn rain covers it with blessings.
They walk with ever growing strength,
they will see the God of gods in Zion.

O Lord God of hosts, hear my prayer,
give ear, O God of Jacob.
Turn your eyes, O God, our shield,
look on the face of your anointed.

One day within your courts
is better than a thousand elsewhere.
The threshold of the house of God
I prefer to the dwellings of the wicked.

For the Lord God is a rampart, a shield;
he will give us his favour and glory.
The Lord will not refuse any good
to those who walk without blame.

Lord, God of hosts,
happy the man who trusts in you!

The universal reign of the true God   Ps 95(96)

*There before the throne, and the four living creatures
and the elders, they were singing a new song (Rev 14:3).*

O sing a new song to the Lord,
sing to the Lord all the earth.
O sing to the Lord, bless his name.

Proclaim his help day by day,
tell among the nations his glory
and his wonders among all the peoples.

The Lord is great and worthy of praise,
to be feared above all gods;
the gods of the heathens are naught.

It was the Lord who made the heavens,
his are majesty and state and power
and splendour in his holy place.

Give the Lord, you families of peoples,
give the Lord glory and power,
give the Lord the glory of his name.

MONDAY MORNING

Bring an offering and enter his courts,
worship the Lord in his temple.
O earth, tremble before him.

Proclaim to the nations: 'God is king.'
The world he made firm in its place;
he will judge the peoples in fairness.

Let the heavens rejoice and earth be glad,
let the sea and all within it thunder praise,
let the land and all it bears rejoice,
all the trees of the wood shout for joy

at the presence of the Lord for he comes,
he comes to rule the earth.
With justice he will rule the world,
he will judge the peoples with his truth.

Ant. Inquire of the Lord while he is present,
  call upon the Lord when he is close at hand.

Word of God   Eph 6:10–18

Find your strength in the Lord, in his mighty power. Put
on all the armour which God provides, so that you may be
able to stand firm against the devices of the devil. For
our fight is not against human foes, but against cosmic
powers, against the authorities and potentates of this
dark world, against the superhuman forces of evil in the
heavens. Therefore, take up God's armour; then you
will be able to stand your ground when things are at their
worst, to complete every task and still to stand. Stand
firm, I say. Fasten on the belt of truth; for coat of mail
put on integrity; let the shoes on your feet be the gospel
of peace, to give you firm footing; and, with all these,
take up the great shield of faith, with which you will be
able to quench all the flaming arrows of the evil one.
Take salvation for helmet; for sword, take that which
the Spirit gives you – the words that come from God.
Give yourselves wholly to prayer and entreaty; pray on
every occasion in the power of the Spirit.

Song of Zechariah

Ant. Praise to the God of Israel,
    whose promise of life is fulfilled in Christ Jesus!
Or as follows:

New Testament Song   1 Cor 13:4–10, 12–13

Ant. Faith, hope and love last for ever,
    but the greatest of them all is love.

Love is patient;
love is kind and envies no one.
Love is never boastful, nor conceited, nor rude;
never selfish, not quick to take offence.
Love keeps no score of wrongs;
does not gloat over other men's sins,
but delights in the truth.
There is nothing love cannot face;
there is no limit to its faith, its hope, and its endurance.

Love will never come to an end.
Are there prophets?
their work will be over.
Are there tongues of ecstasy?
they will cease.
Is there knowledge?
it will vanish away;
for our knowledge and our prophecy alike are partial,
and the partial vanishes when wholeness comes.

My knowledge now is partial;
then it will be whole, like God's knowledge of me.
In a word, there are three things that last for ever:
faith, hope and love;
but the greatest of them all is love.

Ant. Faith, hope and love last for ever,
    but the greatest of them all is love.

Prayers

Loving Father of all, give us patience today with those
who annoy us, sympathy for those in trouble, and the
love which reflects your loving forgiveness for all men.

Father, help us to listen sincerely to other people
in the Spirit of your love.

You have given us the task of building your creation
into a world of love and justice;
bless the work we do today,
may it give you honour and praise.

Holy Spirit of God present in our hearts today,
inspire us to value even the small things of life,
and to meet the great things with generous courage.

Further prayers . . . Our Father . . .

Praise be to God the Father of our Lord Jesus Christ,
who has given us in Christ every spiritual blessing.

Lord God, may your grace inspire all our actions and
sustain them to the end, so that all our prayer and work
may begin in you, and by you be completed, through
Jesus Christ our Lord. Amen.

May the Lord bless us,
may he keep us from all evil
and bring us to life everlasting. Amen.

EVENING PRAYER

Lord, open my lips, and my mouth shall proclaim your praise.
Glory to the Father, and to the Son, and to the Holy Spirit:
as in the beginning, so now, and for ever. Amen, alleluia!

In No Strange Land

O world invisible, we view thee,
O world intangible, we touch thee,
O world unknowable, we know thee,
Inapprehensible, we clutch thee!

Does the fish soar to find the ocean,
The eagle plunge to find the air –
That we ask of the stars in motion
If they have rumour of thee there?

Not where the wheeling systems darken,
And our benumb'd conceiving soars! —

The drift of pinions, would we hearken,
Beats at our own clay-shuttered doors.

The angels keep their ancient places; –
Turn but a stone, and start a wing!
'Tis ye, 'tis your estrangèd faces,
That miss the many-splendour'd thing.

But (when so sad thou canst not sadder)
Cry – and upon thy so sore loss
Shall shine the traffic of Jacob's ladder
Pitched between Heaven and Charing Cross.

Yea, in the night, my Soul, my daughter,
Cry – clinging heaven by the hems;
And lo, Christ walking on the water,
Not of Gennesareth, but Thames!

Francis Thompson

Cry for help: a pilgrimage song   Ps 122(123)

> *Happy are those servants whom the master finds on
> the alert when he comes . . . He will seat them at table,
> and come and wait on them* (Lk 12:37).

Ant. In everything make your requests known to God
in prayer and petition, with thanksgiving.

To you have I lifted up my eyes,
you who dwell in the heavens:
my eyes, like the eyes of slaves
on the hand of their lords.

Like the eyes of a servant
on the hand of her mistress,
so our eyes are on the Lord our God
till he show us his mercy.

Have mercy on us, Lord, have mercy.
We are filled with contempt.
Indeed all too full is our soul
with the scorn of the rich,
with the proud man's disdain.

Thanksgiving for help in crisis Ps 123(124)

Do not be silenced, for I am with you and no one shall attempt to do you harm (Acts 18:9, 10).

'If the Lord had not been on our side,'
this is Israel's song.
'If the Lord had not been on our side
when men rose against us,
then would they have swallowed us alive
when their anger was kindled.

Then would the waters have engulfed us,
the torrent gone over us;
over our head would have swept
the raging waters.'

Blessed be the Lord who did not give us
a prey to their teeth!
Our life, like a bird, has escaped
from the snare of the fowler.

Indeed the snare has been broken
and we have escaped.
Our help is in the name of the Lord,
who made heaven and earth.

Ant. In everything make your requests known to God
in prayer and petition, with thanksgiving.

Word of God Mt 5:3–10

This is the teaching Jesus gave:
'How blest are those who know their need of God;
the kingdom of Heaven is theirs.
How blest are the sorrowful;
they shall find consolation.
How blest are those of a gentle spirit;
they shall have the earth for their possession.
How blest are those who hunger and thirst to see right
     prevail;

they shall be satisfied.
How blest are those who show mercy;
mercy shall be shown to them.
How blest are those whose hearts are pure;
they shall see God.
How blest are the peacemakers;
God shall call them his sons.
How blest are those who have suffered persecution for the
    cause of right;
the kingdom of Heaven is theirs.'

Song of the Virgin Mary

Ant. Your son will be great;
    he will bear the title 'Son of the Most High'.

Or as follows:

New Testament Song
Eph 1:3–10

Ant. Blessed are those whom Christ has called together
    into his kingdom.

Praise be to the God and Father
of our Lord Jesus Christ,
who has bestowed on us in Christ
every spiritual blessing in the heavenly realms.

In Christ he chose us
before the world was founded,
to be dedicated, to be without blemish in his sight,
to be full of love.

He destined us – such was his will and pleasure –
to be accepted as his sons through Jesus Christ,
in order that the glory of his gracious gift,
so graciously bestowed on us in his Beloved,
might redound to his praise.

For in Christ our release is secured
and our sins are forgiven
through the shedding of his blood.
Therein lies the richness of God's grace lavished upon us,
imparting full wisdom and insight.

He has made known to us his hidden purpose
to be put into effect when the time was ripe:
that the universe, all in heaven and on earth,
might be brought into a unity in Christ.

Ant. Blessed are those whom Christ has called together
into his kingdom.

Prayers

Father, may we stand before you with quiet hearts, to
worship you in Spirit and in Truth.

Father, your Son shared his life with men,
he shared with them his joy and his sorrow;
help all who are lonely or dying
to know that Jesus shares his life with them now.

We thank you, Lord God, for the care and the love
you have shown us today;
forgive us each time we fail to care for and love those
around us.

Lord Jesus, even in your suffering you showed us how
to love;
give us strength to bear our troubles
with loving confidence in the Father.

Further prayers . . . Our Father . . .

Stay with us Lord Jesus, for it is nearly evening. Be our
companion on the road, enkindle our hearts and stir up
our hope, so that in the Scripture and in the breaking of
bread we and all our fellow men may learn to know you,
the everlasting King. Amen.

May the Lord bless us,
may he keep us from all evil
and lead us to life everlasting. Amen.

TUESDAY

Lord, open my lips, and my mouth shall proclaim your praise.
To you be glory in the Church and in Christ Jesus
from generation to generation evermore.
Amen, alleluia!

Pied Beauty

Glory be to God for dappled things –
    For skies of couple-colour as a brinded cow;
       For rose-moles all in stipple upon trout that swim;
Fresh-firecoal chestnut-falls; finches' wings;
    Landscape plotted and pieced – fold, fallow, and plough;
      And áll trádes, their gear and tackle and trim.

All things counter, original, spare, strange;
    Whatever is fickle, freckled (who knows how?)
      With swift, slow; sweet, sour; adazzle, dim;
He fathers-forth whose beauty is past change:
                Praise him.
                    Gerard Manley Hopkins

Man the viceroy of God   Ps 8

*He put everything in subjection beneath Christ's feet, and
appointed him as supreme head to the Church (Eph 1:22).*

Ant. Sing thankfully in your hearts to God,
    with psalms and hymns and spiritual songs.

How great is your name, O Lord our God,
through all the earth!

Your majesty is praised above the heavens;
on the lips of children and of babes
you have found praise to foil your enemy,
to silence the foe and the rebel.

When I see the heavens, the work of your hands,
the moon and the stars which you arranged,
what is man that you should keep him in mind,
mortal man that you care for him?

Yet you have made him little less than a god;
with glory and honour you crowned him,
gave him power over the works of your hand,
put all things under his feet.

All of them, sheep and cattle,
yes, even the savage beasts,
birds of the air, and fish
that make their way through the waters.

How great is your name, O Lord our God,
through all the earth!

Harvest Song   Ps 66(67)

*You who once were far off have been brought near through
the shedding of Christ's blood* (Eph 2:13).

O God, be gracious and bless us
and let your face shed its light upon us.
So will your ways be known upon earth
and all nations learn your saving help.

Let the peoples praise you, O God;
let all the peoples praise you.

Let the nations be glad and exult
for you rule the world with justice.
With fairness you rule the peoples,
you guide the nations on earth.

Let the peoples praise you, O God;
let all the peoples praise you.

The earth has yielded its fruit
for God, our God, has blessed us:
May God still give us his blessing
till the ends of the earth revere him.

Let the peoples praise you, O God;
let all the peoples praise you.

Ant. Sing thankfully in your hearts to God,
   with psalms and hymns and spiritual songs.

Word of God
1 Jn. 5:1–5

Everyone who believes that Jesus is the Christ is a child of
God, and to love the parent means to love his child; it follows
that when we love God and obey his commands we love his
children too. For to love God is to keep his commands; and
they are not burdensome, because every child of God is victor
over the godless world. The victory that defeats the world is
our faith, for who is victor over the world but he who
believes that Jesus is the Son of God?

Song of Zechariah

Ant. Blessed be the God of Israel!
   He has raised up for us a mighty saviour
   from the house of his servant David.

Or as follows:

New Testament Song
Mt 11:25–30

Ant. Learn from me, for I am gentle and humble-hearted.

I thank thee, Father, Lord of heaven and earth,
for hiding these things from the learned and wise,
and revealing them to the simple.
Yes, Father, such was thy choice.

Everything is entrusted to me by my Father;
and no one knows the Son but the Father,
and no one knows the Father but the Son
and those to whom the Son may choose to reveal him.

Come to me, all whose work is hard, whose load is heavy,
and I will give you relief.
Bend your necks to my yoke, and learn from me,
for I am gentle and humble-hearted,
and your souls will find relief.
For my yoke is good to bear, my load is light.

Ant. Learn from me, for I am gentle and humble-hearted.

113

Prayers

God our Father, we pray that in your generosity you may
support those who ask for your help: may all who proclaim
you as their Father share the benefits of your new creation.

Father, you never withdraw your love from your sons
and daughters:
may we never fail to love our brothers and sisters in
Christ.

We pray for our family and friends:
keep them safe today
and bring them joy and satisfaction in all they do.

We pray to you, Jesus Christ, as our brother:
as you were part of a family and obedient to your
parents,
so may we find in our family ties the roots of that love
which we are called to show to all men.

Further prayers . . . Our Father . .

Praise God in the heavens, praise him on earth.
Praise God all his children, give praise to God, give
praise.

Heavenly Father, whose Son knew the mutual care and
trust of an earthly home, watch over the homes of your
people and grant that families may be able to hold together in love and godly discipline; through Jesus Christ
our Lord. Amen.

May the Lord bless us,
may he keep us from all evil
and lead us to life everlasting. Amen.

EVENING PRAYER

Lord, open my lips, and my mouth shall proclaim your praise.
Glory to the Father, and to the Son, and to the Holy Spirit:
as in the beginning, so now, and for ever. Amen, alleluia!

From Choruses from *The Rock*, X

O Light Invisible, we praise Thee!
Too bright for mortal vision.
O Greater Light, we praise Thee for the less;
The eastern light our spires touch at morning,
The light that slants upon our western doors at evening,
The twilight over stagnant pools at batflight,
Moon light and star light, owl and moth light,
Glow-worm glowlight on a grassblade.
O Light Invisible, we worship Thee!

We thank Thee for the lights that we have kindled,
The light of altar and of sanctuary;
Small lights of those who meditate at midnight
And lights directed through the coloured panes of windows
And light reflected from the polished stone,
The gilded carven wood, the coloured fresco.
Our gaze is submarine, our eyes look upward
And see the light that fractures through unquiet water.
We see the light but see not whence it comes
O Light Invisible, we glorify Thee!

T. S. Eliot

Prayer for protection and forgiveness   Ps 24(25)I

*You, because you put your faith in God, are under the
protection of his power until salvation comes (1 Pt 1:5).*

Ant. Through Jesus, let us continually offer up to God
the sacrifice of praise, the tribute of lips
which acknowledge his name.

To you, O Lord, I lift up my soul.
I trust you, let me not be disappointed;
do not let my enemies triumph.
Those who hope in you shall not be disappointed,
but only those who wantonly break faith.

Lord, make me know your ways.
Lord, teach me your paths.
Make me walk in your truth, and teach me:
for you are God my saviour.

115

In you I hope all the day long
because of your goodness, O Lord.
Remember your mercy, Lord,
and the love you have shown from of old.
Do not remember the sins of my youth.
In your love remember me.

The Lord is good and upright.
He shows the path to those who stray,
He guides the humble in the right path;
he teaches his way to the poor.

His ways are faithfulness and love
for those who keep his covenant and will.
Lord, for the sake of your name
forgive my guilt, for it is great.

Ps 24(25)II

If anyone fears the Lord
he will show him the path he should choose.
His soul shall live in happiness
and his children shall possess the land.
The Lord's friendship is for those who revere him;
to them he reveals his covenant.

My eyes are always on the Lord;
for he rescues my feet from the snare.
Turn to me and have mercy
for I am lonely and poor.

Relieve the anguish of my heart
and set me free from my distress
See my affliction and my toil
and take all my sins away.

See how many are my foes;
how violent their hatred for me.
Preserve my life and rescue me.
Do not disappoint me, you are my refuge.
May innocence and uprightness protect me:
for my hope is in you, O Lord.

Redeem Israel, O God, from all its distress.

Ant. Through Jesus, let us continually offer up to God
the sacrifice of praise, the tribute of lips
which acknowledge his name.

Word of God   Mt 5:43–48

This is the teaching Jesus gave:
'You have learned that they were told, "Love your neighbour, hate your enemy." But what I tell you is this: Love
your enemies and pray for your persecutors; only so can you
be children of your heavenly Father, who makes his sun rise
on good and bad alike, and sends the rain on the honest and
the dishonest. If you love only those who love you, what
reward can you expect? Surely the tax-gatherers do as much
as that. And if you greet only your brothers. what is there
extraordinary about that? Even the heathen do as much.
There must be no limit to your goodness, as your heavenly
Father's goodness knows no bounds.'

Song of the Virgin Mary

Ant. The Lord God will give your son
the throne of his ancestor David.

Or as follows:

New Testament Song   Rev 4:11;5:9, 10, 12

Ant. To the Lamb be honour and glory and praise!

Thou art worthy, O Lord our God,
to receive glory and honour and power,
because thou didst create all things;
by thy will they were created, and have their being.
Thou art worthy to take the scroll and to break its seals,
for thou wast slain and by thy blood purchased for God
men of every tribe and language, people and nation;
thou hast made of them a royal house,
to serve our God as priests;
and they shall reign upon earth.
Worthy is the Lamb,
the Lamb that was slain,

117

to receive all power and wealth, wisdom and might,
honour and glory and praise!

Ant. To the Lamb be honour and glory and praise!

Prayers

Look kindly on your people, Lord, and free them from all
troubles, so that they may serve you with a generous heart
and always stand firm in your love.

> We pray to you, Father, for all who have died:
> (especially N. and N.)
> They tried to live a good life here with us;
> bring them now into the fullness of life with you.

> Father, your Son noticed the suffering of one woman
> in the midst of a crowd;
> teach us to be attentive
> and to respond to the needs of others.

> Thank you, Father.
> Thank you for our homes and our families;
> thank you for our work and our relaxation.
> May we always enjoy good things with thankfulness.

Further prayers . . . Our Father . . .

Lord God, both night and day belong to you. May the light
of your presence always shine in our hearts, and may we live
in that light for ever. Amen.

May the Lord bless us,
may he keep us from all evil
and lead us to life everlasting. Amen.

WEDNESDAY

MORNING PRAYER

Lord, open my lips, and my mouth shall proclaim your praise.
To you be glory in the Church and in Christ Jesus
from generation to generation evermore.
Amen, alleluia!

The Salutation

These little Limmes,
These Eys and Hands which here I find,
These rosie Cheeks wherwith my Life begins,
Where have ye been ? Behind
What Curtain were ye from me hid so long !
Where was ? in what Abyss, my Speaking Tongue ?

When silent I,
So many thousand thousand yeers,
Beneath the Dust did in a Chaos lie,
How could I Smiles or Tears,
Or Lips or Hands or Eys or Ears perceiv ?
Welcom ye Treasures which I now receiv.

I that so long
Was Nothing from Eternitie,
Did little think such Joys as Ear or Tongue,
To Celebrat or See:
Such Sounds to hear, such Hands to feel, such Feet,
Beneath the Skies, on such a Ground to meet.

New Burnisht Joys !
Which yellow Gold and Pearl excell !
Such Sacred Treasures are the Lims in Boys,
In which a Soul doth Dwell;
Their Organized Joynts, and Azure Veins
More Wealth include, then all the World contains.

From Dust I rise,
And out of Nothing now awake,
These Brighter Regions which salute mine Eys,
A Gift from GOD I take.
The Earth, the Seas, the Light, the Day, the Skies,
The Sun and Stars are mine; if those I prize.

Long time before
I in my Mother's Womb was born,
A GOD preparing did this Glorious Store,
The World for me adorne.
Into this Eden so Divine and fair,

119

So Wide and Bright, I com his Son and Heir.

A Stranger here
Strange Things doth meet, Strange Glories See;
Strange Treasures lodg'd in this fair World appear,
Strange all, and New to me.
But that they mine should be, who nothing was,
That Strangest is of all, yet brought to pass.

Thomas Traherne

God, the source of true happiness   Ps 15(16)

If I go and prepare a place for you, I shall come again and receive you to myself, so that where I am you may be also (Jn 14:3).

Ant. To the only God our Saviour
be glory and majesty, might and authority,
through Jesus Christ our Lord!

Preserve me, God, I take refuge in you.
I say to the Lord: 'You are my God.
My happiness lies in you alone.'

He has put into my heart a marvellous love
for the faithful ones who dwell in his land.
Those who choose other gods increase their sorrows.
Never will I offer their offerings of blood.
Never will I take their name upon my lips.

O Lord, it is you who are my portion and cup;
it is you yourself who are my prize.
The lot marked out for me is my delight:
welcome indeed the heritage that falls to me!

I will bless the Lord who gives me counsel,
who even at night directs my heart.
I keep the Lord ever in my sight:
since he is at my right hand, I shall stand firm.

And so my heart rejoices, my soul is glad;
even my body shall rest in safety.
For you will not leave my soul among the dead,
nor let your beloved know decay.

You will show me the path of life,
the fullness of joy in your presence,
at your right hand happiness for ever.

Praise of God's deity   Ps 145(146)

*Go out quickly into the streets and alleys . . . and bring me
in the poor, the crippled, the blind, and the lame* (Lk 14:21).

My soul, give praise to the Lord;
I will praise the Lord all my days,
make music to my God while I live.

Put no trust in princes,
in mortal men in whom there is no help.
Take their breath, they return to clay
and their plans that day come to nothing.

He is happy who is helped by Jacob's God,
whose hope is in the Lord his God,
who alone made heaven and earth,
the seas and all they contain.

It is he who keeps faith for ever,
who is just to those who are oppressed.
It is he who gives bread to the hungry,
the Lord, who sets prisoners free,

the Lord who gives sight to the blind,
who raises up those who are bowed down,
the Lord, who protects the stranger
and upholds the widow and orphan.

It is the Lord who loves the just
but thwarts the path of the wicked.
The Lord will reign for ever,
Zion's God, from age to age.

Ant. To the only God our Saviour
be glory and majesty, might and authority,
through Jesus Christ our Lord!

Word of God   Rom 12:1-8
I implore you by God's mercy to offer your very selves to
him: a living sacrifice, dedicated and fit for his acceptance,

the worship offered by mind and heart. Adapt yourselves
no longer to the pattern of this present world, but let your
minds be remade and your whole nature thus transformed.
Then you will be able to discern the will of God, and to know
what is good, acceptable, and perfect.

In virtue of the gift that God in his grace has given me I say
to everyone among you: do not be conceited or think too
highly of yourself; but think your way to a sober estimate
based on the measure of faith that God has dealt to each
of you. For just as in a single human body there are many
limbs and organs, all with different functions, so all of us,
united with Christ, form one body, serving individually as
limbs and organs to one another.

The gifts we possess differ as they are allotted to us by God's
grace, and must be exercised accordingly: the gift of inspired
utterance, for example, in proportion to a man's faith;
or the gift of administration, in administration. A teacher
should employ his gift in teaching, and one who has the
gift of stirring speech should use it to stir his hearers. If you
give to charity, give with all your heart; if you are a leader,
exert yourself to lead; if you are helping others in distress,
do it cheerfully.

Song of Zechariah

Ant. He swore to our father Abraham
    to set us free from the hand of our enemies,
    free to worship him without fear.

Or as follows:

New Testament Song   Jn 3:29–36

Ant. He whom God has sent utters the words of God.

It is the bridegroom to whom the bride belongs.
The bridegroom's friend, who stands by and listens to him,
is overjoyed at hearing the bridegroom's voice.

He who comes from above is above all others;
he who is from the earth belongs to the earth
and uses earthly speech.

He who comes from heaven bears witness to what he has
    seen and heard,
yet no one accepts his witness.
To accept his witness is to attest that God speaks the truth;
for he whom God sent utters the words of God,
so measureless is God's gift of the Spirit.

The Father loves the Son
and has entrusted him with all authority;
he who puts his faith in the Son
has hold of eternal life.

Ant. He whom God has sent utters the words of God.

Prayers

Father, we ask you to pour your grace into our hearts, to
overcome our selfishness and make us your true children.

> Lord, listen kindly to our prayer
> when we ask for ourselves
> things we have not been generous enough to give to others.

> We pray to you today, Father, to keep us in peace with
>   other people;
> teach us not to presume on our own strength,
> but instead, to be assured, in our weakness, of the power
>   of your gifts.

> We pray that you will be with those who live alone.
> Bring them warmth and companionship.

Further prayers... Our Father...

May the peace of God which passes all understanding
keep our hearts and our minds
in the knowledge and love of God and of his Son Jesus
    Christ.

God our Saviour, hear our prayer: help us to walk in light
and work for truth, so that we who have been born from you
as children of light may bear witness to you before men.
We ask this through Christ our Lord. Amen.

May the Lord bless us,
may he keep us from all evil
and lead us to life everlasting. Amen.

EVENING PRAYER

Lord, open my lips, and my mouth shall proclaim your praise.
Glory to the Father, and to the Son, and to the Holy Spirit:
as in the beginning, so now, and for ever. Amen, alleluia!

You, neighbour God, if sometimes in the night
I rouse you with loud knocking, I do so
only because I seldom hear you breathe;
I know: you are alone.
And should you need a drink, no one is there
to reach it to you, groping in the dark.
Always I hearken. Give but a small sign.
I am quite near.

Between us there is but a narrow wall,
and by sheer chance; for it would take
merely a call from your lips or from mine
to break it down,
and that without a sound.

The wall is builded of your images.

They stand before you hiding you like names,
And when the light within me blazes high
that in my inmost soul I know you by,
the radiance is squandered on their frames.

And then my senses, which too soon grow lame,
exiled from you, must go their homeless ways.

Rainer Maria Rilke

Triumphant trust in God　　　　　　　　　Ps 26(27)I
  *If God is on our side, who is against us? What can separate
  us from the love of Christ?* (Rom 8:31, 35)

Ant. Continue to pray in the power of the Holy Spirit,
  and keep yourselves in the love of God.

The Lord is my light and my help;
whom shall I fear?
The Lord is the stronghold of my life;
before whom shall I shrink?

Though an army encamp against me
my heart would not fear.
Though war break out against me
even then would I trust.

There is one thing I ask of the Lord,
for this I long,
to live in the house of the Lord,
all the days of my life,
to savour the sweetness of the Lord,
to behold his temple.

For there he keeps me safe in his tent
in the day of evil.
He hides me in the shelter of his tent,
on a rock he sets me safe.

And now my head shall be raised
above my foes who surround me
and I shall offer within his tent
a sacrifice of joy.

I will sing and make music for the Lord.

Ps 26(27)II

O Lord, hear my voice when I call;
have mercy and answer.
Of you my heart has spoken:
'Seek his face.'

It is your face, O Lord, that I seek;
hide not your face.
Dismiss not your servant in anger;
you have been my help.

Do not abandon or forsake me,
O God my help!
Though father and mother forsake me,
the Lord will receive me.

Instruct me, Lord, in your way;
on an even path lead me.
When they lie in ambush protect me
from my enemy's greed.

False witnesses rise against me,
breathing out fury.
I am sure I shall see the Lord's goodness
in the land of the living.
Hope in him, hold firm and take heart.
Hope in the Lord!

Ant. Continue to pray in the power of the Holy Spirit,
and keep yourselves in the love of God.

Word of God
1 Cor 1:18–25

The doctrine of the cross is sheer folly to those on their way
to ruin, but to us who are on the way to salvation it is the
power of God. Scripture says, 'I will destroy the wisdom
of the wise, and bring to nothing the cleverness of the clever.'
Where is your wise man now, your man of learning, or your
subtle debater – limited, all of them, to this passing age?
God has made the wisdom of this world look foolish.
As God in his wisdom ordained, the world failed to find him
by its wisdom, and he chose to save those who have faith
by the folly of the Gospel. Jews call for miracles, Greeks
look for wisdom; but we proclaim Christ – yes, Christ
nailed to the cross; and though this is a stumbling-block
to Jews and folly to Greeks, yet to those who have heard
his call, Jews and Greeks alike, he is the power of God and
the wisdom of God.
Divine folly is wiser than the wisdom of man, and divine
weakness stronger than man's strength.

Song of the Virgin Mary
Ant You shall conceive and bear a son,
who will be king over Israel for ever;
his reign shall never end.

Or as follows:

New Testament Song
Col 1:12–20

Ant Glory to you, Lord, the first to return from the dead!

Give thanks to the Father
who has made you fit to share the heritage of God's people
in the realm of light.

He rescued us from the domain of darkness
and brought us away into the kingdom of his dear Son,
in whom our release is secured and our sins forgiven.

He is the image of the invisible God;
his is the primacy over all created things.
In him everything in heaven and on earth was created,
not only things visible but also the invisible orders
of thrones, sovereignties, authorities, and powers:
the whole universe has been created through him and for
   him.

He exists before everything,
and all things are held together in him.
He is the head of the body, the church.
He is its origin, the first to return from the dead,
to be in all things alone supreme.
For in him the complete being of God came to dwell.

Through him God chose to reconcile the whole universe to
   himself,
making peace through the shedding of his blood upon the
   cross –
to reconcile all things, whether on earth or in heaven,
through him alone.

Ant. Glory to you, Lord, the first to return from the dead!

Prayers

God our Father, grant that as we reject all that offends you,
we may be filled with the joy of doing your will.

   We thank you, Lord, for the joy of human friendship and
      love,
   for the people on whom we depend,
   for peace with you and with each other.

   We pray for all who are homeless today:
   for families searching for a place to live,
   and for refugees driven from their homeland.

   We thank you, Father, for all the good things we enjoy;
   teach us to be grateful and to use them well.

Further prayers . . . Our Father . . .

127

Lord, no eye has seen, no ear has heard, no heart has conceived the things you have prepared for those who love you. Set us ablaze with the fire of the Holy Spirit, that we may love you in and above all things and so receive the rewards you have promised us through Christ our Lord. Amen.

May the Lord bless us,
may he keep us from all evil
rewards you have promised us, through Christ our Lord. Amen.

THURSDAY

Morning Prayer

Lord, open my lips, and my mouth shall proclaim your praise.
To you be glory in the Church and in Christ Jesus,
from generation to generation evermore.
Amen, alleluia!

Who was ever so wake
as this wakening day?
Not just brooklet and brake,
but the roof, too, is gay,

with its tiles that outstand
in the blue of the sky,
as alive as a land
and as full of reply.

Breathing thanks are conveyed.
All nocturnal affliction
had vanished with night,

whose darkness was made
– O pure contradiction! –
from legions of light.   Rainer Maria Rilke

Prayer in desolation   Ps 142(143)

If the Spirit is the source of our life, let the Spirit also direct our course (Gal 5:25).

Ant. Is anyone among you in trouble? He should turn to prayer. Is anyone in good heart? He should sing praises.

Lord, listen to my prayer:
turn your ear to my appeal.
You are faithful, you are just; give answer.
Do not call your servant to judgment
for no one is just in your sight.

The enemy pursues my soul;
he has crushed my life to the ground;
he has made me dwell in darkness
like the dead, long forgotten.
Therefore my spirit fails;
my heart is numb within me.

I remember the days that are past:
I ponder all your works.
I muse on what your hand has wrought
and to you I stretch out my hands.
Like a parched land my soul thirsts for you.

Lord, make haste and give me answer;
for my spirit fails within me.
Do not hide your face
lest I become like those in the grave.

In the morning let me know your love
for I put my trust in you.
Make me know the way I should walk:
to you I lift up my soul.

Rescue me, Lord, from my enemies;
I have fled to you for refuge.
Teach me to do your will
for you, O Lord, are my God.
Let your good spirit guide me
in ways that are level and smooth.

For your name's sake, Lord, save my life;
in your justice save my soul from distress.

Praise to God the giver of life

Ps 146(147)

In Christ Jesus you are being built with all the rest into a spiritual dwelling for God (Eph 2:22).

Praise the Lord for he is good;
sing to our God for he is loving:
to him our praise is due.

The Lord builds up Jerusalem
and brings back Israel's exiles,
he heals the broken-hearted,
he binds up all their wounds.
He fixes the number of the stars;
he calls each one by its name.

Our Lord is great and almighty;
his wisdom can never be measured.
The Lord raises the lowly;
he humbles the wicked to the dust.
Sing to the Lord, giving thanks;
sing psalms to our God with the harp.

He covers the heavens with clouds;
he prepares the rain for the earth,
making mountains sprout with grass
and with plants to serve man's needs.
He provides the beasts with their food
and young ravens that call upon him.

His delight is not in horses
nor his pleasure in warriors' strength.
The Lord delights in those who revere him,
in those who wait for his love.

Ant. Is anyone among you in trouble? He should turn to
prayer. Is anyone in good heart? He should sing praises.

Word of God

Heb 12:1-4, 12-14

We must run with resolution the race for which we are
entered, our eyes fixed on Jesus, on whom faith depends
from start to finish: Jesus who, for the sake of the joy that

lay ahead of him, endured the cross, making light of its disgrace, and has taken his seat at the right hand of the throne of God.

Think of him who submitted to such opposition from sinners: that will help you not to lose heart and grow faint. In your struggle against sin, you have not yet resisted to the point of shedding you blood. Come, then, stiffen your drooping arms and shaking knees, and keep your steps from wavering. Then the disabled limb will not be put out of joint, but regain its former powers. Aim at peace with all men, and a holy life, for without that no one will see the Lord.

Song of Zechariah

Ant. You will go before the Lord to prepare his way, and to give his people knowledge of salvation.

Or as follows:

New Testament Song   1 Tim 3:16; 4:10; 1:17

Ant. In Christ Jesus our Lord we have access to God, alleluia!

Christ Jesus was manifested in the body,
vindicated in the Spirit,
seen by angels, alleluia!

Proclaimed among the nations,
believed in throughout the world,
he is glorified in heaven, alleluia!

We have set our hope on him, the living God,
the Saviour of all men, alleluia!
the Saviour, above all, of believers.

To the king of all worlds,
immortal, invisible, the only true God,
be honour and glory for ever and ever! Amen.

Ant. In Christ Jesus our Lord we have access to God, alleluia!

Prayers

Father, you have promised to be always with your people. Guard us today, so that through our work and recreation we may always be close to you.

Lord, we offer you today everything we do and everything we say,

everything we give and everything we receive.

Help us never to forget those whom you keep under your special care –

the poor, the sick, the oppressed.

We pray for the life of the world:
that every nation may seek the way that leads to peace;
that human rights and freedom may everywhere be respected,
and that the world's resources may be ungrudgingly shared.

Further prayers . . . Our Father . . .

To the God of all grace,
who has called us into his eternal glory in Christ,
belong glory and power for ever and ever!

Eternal Father, your Son gave himself up to death out of love for the world; grant us the grace to spend our lives in the same spirit of love. We ask this through Christ our Lord. Amen.

May the Lord bless us,
may he keep us from all evil
and lead us to life everlasting. Amen.

Evening Prayer

Lord, open my lips, and my mouth shall proclaim your praise.
Glory to the Father, and to the Son, and to the Holy Spirit:
as it was in the beginning, so now, and for ever. Amen, alleluia!

Sailing to Byzantium

That is no country for old men. The young
In one another's arms, birds in the trees
– Those dying generations – at their song,
The salmon-falls, the mackerel–crowded seas,
Fish, flesh, or fowl, commend all summer long
Whatever is begotten, born, and dies.
Caught in that sensual music all neglect
Monuments of unageing intellect.

An aged man is but a paltry thing,
A tattered coat upon a stick, unless
Soul clap its hands and sing, and louder sing
For every tatter in its mortal dress,
Nor is there singing school but studying
Monuments of its own magnificence;
And therefore I have sailed the seas and come
To the holy city of Byzantium.

O sages standing in God's holy fire
As in the gold mosaic of a wall,
Come from the holy fire, perne in a gyre,
And be the singing-masters of my soul.
Consume my heart away; sick with desire
And fastened to a dying animal
It knows not what it is; and gather me
Into the artifice of eternity.

Once out of nature I shall never take
My bodily form from any natural thing,
But such a form as Grecian goldsmiths make
Of hammered gold and gold enamelling
To keep a drowsy Emperor awake;
Or set upon a golden bough to sing
To lords and ladies from Byzantium
Of what is past, or passing, or to come.

W. B. Yeats

Prayer for the king Ps 60(61)

He rescued us from the domain of darkness and brought us away into the kingdom of his dear Son (Col 1:13).

Ant. Persevere in prayer, with mind awake and thankful heart.

O God, hear my cry!
Listen to my prayer!
From the end of the earth I call:
my heart is faint.

On the rock too high for me to reach
set me on high,
O you who have been my refuge,
my tower against the foe.

Let me dwell in your tent for ever
and hide in the shelter of your wings.
For you, O God, hear my prayer
and grant me the heritage of those who fear you.

May you lengthen the life of the king:
may his years cover many generations.
May he ever sit enthroned before God:
bid love and truth be his protection.

So I will always praise your name
and day after day fulfil my vows.

God rescues his people from their foes Ps 124(125)

Peace and mercy upon the whole Israel of God (Gal 6:16).

Those who put their trust in the Lord
are like Mount Zion, that cannot be shaken,
that stands for ever.

Jerusalem! The mountains surround her,
so the Lord surrounds his people
both now and for ever.

For the sceptre of the wicked shall not rest
over the land of the just
for fear that the hands of the just
should turn to evil.

Do good, Lord, to those who are good,
to the upright of heart;
but the crooked and those who do evil,
drive them away!

On Israel, peace!

Ant. Persevere in prayer, with mind awake and thankful heart.

Word of God   Mt 7:7–12

This is the teaching Jesus gave:
'Ask, and you will receive; seek, and you will find; knock,
and the door will be opened. For everyone who asks
receives, he who seeks finds, and to him who knocks, the
door will be opened.
'Is there a man among you who will offer his son a stone
when he asks for bread, or a snake when he asks for fish?
If you, then, bad as you are, know how to give your
children what is good for them, how much more will your
heavenly Father give good things to those who ask him!
'Always treat others as you would like them to treat you:
that is the Law and the prophets.'

Song of the Virgin Mary

Ant. The Holy Spirit will come upon you,
    and the power of the Most High will overshadow you.
Or as follows:

New Testament Song   Rev 11:17–18; 12:10–12

Ant. The Lord our God, the Almighty, reigns.

We give thee thanks, O Lord God,
sovereign over all,
who are and who were,
because thou hast taken thy great power into thy hands
and entered upon thy reign.

The nations raged,
but thy day of retribution has come.
Now is the time for the dead to be judged;
now is the time for recompense
to thy servants the prophets, to thy dedicated people,

135

and all who honour thy name, both great and small.

This is the hour of victory for our God,
the hour of his sovereignty and power,
when his Christ comes to his rightful rule!
For the accuser of our brothers is overthrown,
who day and night accused them before our God.

By the sacrifice of the Lamb
they have conquered him,
and by the testimony which they uttered;
for they did not hold their lives too dear to lay them down.
Rejoice then, you heavens,
and you that dwell in them!

Ant. The Lord our God, the Almighty, reigns.

Prayers

Father, as we wait quietly in your presence, fill our minds
with your thoughts, and our hearts with your desires.

> We thank you, Father, for this day and for all that it has
>   brought us;
> may the work we have done and the people we have met
> bring us closer to you.

> Father, where there is war and conflict,
> where there are great problems to be resolved,
> may men know and understand your will,
> and be your instruments in carrying it out.

> As we come to the end of a day's work,
> let us remember those who must work through the night,
> especially doctors and nurses, pilots and sailors.
>
> Further prayers . . . Our Father . . .

Loving Father, as the day draws to its close, we offer you
thanks and praise. In your mercy forgive whatever sins we
have committed in our weakness, through Christ our Lord.
Amen.

May the Lord bless us,
may he keep us from all evil
and lead us to life everlasting. Amen.

FRIDAY

Lord, open my lips, and my mouth shall proclaim your praise.
To you be glory in the Church and in Christ Jesus
from generation to generation evermore.
Amen, alleluia!

The Face of Christ

The tragic beauty of the face of Christ
shines in the face of man;

the abandoned old live on
in shabby rooms, far from inner comfort.
Outside, in the street
din and purpose, the world like a fiery animal
reined in by youth. Within
a pallid tiring heart
shuffles about its dwelling.

Nothing, or so little, come of life's promise.
Out of broken men, despised minds
what does one make –
a roadside show, a graveyard of the heart?

The Christian God reproves
faithless ranting minds
crushing like upper and lower stones
all life between;
Christ, fowler of street and hedgerow
of cripples and the distempered old
– eyes blind as woodknots,
tongues tight as immigrants –
takes in His gospel net
all the hue and cry of existence.

Heaven, of such imperfection,
wary, ravaged, wild?

Yes. Compel them in.

Daniel Berrigan

Prayer of contrition and trust Ps 50(51)

Jesus, son of the living God, be merciful to me, a sinner.

Ant. Be always joyful: pray continually;
give thanks whatever happens.

Have mercy on me, God, in your kindness.
In your compassion blot out my offence.
O wash me more and more from my guilt
and cleanse me from my sin.

My offences truly I know them;
my sin is always before me.
Against you, you alone, have I sinned;
what is evil in your sight I have done.

That you may be justified when you give sentence
and be without reproach when you judge,
O see, in guilt I was born,
a sinner was I conceived.

Indeed you love truth in the heart;
then in the secret of my heart teach me wisdom.
O purify me, then I shall be clean;
O wash me, I shall be whiter than snow.

Make me hear rejoicing and gladness,
that the bones you have crushed may thrill.
From my sins turn away your face
and blot out all my guilt.

A pure heart create for me, O God,
put a steadfast spirit within me.
Do not cast me away from your presence,
nor deprive me of your holy spirit.

Give me again the joy of your help;
with a spirit of fervour sustain me,
that I may teach transgressors your ways
and sinners may return to you.

O rescue me, God, my helper,
and my tongue shall ring out your goodness.
O Lord, open my lips
and my mouth shall declare your praise.

For in sacrifice you take no delight,
burnt offering from me you would refuse,
my sacrifice, a contrite spirit.
A humbled, contrite heart you will not spurn.

In your goodness, show favour to Zion:
rebuild the walls of Jerusalem.
Then you will be pleased with lawful sacrifice,
burnt offerings wholly consumed,
then you will be offered young bulls on your altar.

Praise to God, creator and shepherd   Ps 99(100)

Let Christ's peace be arbiter in your hearts,
and be filled with gratitude (Col 3:15).

Cry out with joy to the Lord, all the earth.
Serve the Lord with gladness.
Come before him, singing for joy.

Know that he, the Lord, is God.
He made us, we belong to him,
we are his people, the sheep of his flock.

Go within his gates, giving thanks.
Enter his courts with songs of praise.
Give thanks to him and bless his name.

Indeed, how good is the Lord,
eternal his merciful love.
He is faithful from age to age.

Ant. Be always joyful: pray continually;
give thanks whatever happens.

Word of God   2 Cor 5:14–21

The love of Christ leaves us no choice, when once we have
reached the conclusion that one man died for all and
therefore all mankind has died. His purpose in dying for
all was that men, while still in life, should cease to live for
themselves, and should live for him who for their sake died
and was raised to life. With us therefore worldly standards
have ceased to count in our estimate of any man; even if

139

once they counted in our understanding of Christ, they do so now no longer. When anyone is united to Christ, there is a new world; the old order has gone, and a new order has already begun.

From first to last this has been the work of God. He has reconciled us men to himself through Christ, and he has enlisted us in this service of reconciliation. What I mean is, that God was in Christ reconciling the world to himself, no longer holding men's misdeeds against them, and that he has entrusted us with the message of reconciliation. We come therefore as Christ's ambassadors. It is as if God were appealing to you through us: in Christ's name, we implore you, be reconciled to God! Christ was innocent of sin, and yet for our sake God made him one with the sinfulness of men, so that in him we might be made one with the goodness of God himself.

Song of Zechariah

Ant. The Lord has come to his people;
    he has saved them and set them free.

Or as follows:

New Testament Song   Rom 8:28–35, 37

Ant. You did not spare your own Son, but gave him up for
    us all.

In everything God co-operates for good with those who love
    him
and are called according to his purpose.
For God knew his own before ever they were,
and ordained that they should be shaped to the likeness of
    his Son.

It is these, so foreordained, whom he has also called;
and those whom he called he has justified,
and to those whom he justified he has also given his
    splendour.

With all this in mind, what are we to say?
If God is on our side, who is against us?

He did not spare his own Son, but gave him up for us all;
with this gift how can he fail to lavish upon us all he has to
give?

Who will be the accuser of God's chosen ones?
It is God who pronounces acquittal;
then who can condemn?
It is Christ – Christ who died, and was raised from the dead –
who is at God's right hand, and indeed pleads our cause.

Then what can separate us from the love of Christ?
Can affliction or hardship?
Can persecution, hunger, nakedness, peril, or the sword?
In spite of all, overwhelming victory is ours
through him who loved us.

Ant. You did not spare your own Son, but gave him up for
us all.

Prayers

Father in heaven, we have put our hope in you, but we often
lose our way; help us to turn to you afresh, show us where
we are and where we should be, today and always.

Father, your Son was always compassionate to sinners.
Confident of your loving mercy, we ask forgiveness for
our failings.

Lord, help us to work more willingly,
to greet people more warmly,
to put ourselves out for others more readily.

We look for kindness and understanding in others;
may they find your love and care in us.

Further prayers ... Our Father ...

Lord, you have promised us that if a loving mother forgets
her child, you will not forget us. To you be honour, glory
and praise!

Almighty God, by whose grace alone we have been accepted
and called to your service: strengthen us by your Spirit and
make us worthy of our calling, through Jesus Christ our
Lord. Amen.

May the Lord bless us,
may he keep us from all evil
and lead us to life everlasting. Amen.

EVENING PRAYER

Lord, open my lips, and my mouth shall proclaim your praise.
Glory to the Father, and to the Son, and to the Holy Spirit:
as in the beginning, so now, and for ever. Amen, alleluia!

A Song (of Divine Love)

Lord, when the sense of thy sweet grace
Sends up my soul to seek thy face
Thy blessèd eyes breed such desire,
I dy in love's delicious Fire.
   O Love, I am thy Sacrifice.
Be still triumphant, blessèd eyes.
Still shine on me, fair suns! that I
Still may behold, though still I dy.

   Though still I dy, I live again;
Still longing so to be still slain,
So gainful is such losse of breath;
I dy even in desire of death.
   Still live in me this loving strife
Of living Death and dying Life.
For while thou sweetly slayest me
Dead to my selfe, I live in Thee.

Richard Crashaw

God the protector

Ps 120(121)

*They shall never again feel hunger or thirst,
the sun shall not beat on them nor any scorching heat*
(Rev 7:16).

Ant. We do not know how we ought to pray,
but through our inarticulate groans
the Spirit himself is pleading for us.

I lift up my eyes to the mountains:
from where shall come my help?

My help shall come from the Lord
who made heaven and earth.

May he never allow you to stumble!
Let him sleep not, your guard.
No, he sleeps not nor slumbers,
Israel's guard.

The Lord is your guard and your shade;
at your right side he stands.
By day the sun shall not smite you
nor the moon in the night.

The Lord will guard you from evil,
he will guard your soul.
The Lord will guard your going and coming
both now and for ever.

Prayer of a man saved from death   Ps 114(116)

> *To enter the kingdom of God we must pass through many
> hardships* (Acts 14:22).

I love the Lord for he has heard
the cry of my appeal;
for he turned his ear to me
in the day when I called him.

They surrounded me, the snares of death,
with the anguish of the tomb;
they caught me, sorrow and distress.
I called on the Lord's name.

O Lord my God, deliver me!

How gracious is the Lord, and just;
our God has compassion.
The Lord protects the simple hearts;
I was helpless so he saved me.

Turn back, my soul, to your rest
for the Lord has been good;
he has kept my soul from death,
my eyes from tears
and my feet from stumbling.

143

I will walk in the presence of the Lord
in the land of the living.

Ant. We do not know how we ought to pray,
  but through our inarticulate groans
  the Spirit himself is pleading for us.

Word of God   Jn 16:32–17:5

Jesus said to his disciples, 'The hour is coming, has indeed
already come, when you are all to be scattered, each to his
home, leaving me alone. Yet I am not alone, because the
Father is with me. I have told you all this so that in me
you may find peace. In the world you will have trouble.
But courage! The victory is mine; I have conquered the
world.'

After these words Jesus looked up to heaven and said:
'Father, the hour has come. Glorify thy Son, that the Son
may glorify thee. For thou hast made him sovereign over all
mankind, to give eternal life to all whom thou hast given him.
This is eternal life: to know thee who alone art truly God,
and Jesus Christ whom thou hast sent. I have glorified thee
on earth by completing the work which thou gavest me to do;
and now, Father, glorify me in thy own presence with the
glory which I had with thee before the world began.'

Song of the Virgin Mary

Ant. The child to be born will be called 'Son of God.'

Or as follows:

New Testament Song   Rev 15:3–4

Ant. Glory to the Lamb who was slain!
  He is king for ever and ever.

Great and marvellous are thy deeds,
O Lord God, sovereign over all;
just and true are thy ways,
Thou king of the ages.

Who shall not revere thee, Lord,
and do homage to thy name?
For thou alone art holy.

All nations shall come
and worship in thy presence,
for thy just dealings stand revealed.

Ant. Glory to the Lamb who was slain!
He is king for ever and ever.

Prayers

God our Father, you are altogether good, altogether kind.
You have been good to us beyond what we deserve, kind
when we had no right to expect it.

We thank you, Lord God, for the world you have created,
and all the good things in it.
Teach us to use your creation for your greater praise.

We thank you for your patient mercy with our faults and
failings;
help us through the power of Jesus to live in your love.

We thank you for our families and friends,
and for the joys we share together;
grant us strength to overcome difficulties.

Further prayers . . . Our Father . . .

Loving Father, by your will Christ your Son gave his life
for us. Grant us so to live that, by sharing in his sufferings,
we may come to share the power of his resurrection, through
the same Christ our Lord. Amen.

May the Lord bless us,
may he keep us from all evil
and lead us to life everlasting. Amen.

SATURDAY

Lord, open my lips, and my mouth shall proclaim your praise.
To you be glory in the Church and in Christ Jesus
from generation to generation evermore.
Amen, alleluia!

Hymn for the Church Militant

Great God, that bowest sky and star,
  Bow down our towering thoughts to thee,
And grant us in a faltering war
  The firm feet of humility.

Lord, we that snatch the swords of flame,
  Lord, we that cry about thy ear,
We too are weak with pride and shame,
  We too are as our foemen are.

Yea, we are mad as they are mad,
  Yea, we are blind as they are blind,
Yea, we are very sick and sad
  Who bring good news to all mankind.

The dreadful joy thy Son has sent
  Is heavier than any care;
We find, as Cain his punishment,
  Our pardon more than we can bear.

Lord, when we cry thee far and near
  And thunder through all lands unknown
The gospel into every ear,
  Lord, let us not forget our own.

Cleanse us from ire of creed or class,
  The anger of the idle kings;
Sow in our souls, like living grass,
  The laughter of all lowly things.

G. K. Chesterton

Prayer of repentance and trust   Ps 129(130)

He will save his people from their sins (Mt 1:21).

Ant. Give yourselves wholly to prayer and entreaty;
    pray on every occasion in the power of the Spirit.

Out of the depths I cry to you, O Lord,
Lord, hear my voice!
O let your ears be attentive
to the voice of my pleading.

If you, O Lord, should mark our guilt,
Lord, who would survive?
But with you is found forgiveness:
for this we revere you.

My soul is waiting for the Lord,
I count on his word.
My soul is longing for the Lord
more than watchman for daybreak.

Let the watchman count on daybreak
and Israel on the Lord.

Because with the Lord there is mercy
and fullness of redemption,
Israel indeed he will redeem
from all its iniquity.

World-wide call to praise God   Ps 116(117)

*Christ became a servant . . . to give the Gentiles cause to
glorify God for his mercy* (Rom 15:8, 9).

O praise the Lord, all you nations,
acclaim him all you peoples!
Strong is his love for us;
he is faithful for ever.

Ant. Give yourselves wholly to prayer and entreaty;
    pray on every occasion in the power of the Spirit.

Word of God   Jn 15:1–11

Jesus said to his disciples,
'I am the real vine, and my Father is the gardener. Every

barren branch of mine he cuts away; and every fruiting branch he cleans, to make it more fruitful still. You have already been cleansed by the word that I spoke to you. Dwell in me, as I in you. No branch can bear fruit by itself, but only if it remains united with the vine; no more can you bear fruit, unless you remain united with me.

'I am the vine, and you the branches. He who dwells in me, as I dwell in him, bears much fruit; for apart from me you can do nothing. He who does not dwell in me is thrown away like a withered branch. The withered branches are heaped together, thrown on the fire, and burnt.

'If you dwell in me, and my words dwell in you, ask what you will, and you shall have it. This is my Father's glory, that you may bear fruit in plenty and so be my disciples. As the Father has loved me, so I have loved you. Dwell in my love. If you heed my commands, you will dwell in my love, as I have heeded my Father's commands and dwell in his love.

'I have spoken thus to you, so that my joy may be in you, and your joy complete.'

Song of Zechariah

Ant. He will guide our feet into the way of peace.

Or as follows:

Song of the Angels

Ant. Praise be to the God and Father of our Lord Jesus Christ,
  who has bestowed on us in Christ every spiritual blessing
  in the heavenly realms.

Glory to God in the highest,
and peace to his people on earth.

Lord God, heavenly King, almighty God and Father.
We worship you,
we give you thanks,
we praise you for your glory.

Lord Jesus Christ, only Son of the Father.
Lord God, Lamb of God,

you take away the sin of the world,
have mercy on us;
you are seated at the right hand of the Father:
receive our prayer.

For you alone are the Holy One,
you alone are the Lord;
you alone are the Most High, Jesus Christ,
with the Holy Spirit,
in the glory of God the Father.

Ant. Praise be to the God and Father of our Lord Jesus
Christ,
who has bestowed on us in Christ every spiritual blessing
in the heavenly realms.

Prayers

Father, you woke us this morning to a new day. Help us to
seek you and know you in everything we do today, and in
everyone we meet.

Father, free us from all fear,
that we may learn to love all men as you do.

Pour your peace into our hearts
that we may be a source of strength and hope to all we
meet.

Father, fill our hearts with your love,
that our day may be spent in giving to all those around us.

Further prayers ... Our Father ...

Praise to our God! Wonderful are his works! Straight his
paths!

Lord, all that we are and all that we have is your gift to us.
With our lives and all that is in us we praise you; make us
whole in your Spirit, so that everything we do today may
be a prayer to you. We ask this through Christ our Lord.

May the Lord bless us,
may he keep us from evil
and lead us to life everlasting. Amen.

EVENING PRAYER

Lord, open my lips, and my mouth shall proclaim your praise.
Glory to the Father, and to the Son, and to the Holy Spirit:
as in the beginning, so now, and for ever. Amen, alleluia!

Peace

My soul, there is a country
Far beyond the stars,
Where stands a winged sentry
All skilful in the wars:
There, above noise and danger,
Sweet Peace sits crowned with smiles,
And One born in a manger
Commands the beauteous files,
He is thy gracious Friend,
And – O my soul, awake! –
Did in pure love descend
To die here for thy sake,
If thou canst get but thither,
There grows the flower of Peace,
The Rose that cannot wither,
Thy fortress, and thy ease.
Leave then thy foolish ranges;
For none can thee secure
But One who never changes –
Thy God, thy life, thy cure.

Henry Vaughan

The problem of innocent suffering   Ps 72(73)I

*This is eternal life: to know you who alone are truly God,
and Jesus Christ whom you have sent* (Jn 17:3).

Ant. God's grace be with all who love our Lord Jesus Christ,
grace and immortality.

How good God is to Israel,
to those who are pure of heart.
Yet my feet came close to stumbling,
my steps had almost slipped
for I was filled with envy of the proud
when I saw how the wicked prosper.

150

For them there are no pains;
their bodies are sound and sleek.
They have no share in men's sorrows;
they are not stricken like others.

So they wear their pride like a necklace,
they clothe themselves with violence.
Their hearts overflow with malice,
their minds seethe with plots.

They scoff; they speak with malice;
from on high they plan oppression.
They have set their mouths in the heavens
and their tongues dictate to the earth.

So the people turn to follow them
and drink in all their words.
They say: 'How can God know?
Does the Most High take any notice?'
Look at them, such are the wicked,
but untroubled, they grow in wealth.

How useless to keep my heart pure
and wash my hands in innocence,
when I was stricken all day long,
suffered punishment day after day.

Then I said: 'If I should speak like that
I should betray the race of your sons.'

Ps 72(73)II

I strove to fathom this problem,
too hard for my mind to understand,
until I pierced the mysteries of God
and understood what becomes of the wicked.

How slippery the paths on which you set them;
you make them slide to destruction.
How suddenly they come to their ruin,
wiped out, destroyed by terrors.
Like a dream one wakes from, O Lord,
when you wake you dismiss them as phantoms.

151

And so when my heart grew embittered
and when I was cut to the quick,
I was stupid and did not understand,
no better than a beast in your sight.

Yet I was always in your presence;
you were holding me by my right hand.
You will guide me by your counsel
and so you will lead me to glory.

What else have I in heaven but you?
Apart from you I want nothing on earth.
My body and my heart faint for joy;
God is my possession for ever.

All those who abandon you shall perish;
you will destroy all those who are faithless.
To be near God is my happiness.
I have made the Lord God my refuge.
I will tell of all your works
at the gates of the city of Zion.

Ant. God's grace be with all who love our Lord Jesus Christ,
grace and immortality.

Word of God   Jn 17:12–17

Jesus looked up to heaven and said: 'When I was with them,
I protected by the power of thy name those whom thou hast
given me, and kept them safe. Not one of them is lost
except the man who must be lost, for Scripture has to be
fulfilled.
'And now I am coming to thee; but while I am still in the
world I speak these words, so that they may have my joy
within them in full measure. I have delivered thy word
to them, and the world hates them because they are strangers
in the world, as I am. I pray thee, not to take them out of the
world, but to keep them from the evil one. They are strangers
in the world, as I am. Consecrate them by the truth; thy
word is truth.'

Song of the Virgin Mary

Ant. I am the Lord's servant;
  as you have spoken, so be it.

Or as follows:

New Testament Song   Phil 2:6–11

Ant. He humbled himself, and in obedience accepted even
  death – death on a cross.

The divine nature was Christ's from the first;
yet he did not think to snatch at equality with God,
but made himself nothing,
assuming the nature of a slave.

Bearing the human likeness,
revealed in human shape,
he humbled himself,
and in obedience accepted even death –
death on a cross.

Therefore God raised him to the heights
and bestowed on him the name above all names,
that at the name of Jesus every knee should bow –
in heaven, on earth, and in the depths –
and every tongue confess, 'Jesus Christ is Lord',
to the glory of God the Father.

Ant. He humbled himself, and in obedience accepted even
  death – death on a cross.

Prayers

We thank you, Lord and Father, for all you have given us
in the past week. We offer you all that has happened;
forgive us our failings, and give us new strength for the
future.

  Father, in Mary you have given all Christians
  an example for their own lives;
  help us, too, to bring your Son into the world.

Father, we pray to you for our own country;
help us to contribute to its true growth and well-being
in the Spirit of your Son.

May we experience your action ever more intimately,
may your presence grow ever more vivid
in us and everywhere around us.

Further prayers ... Our Father ...

May the love and peace of God our Father remain with us
for ever.

Almighty God, who after the creation of the world rested from all your work and made holy a day of rest for your creatures, grant that our rest here on earth may prepare us for the eternal rest promised to your children in heaven, through Christ our Lord. Amen.

May the Lord bless us,
may he keep us from all evil
and lead us to life everlasting. Amen.

Season of Lent

SUNDAY

Lord, open my lips, and my mouth shall proclaim your praise.
To you be glory in the Church and in Christ Jesus,
from generation to generation evermore. Amen.

O Deus Ego Amo Te

O God, I love thee, I love thee –
Not out of hope of heaven for me
Nor fearing not to love and be
   In the everlasting burning.
Thou, thou, my Jesus, after me
   Didst reach thine arms out dying,
For my sake sufferedst nails and lance,
Mocked and marrèd countenance,
   Sorrows passing number,
   Sweat and care and cumber,
Yea and death, and this for me,
   And thou couldst see me sinning:
Then I, why should not I love thee,
Jesu, so much in love with me?
Not for heaven's sake; not to be
Out of hell by loving thee;
Not for any gains I see;
But just the way that thou didst me
I do love and I will love thee;
What must I love thee, Lord, for then?
For being my king and God. Amen.

Gerard Manley Hopkins

The joy of being forgiven Ps 31(32)

Nor do I condemn you. You may go; do not sin again
(Jn. 8:11).

Ant. If we confess our sins, he is just, and may be trusted
to cleanse us from every kind of wrong.

Happy the man whose offence is forgiven,
whose sin is remitted.
O happy the man to whom the Lord
imputes no guilt,
in whose spirit is no guile.

I kept it secret and my frame was wasted.
I groaned all the day long
for night and day your hand
was heavy upon me.
Indeed, my strength was dried up
as by the summer's heat.

But now I have acknowledged my sins;
my guilt I did not hide.
I said: 'I will confess
my offence to the Lord.'
And you, Lord, have forgiven
the guilt of my sin.

So let every good man pray to you
in the time of need.
The floods of water may reach high
but him they shall not reach.
You are my hiding place, O Lord;
you save me from distress.
You surround me with cries of deliverance.

Rejoice, rejoice in the Lord,
exult, you just!
O come, ring out your joy,
all you upright of heart.

Ant. If we confess our sins, he is just, and may be trusted
to cleanse us from every kind of wrong.

Joy in the Lord   Ps 149

Rejoice, rejoice, my spirit, in God my saviour (Lk 1:47).

Ant. I will exult in the Lord
and rejoice in the God of my deliverance.

Sing a new song to the Lord,
his praise in the assembly of the faithful.
Let Israel rejoice in its Maker,
let Zion's sons exult in their king.
Let them praise his name with dancing
and make music with timbrel and harp.

For the Lord takes delight in his people.
He crowns the poor with salvation.
Let the faithful rejoice in their glory,
shout for joy and take their rest.

Ant. I will exult in the Lord
and rejoice in the God of my deliverance.

Word of God   Gen 2:5–9, 15–17

When the Lord God made earth and heaven, there was
neither shrub nor plant growing wild upon the earth,
because the Lord God had sent no rain on the earth; nor
was there any man to till the ground. A flood used to rise
out of the earth and water all the surface of the ground.
Then the Lord God formed a man from the dust of the
ground and breathed into his nostrils the breath of life.
Thus the man became a living creature. Then the Lord God
planted a garden in Eden away to the east, and there he
put the man whom he had formed. The Lord God made
trees spring from the ground, all trees pleasant to look at
and good for food; and in the middle of the garden he set
the tree of life and the tree of the knowledge of good and evil.
The Lord God took the man and put him in the garden
of Eden to till it and care for it. He told the man, 'You
may eat from every tree in the garden, but not from the
tree of the knowledge of good and evil; for on the day that
you eat from it, you will certainly die.'

157

Song of Zechariah

Ant. The first man, Adam, became an animate being,
the last Adam has become a life-giving spirit.

Or as follows:

Old Testament Song   Jer 31:10–14

*As High Priest, Caiaphas was prophesying that Jesus would
die to gather together the scattered children of God
(Jn 11:51, 52).*

Ant. He shall watch over them as a shepherd watches his
flock.

Listen to the word of the Lord, you nations,
announce it, make it known to coasts and islands far away:
He who scattered Israel shall gather them again
and watch over them as a shepherd watches his flock.
For the Lord has ransomed Jacob
and redeemed him from a foe too strong for him.

They shall come with shouts of joy to Zion's height,
shining with happiness at the bounty of the Lord,
the corn, the new wine, and the oil,
the young of flock and herd.

They shall become like a watered garden
and they shall never want again.
Then shall the girl show her joy in the dance,
young men and old shall rejoice.

I will turn their mourning into gladness,
I will relent and give them joy to outdo their sorrow.
I will satisfy the priests with the fat of the land
and fill my people with my bounty.

Ant. He shall watch over them as a shepherd watches his
flock.

Prayers

Almighty God, we ask that through this season of Lent
we may follow in our lives the suffering, death and resurrection of your Son Jesus, and so come to share in his glory.

Father, when we suffer in any way,
you are asking us to carry our cross;
grant us the strength to bear it for love of you.

We pray that when weakness overcomes us
we may realise that our strength is in you alone;
we trust in you completely.

Christ, our loving Master,
in your kindness be with the sick and the poor,
the weak and the dying,
to comfort them.

Further prayers . . . Our Father . . .

Almighty God, we pray that through the observance of Lent
we may penetrate more deeply into the mystery of Christ,
and obtain its fruits by the worthy conduct of our lives. We
ask this through Christ our Lord. Amen.

May the Lord bless us,
may he keep us from all evil
and lead us to life everlasting. Amen.

EVENING PRAYER

Lord, open my lips, and my mouth shall proclaim your praise.
Glory to the Father, and to the Son, and to the Holy Spirit:
as in the beginning, so now, and for ever. Amen.

The Pillar of the Cloud

Lead, kindly Light, amid the encircling gloom,
   Lead thou me on;
The night is dark, and I am far from home,
   Lead thou me on.
Keep thou my feet: I do not ask to see
The distant scene; one step enough for me.

I was not ever thus, nor prayed that thou
   Shouldst lead me on;
I loved to choose and see my path; but now
   Lead thou me on.
I loved the garish day, and, spite of fears,
Pride ruled my will: remember not past years.

So long thy power hath blest me, sure it still
   Will lead me on,

O'er moor and fen, o'er crag and torrent, till
    The night is gone,
And with the morn those angel faces smile
Which I have loved long since, and lost a while.

                                        John Henry Newman

The Messiah, king, priest and judge   Ps 109(110)

*Son though he was, he learned obedience in the school
of suffering, and became the source of eternal salvation
for all who obey him, named by God high priest in the
succession of Melchizedek (Heb 5:8–10).*

Ant. You are a priest for ever,
    a priest like Melchizedek of old.

The Lord's revelation to my Master:
'Sit on my right:
I will put your foes beneath your feet.'

The Lord will send from Zion
your sceptre of power:
rule in the midst of all your foes.

A prince from the day of your birth
on the holy mountains;
from the womb before the daybreak I begot you.

The Lord has sworn an oath he will not change.
'You are a priest for ever,
a priest like Melchizedek of old.'

He shall drink from the stream by the wayside
and therefore he shall lift up his head.

Ant. You are a priest for ever,
    a priest like Melchizedek of old.

Hymn to the one true God   Ps 113B(115)

*You turned from idols to be servants of the living and
true God (1 Thess 1:9).*

Ant. The Lord is the shield that guards you.

Not to us, Lord, not to us,
but to your name give the glory
for the sake of your love and your truth,
lest the heathen say: 'Where is their God?'

But our God he is in the heavens;
he does whatever he wills.
Their idols are silver and gold,
the work of human hands.

They have mouths but they cannot speak;
they have eyes but they cannot see;
they have ears but they cannot hear;
they have nostrils but they cannot smell.

With their hands they cannot feel;
with their feet they cannot walk.
No sound comes from their throats.
Their makers will become like them:
so will all who trust in them.

Sons of Israel, trust in the Lord;
he is their help and their shield.
Sons of Aaron, trust in the Lord;
he is their help and their shield.

You who fear him, trust in the Lord;
he is their help and their shield.
He remembers us, will give us his blessing;
he will bless the sons of Israel.
He will bless the sons of Aaron.

The Lord will bless those who fear him,
the little no less than the great:
to you may the Lord grant increase,
to you and all your children.

May you be blessed by the Lord,
the maker of heaven and earth.
The heavens belong to the Lord
but the earth he has given to men.

161

The dead shall not praise the Lord,
nor those who go down into the silence.
But we who live bless the Lord
now and for ever. Amen.

Ant. The Lord is the shield that guards you.

Word of God   2 Cor 6:1–6

We urge this appeal upon you: you have received the grace
of God; do not let it go for nothing. God's own words are:

'In the hour of my favour I gave heed to you;
on the day of deliverance I came to your aid.'

The hour of favour has now come; now, I say, has the day
of deliverance dawned.

In order that our service may not be brought into discredit,
we avoid giving offence in anything. As God's servants,
we try to recommend ourselves in all circumstances by our
steadfast endurance: in distress, hardships, and dire straits;
flogged, imprisoned, mobbed; overworked, sleepless, starving.
We recommend ourselves by the innocence of our behaviour,
our grasp of truth, our patience and kindliness; by gifts of
the Holy Spirit, by sincere love, by declaring the truth, by
the power of God.

Song of the Virgin Mary

Ant. Wherever we go we carry death with us in our body,
the death that Jesus died,
that in this body also life may reveal itself,
the life that Jesus lives.

Or as follows:

New Testament Song   1 Pt 2:21–25

Ant. By his wounds you have been healed.

Christ suffered on your behalf.
and thereby left you an example;
it is for you to follow in his steps.

He committed no sin,
he was convicted of no falsehood;

162

when he was abused he did not retort with abuse,
when he suffered he uttered no threats,
but committed his cause to the One who judges justly.

In his own person he carried our sins to the gibbet,
so that we might cease to live for sin
and begin to live for righteousness.

By his wounds you have been healed.
You were straying like sheep,
but now you have turned
towards the Shepherd and Guardian of your souls.

Ant. By his wounds you have been healed.

Prayers

Father, Son and Holy Spirit, we praise you for your creation,
for its beauty and wonders, and thank you for our task of
consecrating it to you.

We thank you for the strength and love you have given
to those who work to relieve suffering:
bless them and draw them close to you.

Lord, may all who are suffering
because of the sins of men,
find you and come close to you in their suffering.

God our Father, as we prepare for Easter,
may our lives show to men
the joy of the risen Christ.

Further prayers ... Our Father ...

Almighty, eternal God, by whose will our Saviour became
man and suffered on the cross to show us the meaning of
obedient love, grant that we may learn from his meekness
and share in his resurrection who lives and reigns with you
for ever. Amen.

May the Lord bless us,
may he keep us from all evil
and lead us to life everlasting. Amen.

MONDAY

Lord, open my lips . .
To you be glory . . .

Trinitie Sunday

Lord, who hast form'd me out of mud,
 And hast redeem'd me through thy bloud,
 And sanctifi'd me to do good;

Purge all my sinnes done heretofore:
 For I confesse my heavie score,
 And I will strive to sinne no more.

Enrich my heart, mouth, hands in me,
 With faith, with hope, with charitie;
 That I may runne, rise, rest with thee.

George Herbert

Acknowledgement of guilt   Ps 37(38)

We paid due respect to the earthly fathers who disciplined us, should we not submit even more readily to our spiritual Father, and so attain life? (Heb 12:9).

Ant. Correct us, O Lord, but with justice, not in anger.

O Lord, do not rebuke me in your anger;
do not punish me, Lord, in your rage.
My guilt towers higher than my head;
it is a weight too heavy to bear.

O Lord, you know all my longing:
my groans are not hidden from you.
My heart throbs, my strength is spent;
the very light has gone from my eyes.

I count on you, O Lord:
it is you, Lord God, who will answer.
I confess that I am guilty
and my sin fills me with dismay.

O Lord, do not forsake me!
My God, do not stay afar off!
Make haste and come to my help,
O Lord, my God, my saviour!

Ant. Correct us, O Lord, but with justice, not in anger.

Thanksgiving for God's gifts   Ps 64(65)

The universe itself is to be freed from the shackles of mortality and enter upon the liberty and splendour of the children of God (Rom 8:21).

Ant. Compassion and forgiveness belong to the Lord our God.

To you our praise is due
in Zion, O God.
To you we pay our vows,
you who hear our prayer.

To you all flesh will come
with its burden of sin.
Too heavy for us, our offences,
but you wipe them away.

Blessed he whom you choose and call
to dwell in your courts.
We are filled with the blessings of your house,
of your holy temple.

You keep your pledge with wonders,
O God our saviour,
the hope of all the earth
and of far distant isles.

You uphold the mountains with your strength,
you are girded with power.
You still the roaring of the seas,
the roaring of their waves
and the tumult of the peoples.

The ends of the earth stand in awe
at the sight of your wonders.

The lands of sunrise and sunset
you fill with your joy.

You care for the earth, give it water,
you fill it with riches.
Your river in heaven brims over
to provide its grain.

And thus you provide for the earth;
You drench its furrows,
you level it, soften it with showers,
you bless its growth.

You crown the year with your goodness.
Abundance flows in your steps,
in the pastures of the wilderness it flows.

The hills are girded with joy,
the meadows covered with flocks,
the valleys are decked with wheat.
They shout for joy, yes, they sing.

Ant. Compassion and forgiveness belong to the Lord our
God.

Word of God   Gen 3:1–7

The serpent was more crafty than any wild creature that
the Lord God had made. He said to the woman, 'Is it
true that God has forbidden you to eat from any tree in
the garden?' The woman answered the serpent, 'We may
eat the fruit of any tree in the garden, except for the tree in
the middle of the garden; God has forbidden us either to
eat or to touch the fruit of that; if we do, we shall die ' The
serpent said, 'Of course you will not die. God knows that
as soon as you eat it, your eyes will be opened and you will
be like gods knowing both good and evil.' When the woman
saw that the fruit of the tree was good to eat, and that it
was pleasing to the eye and tempting to contemplate, she
took some and ate it. She also gave her husband some
and he ate it. Then the eyes of both of them were opened
and they discovered that they were naked; so they stitched
fig-leaves together and made themselves loincloths.

Song of Zechariah

Ant. God created man for immortality
and made him the image of his own eternal self.

Or as follows:

Old Testament Song   Dan: The Song of the Three Children
3, 4, 6, 11, 16–18

*Repent and turn to God, so that your sins may be wiped
out* (Acts 3:19).

Ant. We come to thee, Lord, with contrite heart and humbled
spirit.

Blessed art thou, O Lord, the God of our fathers,
thy name is worthy of praise and glorious for ever.
Thou art just in all thy deeds and true in all thy works:
straight are thy paths, and all thy judgments just.

We sinned and broke thy law in rebellion against thee,
in all we did we sinned;
for thy honour's sake do not abandon us for ever;
do not annul thy covenant.

But because we come with contrite heart and humbled
spirit, accept us.
Accept our pledge of loyalty to thee,
for no shame shall come to those who put their trust in thee.

Now we will follow thee
with our whole heart and fear thee.
We seek thy presence;
do not put us to shame.

Ant. We come to thee, Lord, with contrite heart and
humbled spirit.

Prayers

Now is the acceptable time! Now is the day of salvation!
Father, give us eyes to see and strength to respond.

Grant us, Lord, to know when we fail:
aware of our own weakness,
may we not judge others harshly.

Father, give to all men the light that comes from your
    Spirit;
as they follow the example of Jesus in self-sacrifice,
give them strength to persevere.

Father, as we draw closer to the celebration
of the passion, death and rising of Christ,
help us to take up our cross and follow him.

Further prayers ... Our Father ...

Holy Father, whose Son Jesus Christ fasted forty days in the
desert, give us grace to discipline ourselves in humble sub-
mission to your Spirit, that we may lead upright and holy
lives to your honour and glory, through the same Jesus
Christ our Lord. Amen.

May the Lord bless us,
may he keep us from all evil
and lead us to life everlasting. Amen.

EVENING PRAYER

Lord, open my lips ...
Glory to the Father ...

Divine Meditations 14

Batter my heart, three person'd God; for, you
As yet but knocke, breathe, shine, and seeke to mend;
That I may rise, and stand, o'erthrow mee, and bend
Your force, to breake, blowe, burn and make me new.
I, like an usurpt towne, to another due,
Labour to admit you, but Oh, to no end,
Reason your viceroy in mee, mee should defend,
But is captiv'd, and proves weake or untrue.
Yet dearely I love you, and would be loved faine,
But am betroth'd unto your enemie:
Divorce mee, untie, or breake that knot againe,
Take mee to you, imprison mee, for I
Except you enthrall mee, never shall be free,
Nor ever chast, except you ravish mee.

John Donne

The fools   Ps 13(14)

> *Where sin was multiplied, grace immeasurably exceeded it* (Rom 5:20).

Ant. O that Israel's salvation might come from Zion!

The fool has said in his heart:
'There is no God above.'
Their deeds are corrupt, depraved;
not a good man is left.

From heaven the Lord looks down
on the sons of men
to see if any are wise,
if any seek God.

All have left the right path,
depraved, every one:
there is not a good man left,
no, not even one.

Will the evil-doers not understand?
They eat up my people
as though they ate bread:
they never pray to the Lord.

See how they tremble with fear
without cause for fear:
for God is with the just.
You may mock the poor man's hope,
but his refuge is the Lord.

O that Israel's salvation might come from Zion!
When the Lord delivers his people from bondage,
then Jacob will be glad and Israel rejoice.

Ant. O that Israel's salvation might come from Zion!

Reflections on good and evil   Ps 36(37)

> *How blest are those of a gentle spirit; they shall have the earth for their possession* (Mt 5:5).

Ant. Wait for the Lord, keep to his way.

Do not fret because of the wicked;
do not envy those who do evil:
for they wither quickly like grass
and fade like the green of the fields.

If you trust in the Lord and do good,
then you will live in the land and be secure.
If you find your delight in the Lord,
he will grant your heart's desire.

Commit your life to the Lord,
trust in him and he will act,
so that your justice breaks forth like the light,
your cause like the noon-day sun.

Be still before the Lord and wait in patience;
do not fret at the man who prospers;
a man who makes evil plots
to bring down the needy and the poor.

Calm your anger and forget your rage;
do not fret, it only leads to evil.
For those who do evil shall perish;
the patient shall inherit the land.

Ant. Wait for the Lord, keep to his way.

Word of God   Rom 5:12–17

It was through one man that sin entered the world, and
through sin death, and thus death pervaded the whole human
race, inasmuch as all men have sinned. For sin was already
in the world before there was law, though in the absence
of law no reckoning is kept of sin. But death held sway
from Adam to Moses, even over those who had not sinned
as Adam did, by disobeying a direct command – and Adam
foreshadows the Man who was to come.
But God's act of grace is out of all proportion to Adam's
wrongdoing. For if the wrongdoing of that one man brought
death upon so many, its effect is vastly exceeded by the
grace of God and the gift that came to so many by the
grace of the one man, Jesus Christ. And again, the gift of
God is not to be compared in its effect with that one man's
sin; for the judicial action, following upon the one offence,
issued in a verdict of condemnation, but the act of grace,
following upon so many misdeeds, issued in a verdict of
acquittal. For if by the wrongdoing of that one man death

170

established its reign, through a single sinner, much more shall those who receive in far greater measure God's grace, and his gift of righteousness, live and reign through the one man, Jesus Christ.

Song of the Virgin Mary

Ant. God gives freely, and his gift is eternal life in Christ Jesus.

Or as follows:

New Testament Song   Mt 11:25–30

Ant. Come to me, and I will give you relief.

I thank thee, Father, Lord of heaven and earth,
for hiding these things from the learned and wise,
and revealing them to the simple.
Yes, Father, such was thy choice.

Everything is entrusted to me by my Father;
and no one knows the Son but the Father,
and no one knows the Father but the Son
and those to whom the Son may choose to reveal him.

Come to me, all whose work is hard, whose load is heavy;
and I will give you relief.
Bend your necks to my yoke, and learn from me,
for I am gentle and humble-hearted;
and your souls will find relief.
For my yoke is good to bear, my load is light.

Ant. Come to me, and I will give you relief.

Prayers

Father, you willed that by baptism we should die and rise with your Son; renew in us the spirit of our baptism.

We pray for all who have suffered today,
and ask you to be near to them.

Bless those men and women who are working
to bring the basic necessities of life
to the millions who do not possess them;
help them to find strength in your love.

Lord God, all that we have comes from you;
teach us that only in coming to know and love you
can we live a fully human life.

Further prayers . . . Our Father . . .

Almighty God, grant that we who fail through human
weakness may find new strength through the pleading of
your crucified Son, through whom we offer these prayers
and who lives and reigns with you for ever. Amen.

May the Lord bless us,
may he keep us from all evil
and lead us to life everlasting. Amen.

TUESDAY

MORNING PRAYER

Lord, open my lips . . .
To you be glory . . .

Discipline

Throw away the rod,
Throw away thy wrath:
   O my God,
Take the gentle path.

For my heart's desire
Unto thine is bent:
   I aspire
To a full consent.

Though I fail, I weep:
Though I halt in pace,
   Yet I creep
To the throne of grace.

Then let wrath remove;
Love will do the deed:
   For with love
Stonie hearts will bleed.

Love is swift of foot;
Love's a man of warre,
   And can shoot,
And can hit from farre.

Who can scape his bow?
That which wrought on thee,
   Brought thee low,
Needs must work on me.

Throw away thy rod;
Though man frailties hath,
   Thou art God:
Throw away thy wrath.   George Herbert

Prayer of repentance and trust   Ps 129(130)

He will save his people from their sins (Mt 1:21).

Ant. With the Lord there is mercy and fullness of redemption.

Out of the depths I cry to you, O Lord,
Lord, hear my voice!
O let your ears be attentive
to the voice of my pleading.

If you, O Lord, should mark our guilt,
Lord, who would survive?
But with you is found forgiveness:
for this we revere you.

My soul is waiting for the Lord,
I count on his word.
My soul is longing for the Lord
more than watchman for daybreak.

Let the watchman count on daybreak
and Israel on the Lord.
Because with the Lord there is mercy
and fullness of redemption,
Israel indeed he will redeem
from all its iniquity.

Ant. With the Lord there is mercy and fullness of redemption.

Praise of God's fidelity   Ps 145(146)

The Lord is to be trusted, and he will fortify you and guard you from the evil one (2 Thess 3:3).

Ant. It is the Lord who keeps faith for ever.

My soul, give praise to the Lord;
I will praise the Lord all my days,
make music to my God while I live.

Put no trust in princes,
in mortal men in whom there is no help.
Take their breath, they return to clay
and their plans that day come to nothing.

He is happy who is helped by Jacob's God,
whose hope is in the Lord his God,
who alone made heaven and earth,
the seas and all they contain.

It is he who keeps faith for ever,
who is just to those who are oppressed.
It is he who gives bread to the hungry,
the Lord, who sets prisoners free,

the Lord who gives sight to the blind,
who raises up those who are bowed down,
the Lord, who protects the stranger
and upholds the widow and orphan.

It is the Lord who loves the just
but thwarts the path of the wicked.
The Lord will reign for ever,
Zion's God, from age to age.

Ant. It is the Lord who keeps faith for ever.

Word of God   Gen 12:1–7

The Lord said to Abram, 'Leave your own country, your kinsmen, and your father's house, and go to a country that I will show you. I will make you into a great nation, I will
174

bless you and make your name so great that it shall be used in blessings:

> Those that bless you I will bless,
> those that curse you, I will execrate.
> All the families on earth
> will pray to be blessed as you are blessed.

And so Abram set out as the Lord had bidden him, and Lot went with him. Abram was seventy-five years old when he left Harran. He took his wife Sarai, his nephew Lot, all the property they had collected, and all the dependants they had acquired in Harran, and they started on their journey to Canaan. When they arrived, Abram passed through the country to the sanctuary at Shechem, the terebinth-tree of Moreh. At that time the Canaanites lived in this land. There the Lord appeared to Abraham and said, 'I give this land to your descendants.'

Song of Zechariah

Ant. By faith Abraham obeyed the call,
  for he was looking forward to the city with firm
    foundations,
  whose architect and builder is God.

Or as follows:

Old Testament Song   Jer 14:17–21

*The kingdom of God is upon you. Repent and believe the
  Gospel (Mk 1:15).*

Ant. Lord, we have sinned against you. Lord, have mercy.

Let my eyes stream with tears,
ceaselessly, day and night.
For the virgin daughter of my people
has been broken in pieces,
struck by a cruel blow.

If I go into the country,
I see men slain by the sword;
if I enter the city, I see the ravages of famine;
prophet and priest alike
go begging round the land and are never at rest.

Hast thou spurned Judah utterly?
Dost thou loathe Zion?
Why hast thou wounded us, and there is no remedy;
why let us hope for better days, and we find nothing good,
for a time of healing, and all is disaster?

We acknowledge our wickedness,
the guilt of our forefathers;
O Lord, we have sinned against thee,
Do not despise the place where thy name dwells
nor bring contempt on the throne of thy glory.

Ant. Lord, we have sinned against thee. Lord, have mercy.

Prayers

Almighty God, you called Abraham to set out with confidence along the path of faith; deepen our faith and trust in you this Lent.

> Father, too many have known the ravages of war and hatred;
> draw men together at last in peace and harmony.

> During this Lent may we practise genuine self-denial
> in the service of others.

> Lord Jesus Christ, grant to all Christians
> the unity for which you prayed;
> being one, may we draw all men to you.

Further prayers ... Our Father ...

Almighty and eternal God, grant us so to celebrate the mysteries of your Son's passion, that we may be worthy to receive the forgiveness of our sins. We ask this through the same Christ our Lord. Amen.

May the Lord bless us,
may he keep us from all evil
and lead us to life everlasting. Amen.

EVENING PRAYER

Lord, open my lips . . .
Glory to the Father . . .

Procession

God, my God, before you I stand in my distress,
Look on my destitution, turn not away.

I rise and follow, your call I hear,
Stay me and keep my heart from all fear.

Step by step I advance in the dark,
Let me feel your hand, let me hear your voice.

Dwell in my heart and make it pure,
Strong God, on your pathways keep me secure.

I follow, I follow you on the hills,
In the shade of your cross I walk with mine.

Up the steps of your mercy climb – from fall to fall,
Learn in my sins to know your humble heart,

Your unbearable gentleness, Lamb of God,
Whose touch dissolves, or destroys like fire.

I am yours, I am yours – what am I in your sight?
I would know myself, but in your life-giving light.

O make haste your face on mine to impress,
That you find in me no unshapeliness

When you judge me with your clemency
For eternity.

Raissa Maritain

The Hound of Heaven   Ps 138(139) I

There is nothing in creation that can hide from him
(Heb 4:13).

Ant. O depth of wealth, wisdom, and knowledge in God!
How unsearchable his judgments, how untraceable his
ways!

O Lord, you search me and you know me,
you know my resting and my rising,

you discern my purpose from afar.
You mark when I walk or lie down,
all my ways lie open to you.

Before ever a word is on my tongue
you know it, O Lord, through and through.
Behind and before you besiege me,
your hand ever laid upon me.
Too wonderful for me, this knowledge,
too high, beyond my reach.

O where can I go from your spirit,
or where can I flee from your face?
If I climb the heavens, you are there.
If I lie in the grave, you are there.

If I take the wings of the dawn
and dwell at the sea's furthest end,
even there your hand would lead me,
your right hand would hold me fast.

If I say: 'Let the darkness hide me
and the light around me be night,'
even darkness is not dark for you
and the night is as clear as the day.

Ps 138(139)II

For it was you who created my being,
knit me together in my mother's womb.
I thank you for the wonder of my being,
for the wonders of all your creation.

Already you knew my soul,
my body held no secret from you
when I was being fashioned in secret
and moulded in the depths of the earth.

Your eyes saw all my actions,
they were all of them written in your book;
every one of my days was decreed
before one of them came into being.

To me, how mysterious your thoughts,
the sum of them not to be numbered!

If I count them, they are more than the sand;
to finish, I must be eternal, like you.

O search me, God, and know my heart.
O test me and know my thoughts.
See that I follow not the wrong path
and lead me in the path of life eternal.

Ant. O depth of wealth, wisdom, and knowledge in God!
How unsearchable his judgments, how untraceable his
ways!

Word of God   2 Cor 4:8–17

Hard-pressed on every side, we are never hemmed in;
bewildered, we are never at our wits' end; hunted, we are
never abandoned to our fate; struck down, we are not left
to die. Wherever we go we carry death with us in our body,
the death that Jesus died, that in this body also life may
reveal itself, the life that Jesus lives. For continually, while
still alive, we are being surrendered into the hands of death,
for Jesus' sake, so that the life of Jesus also may be revealed
in this mortal body of ours. Thus death is at work in us,
and life in you.

But Scripture says, 'I believed, and therefore I spoke out',
and we too, in the same spirit of faith, believe and therefore
speak out; for we know that he who raised the Lord Jesus
to life will with Jesus raise us too, and bring us to his
presence, and you with us. Indeed, it is for your sake that all
things are ordered, so that, as the abounding grace of God
is shared by more and more, the greater may be the chorus
of thanksgiving that ascends to the glory of God.

No wonder we do not lose heart! Though our outward
humanity is in decay, yet day by day we are inwardly
renewed. Our troubles are slight and short-lived; and their
outcome an eternal glory which outweighs them far.

Song of the Virgin Mary

Ant. The sufferings we now endure bear no comparison
with the splendour, as yet unrevealed, which is in store for
us.

Or as follows:

Old Testament Song Ez 36:24–28

No one can enter the kingdom of God without being born from water and spirit (Jn 3:5).

Ant. I will put my spirit into you, and I will become your
   God.

I will take you out of the nations
and gather you from every land
and bring you to your own soil.
I will sprinkle clean water over you,
and you shall be cleansed from all that defiles you.

I will give you a new heart
and put a new spirit within you;
I will take the heart of stone from your body
and give you a heart of flesh.

I will put my spirit into you
and make you conform to my statutes,
keep my laws and live by them.
You shall become my people,
and I will become your God.

Ant. I will put my spirit into you, and I will become your
   God.

Prayers

Lord, you are our God, we are your people; renew in us that
new heart and new spirit which is the fruit of our baptism.

   We pray for all Heads of State,
   that they may work for peace and harmony
   in the world.

   Father, all true peace comes from your Spirit;
   during this Lent, cleanse our hearts
   of prejudice and selfishness.

   We pray especially for peace in family life,
   and for those orphaned and homeless;
   comfort them in your love.

                 Further prayers . . . Our Father . . .

Loving Father, turn our hearts to you and enable us always
to seek the one thing necessary, to know you and the Lord

Jesus whom you sent and who lives and reigns with you for
ever. Amen.

May the Lord bless us,
may he keep us from all evil
and lead us to life everlasting. Amen.

WEDNESDAY

Morning Prayer

Lord, open my lips ...
To you be glory ...

To Keep a True Lent

Is this a Fast, to keep
   The Larder leane?
    And cleane
From fat of Veales and Sheep?

Is it to quit the dish
   Of Flesh, yet still
    To fill
The platter high with Fish?

Is it to faste an houre,
   Or ragg'd to go,
    Or show
A downcast look, and sowre?

No: 'tis a Fast, to dole
   Thy sheaf of wheat
    And meat
Unto the hungry Soule.

It is to fast from strife,
   From old debate,
    And hate;
To circumcise thy life.

To shew a heart grief-rent;
   To starve thy sin,
    Not Bin;
And that's to keep thy Lent.

Robert Herrick

181

Prayer in desolation Ps 142(143)

Behold the Man! For my part I find no case against him (Jn 19:5, 7).

Ant. The enemy pursues my soul;
  he has crushed my life to the ground.

Lord, listen to my prayer:
turn your ear to my appeal.
You are faithful, you are just; give answer.
Do not call your servant to judgment
for no one is just in your sight.

The enemy pursues my soul;
he has crushed my life to the ground;
he has made me dwell in darkness
like the dead, long forgotten.

Therefore my spirit fails;
my heart is numb within me.

I remember the days that are past:
I ponder all your works.
I muse on what your hand has wrought
and to you I stretch out my hands.
Like a parched land my soul thirsts for you.

Lord, make haste and give me answer;
for my spirit fails within me.
Do not hide your face
lest I become like those in the grave.

In the morning let me know your love
for I put my trust in you.
Make me know the way I should walk:
to you I lift up my soul.

Rescue me, Lord, from my enemies;
I have fled to you for refuge.
Teach me to do your will
for you, O Lord, are my God.
Let your good spirit guide me
in ways that are level and smooth.

For your name's sake, Lord, save my life;
in your justice save my soul from distress,
for I am your servant, O Lord.

Ant. The enemy pursues my soul;
   he has crushed my life to the ground.

World-wide call to praise God   Ps 116(117)

*Christ became a servant . . . to give the Gentiles cause to
glorify God for his mercy* (Rom 15:8).

Ant. O praise the Lord, all you peoples of the earth.

O praise the Lord, all you nations,
acclaim him all you peoples.

Strong is his love for us;
he is faithful for ever.

Ant. O praise the Lord, all you peoples of the earth.

Word of God   Gen 22:1–2, 9–13

The time came when God put Abraham to the test. 'Abraham,' he called, and Abraham replied, 'Here I am.' God
said, 'Take your son Isaac, your only son, whom you love,
and go to the land of Moriah. There you shall offer him as a
sacrifice on one of the hills which I will show you.'
And the two of them went on together and came to the
place of which God had spoken. There Abraham built an
altar and arranged the wood. He bound his son Isaac and
laid him on the altar on top of the wood. Then he stretched
out his hand and took the knife to kill his son; but the angel
of the Lord called to him from heaven, 'Abraham, Abraham.'
He answered, 'Here I am.' The angel of the Lord said,
'Do not raise your hand against the boy; do not touch him.
Now I know that you are a God-fearing man. You have not
withheld from me your son, your only son.' Abraham looked
up, and there he saw a ram caught by its horns in a thicket.
So he went and took the ram and offered it as a sacrifice
instead of his son.

Song of Zechariah

Ant. Carrying his own cross, Jesus went out to the
   Place of the Skull, where they crucified him.

Or as follows:

Old Testament Song   Jer 11:18–20

*They did indeed make common cause in this very city
against Jesus whom you anointed as Messiah* (Acts 4:27).

Ant. Lord of Hosts, I have committed my cause to thee.

It was the Lord who showed me, and so I knew;
he opened my eyes to what they were doing.

I had been like a sheep led obedient to the slaughter;
I did not know that they were hatching plots against me
and saying, 'Let us cut down the tree while the sap is in it;
let us destroy him out of the living,
so that his very name shall be forgotten.'

O Lord of Hosts, who art a righteous judge,
testing the heart and mind,
I have committed my cause to thee;
let me see thy vengeance upon them.

Ant. Lord of Hosts, I have committed my cause to thee.

Prayers

Father, in the eucharist we renew our baptism; may we offer
ourselves to Christ, a living sacrifice, dedicated and fit for
your acceptance, a worship offered in spirit and in truth.

   Let us pray for time to be silent,
   time to find the will of God,
   so that we may make it our own.

   Father in heaven, your Son is an example
   of how we should live;
   fill us with your Spirit,
   so that our lives may show you to all men.

Many people are going to die today;
where there is darkness, fear or doubt,
may the light of Christ bring comfort and calm.

Further prayers . . . Our Father . . .

Almighty God, whose Son entered into his kingdom when he
was lifted up on the Cross: train us to be faithful in the
fellowship of his sufferings, that we may follow him to his
triumph; through Jesus Christ our Lord. Amen.

May the Lord bless us,
may he keep us from all evil
and lead us to life everlasting. Amen.

EVENING PRAYER

Lord, open my lips . . .
To you be glory . . .

Divine Meditations 5

I am a little world made cunningly
Of Elements, and an Angelike spright,
But black sinne hath betraid to endlesse night
My worlds both parts, and (oh) both parts must die.
You which beyond that heaven which was most high
Have found new sphears, and of new lands can write,
Powre new seas in mine eyes, that so I might
Drowne my world with my weeping earnestly,
Or wash it if it must be drown'd no more:
But oh it must be burnt! alas the fire
Of lust and envie have burnt it heretofore,
And made it fouler; Let their flames retire,
And burn me O Lord, with a fiery zeale
Of thee and thy house, which doth in eating heale.

John Donne

Confident prayer in distress Ps 30(31)I

Father, into your hands I commit my spirit (Lk 23:46)

Ant. See what reproaches I endure for your sake,
Lord God of hosts!

In you, O Lord, I take refuge.
Let me never be put to shame.
In your justice, set me free,
hear me and speedily rescue me.

Be a rock of refuge for me,
a mighty stronghold to save me,
for you are my rock, my stronghold.
For your name's sake, lead me and guide me

Release me from the snares they have hidden
for you are my refuge, Lord.
Into your hands I commend my spirit.
It is you who will redeem me, Lord.

O God of truth, you detest
those who worship false and empty gods.
As for me, I trust in the Lord:
let me be glad and rejoice in your love.

You who have seen my affliction
and taken heed of my soul's distress,
have not handed me over to the enemy,
but set my feet at large.

But as for me, I trust in you, Lord,
I say: 'You are my God.
Let your face shine on your servant.
Save me in your love.'

Ps 30(31)II

How great is the goodness, Lord,
that you keep for those who fear you,
that you show to those who trust you
in the sight of men.

You hide them in the shelter of your presence
from the plotting of men:
you keep them safe within your tent
from disputing tongues.

Blessed be the Lord who has shown me
the wonders of his love
in a fortified city.

'I am far removed from your sight'
I said in my alarm.
Yet you heard the voice of my plea
when I cried for help.

Love the Lord, all you saints.
He guards his faithful
but the Lord will repay to the full
those who act with pride.

Be strong, let your heart take courage,
all who hope in the Lord.

Ant. See what reproaches I endure for your sake,
Lord God of hosts!

Word of God
Rom 12:1-2, 9-12

My brothers, I implore you by God's mercy to offer your
very selves to him: a living sacrifice, dedicated and fit for his
acceptance, the worship offered by mind and heart. Adapt
yourselves no longer to the pattern of this present world,
but let your minds be remade and your whole nature thus
transformed. Then you will be able to discern the will of
God, and to know what is good, acceptable, and perfect.
Love in all sincerity, loathing evil and clinging to the
good. Let love for our brotherhood breed warmth of mutual
affection. Give pride of place to one another in esteem.
With unflagging energy, in ardour of spirit, serve the Lord
Let hope keep you joyful; in trouble stand firm; persist in
prayer.

Song of the Virgin Mary

Ant. Live in love, as Christ loved you
and gave himself up on your behalf.

Or as follows:

Old Testament Song

Is 49:7–10

The water that I shall give will be an inner spring always welling up for eternal life (Jn 4:14).

Ant. I helped you on the day of deliverance.

Thus says the Holy One, the Lord who ransoms Israel,
to one who thinks little of himself,
whom every nation abhors,
the slave of tyrants:
When they see you kings shall rise,
princes shall rise and bow down,
because of the Lord who is faithful,
because of the Holy One of Israel who has chosen you.

Thus says the Lord:
In the hour of my favour I answered you,
and I helped you on the day of deliverance,
putting the land to rights
and sharing out afresh its desolate fields;
I said to the prisoners, 'Go free,'
and to those in darkness, 'Come out and be seen.'
They shall find pasture in the desert sands
and grazing on all the dunes.
They shall neither hunger nor thirst,
no scorching heat or sun shall distress them;
for one who loves them shall lead them
and take them to water at bubbling springs.

Ant. I helped you on the day of deliverance.

Prayers

Heavenly Father, we thank you for all that you have given us; it is by your grace that we come to you in faith.

We pray for all who preach the good news of Christ
to those who do not know him;
may he be in their hearts and on their lips.

Give us vigour and hope when we find our faith difficult,
when we are downcast or depressed,
when we are tempted to lose faith in your mercy.

Faith is your gift.
May we have the generosity to receive it.

Further prayers ... Our Father ...

God of mercy and compassion, it was your will that your
Son should suffer for our sake, in order to break the power
of the enemy over us; grant that we may obtain the grace of
rising again with him, Christ our Lord, who lives and reigns
with you for ever. Amen.

May the Lord bless us,
may he keep us from all evil
and lead us to life everlasting. Amen.

THURSDAY

MORNING PRAYER

Lord, open my lips ...
To you be glory ...

Night Thought

My soul and I last night
Looked down together.
I said, 'Here we are come
'To the worst. Look down
'That chasm where all has fallen,
'The rose-bush and the garden
'And the ancestral hills,
'Every remembered stone.
'Of that first house
'There is no trace, none.
'You'll never cross that burn
'Again, nor the white strand
'Where lifted from the deep
'Shells lie upon the sand
'Or among sea-pinks blown,
'Never hear again
'Those wild sea-voices call,
'Eider and gull rejoicing.
'Turn away, turn
'From the closed door of home,
'You live there no longer,
'Nor shall again.

'You have no place at all
'Anywhere on earth
'That is your own, and none
'Calls you back again.'
Soul said, 'Before you were
'I spanned the abyss:
'Freedom it is, unbounded,
'Unbounded laughter. Come!'

Kathleen Raine

Lament in suffering and persecution · Ps 85(86)I

Since Christ himself has passed through the test of suffering he is able to help those who are meeting their test now (Heb 2:18).

Ant. In the day of distress I will call: surely you will reply.

Turn your ear, O Lord, and give answer
for I am poor and needy.
Preserve my life, for I am faithful:
save the servant who trusts in you.

You are my God, have mercy on me, Lord,
for I cry to you all the day long.
Give joy to your servant, O Lord,
for to you I lift up my soul.

O Lord, you are good and forgiving,
full of love to all who call.
Give heed, O Lord, to my prayer
and attend to the sound of my voice.

In the day of distress I will call
and surely you will reply.
Among the gods there is none like you, O Lord,
nor work to compare with yours.

All the nations shall come to adore you
and glorify your name, O Lord:
for you are great and do marvellous deeds,
you who alone are God.

Show me, Lord, your way
so that I may walk in your truth.
Guide my heart to fear your name.

I will praise you, Lord my God, with all my heart
and glorify your name for ever;
for your love to me has been great:
you have saved me from the depths of the grave.

The proud have risen against me;
ruthless men seek my life:
to you they pay no heed.

But you, God of mercy and compassion,
slow to anger, O Lord,
abounding in love and truth,
turn and take pity on me.

O give your strength to your servant
and save your handmaid's son.
Show me a sign of your favour
that my foes may see to their shame
that you console me and give me your help.

Ant. In the day of distress I will call: surely you will reply.

Word of God   Ex 2:24–3:7, 10

The Lord remembered his covenant with Abraham, Isaac and
Jacob; he saw the plight of Israel, and he took heed of it.
Moses was minding the flock of his father-in-law Jethro,
priest of Midian. He led the flock along the side of the
wilderness and came to Horeb, the mountain of God. There
the angel of the Lord appeared to him in the flame of a
burning bush. Moses noticed that, although the bush was on
fire, it was not being burnt up; so he said to himself, 'I
must go across to see this wonderful sight. Why does not
the bush burn away?' When the Lord saw that Moses had
turned aside to look, he called to him out of the bush,
'Moses, Moses.' And Moses answered, 'Yes, I am here.'
God said, 'Come no nearer; take off your sandals; the place

191

where you are standing is holy ground.' Then he said, 'I am the God of your forefathers, the God of Abraham, the God of Isaac, the God of Jacob.' Moses covered his face, for he was afraid to gaze on God.

The Lord said, 'I have indeed seen the misery of my people in Egypt.

Come now; I will send you to Pharoah and you shall bring my people Israel out of Egypt.'

Song of Zechariah

Ant. God will raise up a prophet for you
from among yourselves, as he raised me.

Or as follows:

Old Testament Song   Is 49:1–6

Father, glorify me in your own presence with the glory which I had with you before the world began (Jn 17:5).

Ant. My cause is with the Lord, my reward is in God's hands.

Listen to me, you coasts and islands,
pay heed, you peoples far away:
from birth the Lord called me,
he named me from my mother's womb.

He made my tongue his sharp sword
and concealed me under cover of his hand;
he made me a polished arrow
and hid me out of sight in his quiver.

He said to me, 'You are my servant,
Israel through whom I shall win glory';
so I rose to honour in the Lord's sight
and my God became my strength.

Once I said, 'I have laboured in vain;
I have spent my strength for nothing, to no purpose';
yet in truth my cause is with the Lord
and my reward is in God's hands.

And now the Lord who formed me in the womb to be his
servant,

to bring Jacob back to him
that Israel should be gathered to him,
now the Lord calls me again:
it is too slight a task for you, as my servant,
to restore the tribes of Jacob,
to bring back the descendants of Israel:
I will make you a light to the nations,
to be my salvation to earth's farthest bounds.

Ant. My cause is with the Lord, my reward is in God's hands.

Prayers

Lord, you sent Jesus Christ to us as once you sent Moses to bring freedom to your people; free us from our sins, and grant us the faith to pray constantly: Come, Lord Jesus.

Let us pray for all who are a sign of hope to men;
may they bring them to a knowledge of the source of all hope.

Let us pray for all Christian leaders, the ministers of your Church,
and for all Christians, that they may show in their lives the love of God our Father.

Heavenly Father, give hope and peace to those who despair;
may they find meaning for their lives in Jesus your Son.

Further prayers . . . Our Father . . .

Lord God, you love innocence and only you can restore it. Draw to yourself the hearts of your faithful, so that inspired by your Spirit they may remain firm in faith and active in your service. We ask this through our Lord Jesus Christ, who lives and reigns with you for ever. Amen.

May the Lord bless us,
may he keep us from all evil
and lead us to life everlasting. Amen.

193

Evening Prayer

Lord, open my lips . . .
Glory to the Father . . .

Psalm Ninety – New Style

Those who go on the dark ways of our healing,
leave themselves behind to join the self in lost worlds,
know only meeting, and find in the darkness a song.

For them there is no snare but only freedom,
no refuge but only the truth of us.
Neither the arrow by day, nor the sick mind of night
shall be unknown to them, for they shall know, in truth, a
    larger protection
where every wound opens to the dawn, and every fall is an
    entry into fuller time.

This is a way which starts with man as we know him
and pulls him apart, his dignity from his being.
For man clothed in his dignity is a small thing,
his world a small world ruled by what people say.

He will learn in nakedness the message of the shuddering
    stars:
he will learn who he is when at last, divested of seeming,
he is clothed in love, his body given and shared.

The darkness you will find peopled with thousands and tens
    of thousands
unknowing but touched with the heart made one in darkness
and you who once said to the Lord 'my refuge'
will sing with us a new song when praise at last has no
    bounds
and the heart's single word is found at the furthest reaches
and lost worlds are home of the heart's healing.

Sebastian Moore

Appeal for vindication   Ps 34(35)I

When he was abused, he did not retort with abuse (1 Pt 3:23).

Ant. He submitted to be struck down
    and did not open his mouth.

O Lord, plead my cause against my foes;
fight those who fight me.
Take up your buckler and shield;
arise to help me.

Take up the javelin and the spear
against those who pursue me.
O Lord, say to my soul:
'I am your salvation.'

But my soul shall be joyful in the Lord
and rejoice in his salvation.
My whole being will say:
'Lord, who is like you
who rescue the weak from the strong
and the poor from the oppressor?'

Lying witnesses arise
and accuse me unjustly.
They repay me evil for good:
my soul is forlorn.

Ps 34(35)II

When they were sick I went into mourning,
afflicted with fasting.
My prayer was ever on my lips,
as though for a brother, a friend.
I went as though mourning a mother,
bowed down with grief.

Now that I am in trouble they gather,
they gather and mock me.
They take me by surprise and strike me
and tear me to pieces.
They provoke me with mockery on mockery
and gnash their teeth.

O Lord, how long will you look on?
Come to my rescue!
I will thank you in the great assembly
and praise you amid the throng.

O Lord, you have seen, do not be silent,
do not stand afar off!
Awake, stir to my defence,
to my cause, O God!

Let there be joy for those who love my cause.
Let them say without end:
'Great is the Lord who delights
in the peace of his servant.'
Then my tongue shall speak of your justice
and all the day long of your praise.

Ant. He submitted to be struck down
and did not open his mouth.

Word of God   Rom 5:6–11

At the very time when we were still powerless, then Christ
died for the wicked. Even for a just man one of us would
hardly die, though perhaps for a good man one might
actually brave death; but Christ died for us while we were
yet sinners, and that is God's own proof of his love towards
us. And so, since we have now been justified by Christ's
sacrificial death, we shall all the more certainly be saved
through him from final retribution. For if, when we were
God's enemies, we were reconciled to him through the death
of his Son, how much more, now that we are reconciled,
shall we be saved by his life! But that is not all: we also
exult in God through our Lord Jesus, through whom we
have now been granted reconciliation.

Song of the Virgin Mary

Ant. There is no greater love than this,
that a man should lay down his life for his friends.

Or as follows:

Old Testament Song   Is 50:4–8

When he suffered he uttered no threats (1 Pt 3:23).

Ant. I offered my back to the lash,
I did not hide my face from spitting and insult.

The Lord God has given me
the tongue of a teacher
and skill to console the weary
with a word in the morning;
he sharpened my hearing
that I might listen like one who is taught.

The Lord God opened my ears
and I did not disobey or turn back in defiance.
I offered my back to the lash,
and let my beard be plucked from my chin,
I did not hide my face from spitting and insult;
but the Lord God stands by to help me;
therefore no insult can wound me.

I have set my face like flint,
for I know that I shall not be put to shame,
because one who will clear my name is at my side.

Ant. I offered my back to the lash,
I did not hide my face from spitting and insult.

Prayers

We thank you, Holy Father, for the gift of belief in you.
May we never lose it.

Father, give us that wholehearted love of people
which does not count the cost and does not draw back,
because it is rooted in you.

We pray for all those in industry;
may they work in harmony and justice
for the good of the whole community.

Lord Jesus, in Gethsemane you showed us
how we should trust completely in our Father;
like you, may we do his will, not our own.

Further prayers . . . Our Father . . .

Lighten our darkness, Lord, we pray; and in your great
mercy defend us from all perils and dangers of this night; for
the love of your only Son, Jesus Christ, who lives and reigns
with you for ever. Amen.

May the Lord bless us,
may he keep us from all evil
and lead us to life everlasting. Amen.

FRIDAY

MORNING PRAYER

Lord, open my lips . . .
To you be glory . . .

Christ to the Sufferer

'Lament not thy path of woe,　　O loved man –
it is not unbearable.　　I hold thee dear,
and will set my guard　　in power about thee.
My might is above all　　on this mid-earth,
victory speeds me . . .
See now the path　　where thy blood poured down,
the road dark-stained　　by thy bone-breaking
and thy body bruises.　　No more may their blows
harm thee, who hast borne　　their hard hate.'

The beloved champion　　looked backward then,
hearkening to the words　　of the Glory-King;
he saw groves standing,　　fair, green-blowing,
bright with blossoms　　where his blood had fallen.

From the 9th cent. poem *Andreas*

Prayer of contrition　　Ps 50(51)I

Jesus, Son of the living God, be merciful to me, a sinner.
Ant. The Lord laid upon him the guilt of us all.

Have mercy on me, God, in your kindness.
In your compassion blot out my offence.
O wash me more and more from my guilt
and cleanse me from my sin.

My offences truly I know them;
my sin is always before me.
Against you, you alone, have I sinned;
what is evil in your sight I have done,

198

that you may be justified when you give sentence
and be without reproach when you judge.
O see, in guilt I was born,
a sinner was I conceived.

Indeed you love truth in the heart;
then in the secret of my heart teach me wisdom.
O purify me, then I shall be clean;
O wash me, I shall be whiter than snow.

Make me hear rejoicing and gladness,
that the bones you have crushed may thrill.
From my sins turn away your face
and blot out all my guilt.

Ps 50(51)II

A pure heart create for me, O God,
put a steadfast spirit within me.
Do not cast me away from your presence,
nor deprive me of your holy spirit.

Give me again the joy of your help;
with a spirit of fervour sustain me,
that I may teach transgressors your ways
and sinners may return to you.

O rescue me, God, my helper,
and my tongue shall ring out your goodness.
O Lord, open my lips
and my mouth shall declare your praise.

For in sacrifice you take no delight,
burnt offering from me you would refuse,
my sacrifice, a contrite spirit.
A humble, contrite heart you will not spurn.

In your goodness, show favour to Zion:
rebuild the walls of Jerusalem.
Then you will be pleased with lawful sacrifice,
burnt offerings wholly consumed,
then you will be offered young bulls on your altar.

Ant. The Lord laid upon him the guilt of us all.

Praise to God, creator and shepherd   Ps 99(100)
The good shepherd lays down his life for the sheep (Jn 10:11)

Ant. I will allot him a portion with the great,
    because he exposed himself to face death,
    because he bore the sin of many.

Cry out with joy to the Lord, all the earth.
Serve the Lord with gladness.
Come before him, singing for joy.

Know that he, the Lord, is God.
He made us, we belong to him,
we are his people, the sheep of his flock.

Go within his gates, giving thanks.
Enter his courts with songs of praise.
Give thanks to him and bless his name.

Indeed, how good is the Lord,
eternal his merciful love.
He is faithful from age to age.

Ant. I will allot him a portion with the great,
    because he exposed himself to face death,
    because he bore the sin of many.

Word of God   Ex 14:13–14, 21–22, 26, 28–31

Moses said to the people,
'Have no fear, stand firm and see the deliverance that the
Lord will bring you this day; for as sure as you see the
Egyptians now, you will never see them again. The Lord
will fight for you; so hold your peace.'
Then Moses stretched out his hand over the sea, and the
Lord drove the sea away all night with a strong east wind
and turned the sea-bed into dry land. The waters were
torn apart, and the Israelites went through the sea on the
dry ground, while the waters made a wall for them to right
and to left.
Then the Lord said to Moses, 'Stretch out your hand over
the sea, and let the water flow back over the Egyptians,
their chariots and their cavalry.'
The water flowed back and covered all Pharaoh's army, the

chariots and the cavalry, which had pressed the pursuit
into the sea. Not one man was left alive. Meanwhile the
Israelites had passed along the dry ground through the sea,
with the water making a wall for them to right and to left.
That day the Lord saved Israel from the power of Egypt,
and the Israelites saw the Egyptians lying dead on the sea-
shore. When Israel saw the great power which the Lord
had put forth against Egypt, all the people feared the Lord,
and they put their faith in him and in Moses his servant.

Song of Zechariah

Ant. Our ancestors passed through the Red Sea,
and so received baptism into the fellowship of Moses;
they all drank from the supernatural rock
that accompanied their travels – and that rock was Christ.

Or as follows:

Old Testament Song   Is 52:13–53:6

*Christ was innocent of sin, and yet for our sake God made
him one with the sinfulness of men* (1 Cor 5:21).

Ant. On himself he bore our sufferings, our torments he
endured.

Behold, my servant shall prosper,
he shall be lifted up, exalted to the heights.

Time was when many were aghast at you, my people;
so now many nations recoil at sight of him,
and kings curl their lips in disgust.

For they see what they had never been told
and things unheard before fill their thoughts.

Who could have believed what we have heard,
and to whom has the power of the Lord been revealed?

He grew up before the Lord like a young plant
whose roots are in parched ground;
he had no beauty, no majesty to draw our eyes,
no grace to make us delight in him;
his form, disfigured, lost all the likeness of a man,
his beauty changed beyond human semblance.

He was despised, he shrank from the sight of men,
tormented and humbled by suffering;
we despised him, we held him of no account,
a thing from which men turn away their eyes.

Yet on himself he bore our sufferings,
our torments he endured,
while we counted him smitten by God,
struck down by disease and misery;
but he was pierced for our transgressions,
tortured for our iniquities;
the chastisement he bore is health for us
and by his scourging we are healed.

We had all strayed like sheep,
each of us had gone his own way;
but the Lord laid upon him
the guilt of us all.

Ant. On himself he bore our sufferings, our torments he
endured.

Prayers

Father, purify our hearts and cleanse us from our sin; may
all our words and actions be a worthy offering to you.

We pray for humility to serve,
strength to be detached,
and patience to bear suffering.

We pray for those who suffer helplessly;
may they find patience, comfort and hope
in Jesus Christ your Son.

We pray that through our own troubles
we may learn to be sensitive to the sufferings of others
and never fail to be ready
to make the sacrifices demanded of us.

Further prayers . . . Our Father . . .

Almighty and Holy God, whose love reaches out even
when you must condemn, and whose mercy is shown to all
who truly repent, instil in us a new and contrite spirit that

we may admit our guilt and receive from you perfect
forgiveness, through Jesus Christ our Lord. Amen.

May the Lord bless us,
may he keep us from all evil
and lead us to life everlasting. Amen.

Evening Prayer

Lord, open my lips . . .
Glory to the Father . . .

East Coker IV

The wounded surgeon plies the steel
That questions the distempered part;
Beneath the bleeding hands we feel
The sharp compassion of the healer's art
Resolving the enigma of the fever chart.

Our only health is the disease
If we obey the dying nurse
Whose constant care is not to please
But to remind of our, and Adam's curse,
And that, to be restored, our sickness must grow worse.

The whole earth is our hospital
Endowed by the ruined millionaire,
Wherein, if we do well, we shall
Die of the absolute paternal care
That will not leave us, but prevents us everywhere.

The chill ascends from feet to knees,
The fever sings in mental wires.
If to be warmed, then I must freeze
And quake in frigid purgatorial fires
Of which the flame is roses, and the smoke is briars.

The dripping blood our only drink,
The bloody flesh our only food:
In spite of which we like to think
That we are sound, substantial flesh and blood –
Again, in spite of that, we call this Friday good.

T. S. Eliot

Prayer of the suffering servant Ps 21(22)I

*Was the Messiah not bound to suffer thus before entering
upon his glory? (Lk 24:26)*

Ant. They tear holes in my hands and my feet,
they lay me in the dust of death.

My God, my God, why have you forsaken me?
You are far from my plea and the cry of my distress.
O my God, I call by day and you give no reply;
I call by night and I find no peace.

Yet you, O God, are holy.
enthroned on the praises of Israel.
In you our fathers put their trust;
they trusted and you set them free.
When they cried to you, they escaped.
In you they trusted and never in vain.

But I am a worm and no man,
the butt of men, laughing-stock of the people.
All who see me deride me.
They curl their lips, they toss their heads.
'He trusted in the Lord, let him save him;
let him release him if this is his friend.'

Yes, it was you who took me from the womb,
entrusted me to my mother's breast.
To you I was committed from my birth,
from my mother's womb you have been my God.
Do not leave me alone in my distress;
come close, there is none else to help.

Many bulls have surrounded me,
fierce bulls of Bashan close me in.
Against me they open wide their jaws,
like lions, rending and roaring.

Like water I am poured out,
disjointed are all my bones.
My heart has become like wax,
it is melted within my breast.
Parched as burnt clay is my throat,
my tongue cleaves to my jaws.

Many dogs have surrounded me,
a band of the wicked beset me.
They tear holes in my hands and my feet
and lay me in the dust of death.

I can count every one of my bones.
These people stare at me and gloat;
they divide my clothing among them.
They cast lots for my robe.

O Lord, do not leave me alone,
my strength, make haste to help me!
Rescue my soul from the sword,
my life from the grip of these dogs.
Save my life from the jaws of these lions,
my poor soul from the horns of these oxen.

Ps 21(22) II

I will tell of your name to my brethren
and praise you where they are assembled.
'You who fear the Lord give him praise;
all sons of Jacob, give him glory.
Revere him, Israel's sons.

For he has never despised
nor scorned the poverty of the poor.
From him he has not hidden his face,
but he heard the poor man when he cried.'

You are my praise in the great assembly.
My vows I will pay before those who fear him.
The poor shall eat and shall have their fill.
They shall praise the Lord, those who seek him.
May their hearts live for ever and ever!

All the earth shall remember and return to the Lord,
all families of the nations worship before him
for the kingdom is the Lord's; he is ruler of the nations.
They shall worship him, all the mighty of the earth;
before him shall bow all who go down to the dust.

And my soul shall live for him, my children serve him.
They shall tell of the Lord to generations yet to come,

declare his faithfulness to peoples yet unborn:
'These things the Lord has done.'

Ant. They tear holes in my hands and my feet,
  they lay me in the dust of death.

Word of God
Phil 3:8–11

I count everything sheer loss, because all is far outweighed
by the gain of knowing Christ Jesus my Lord, for whose sake
I did in fact lose everything. I count it so much garbage, for
the sake of gaining Christ and finding myself incorporate in
him, with no righteousness of my own, no legal rectitude,
but the righteousness which comes from faith in Christ,
given by God in response to faith. All I care for is to know
Christ, to experience the power of his resurrection, and to
share his sufferings, in growing conformity with his death,
if only I may finally arrive at the resurrection from the dead.

Song of the Virgin Mary

Ant. By baptism we were buried with him, and lay dead,
  in order that, as Christ was raised from the dead in the
    splendour of the Father,
  so also we might set our feet upon the new path of life.
Or as follows:

Old Testament Song
Is 53:7–12

*Through the obedience of the one man the many will be
made righteous* (Rom. 5:19).

Ant. He was led like a sheep to the slaughter,
  like a ewe that is dumb before the shearers.

He was afflicted, he submitted to be struck down
and did not open his mouth;
he was led like a sheep to the slaughter,
like a ewe that is dumb before the shearers.

Without protection, without justice, he was taken away;
and who gave a thought to his fate,
how he was cut off from the world of living men,
stricken to the death for my people's transgression?

206

He was assigned a grave with the wicked,
a burial-place among the refuse of mankind,
though he had done no violence
and spoken no word of treachery.

Yet the Lord took thought for his tortured servant
and healed him who had made himself a sacrifice for sin;
so shall he enjoy long life and see his children's children,
and in his hand the Lord's cause shall prosper.

After all his pains he shall be bathed in light,
after his disgrace he shall be fully vindicated;
so shall he, my servant, vindicate many,
himself bearing the penalty of their guilt.

Therefore I will allot him a portion with the great,
and he shall share the spoil with the mighty,
because he exposed himself to face death
and was reckoned among transgressors,
because he bore the sin of many
and interceded for their transgressions.

Ant. He was led like a sheep to the slaughter,
like a ewe that is dumb before the shearers.

Prayers

Loving Father, your Son came to serve not to be served;
give us your Spirit, that we may be ready to give ourselves
in helping other people.

As we pray on the day your Son died for all mankind,
may we see what is important in our lives,
and how to remain faithful to it.

Lord Jesus, you are our example;
help us to see the needs of others
and be quick to offer them our help.

Jesus, our Lord and teacher,
give wisdom and guidance
to all who teach and instruct others.

Further prayers . . . Our Father . . .

207

Crucified and Risen Lord, through your passion turn our hearts to you, and make us share more fully in the life of your resurrection. Amen.

May the Lord bless us,
may he keep us from all evil
and lead us to life everlasting. Amen.

SATURDAY

Morning Prayer

Lord, open my lips . . .
To you be glory . . .

Phoenix

Are you willing to be sponged out, erased, cancelled,
    made nothing?
Are you willing to be made nothing?
dipped into oblivion?

If not, you will never really change.

The phoenix renews her youth
only when she is burnt, burnt alive, burnt down
to hot and flocculent ash.
Then the small stirring of a new small bub in the nest
with strands of down like floating ash
Shows that she is renewing her youth like the eagle,
Immortal bird.

D. H. Lawrence

Prayer in distress   Ps 101(102)

Christ, the just, suffered for the unjust, to bring us to God
(1 Pt 3:18).

Ant. He has broken my strength in mid-course,
    he has shortened the days of my life.

O Lord, listen to my prayer
and let my cry for help reach you.
Do not hide your face from me
in the day of my distress.
Turn your ear towards me
and answer me quickly when I call.

For my days are vanishing like smoke,
my bones burn away like a fire.
My heart is withered like the grass.
I forget to eat my bread.
I cry with all my strength
and my skin clings to my bones.

I have become like a pelican in the wilderness,
like an owl in desolate places.
I lie awake and I moan
like some lonely bird on a roof.
All day long my foes revile me;
those who hate me use my name as a curse.

The bread I eat is ashes;
my drink is mingled with tears.
In your anger, Lord, and your fury
you have lifted me up and thrown me down.
My days are like a passing shadow
and I wither away like the grass.

He has broken my strength in mid-course;
he has shortened the days of my life.
I say to God: 'Do not take me away
before my days are complete,
you, whose days last from age to age.

Long ago you founded the earth
and the heavens are the work of your hands.
They will perish but you will remain.
They will all wear out like a garment.
You will change them like clothes that are changed.
But you neither change, nor have an end.'

Ant. He has broken my strength in mid-course,
   he has shortened the days of my life.

Prayer for victory Ps 107(108)

It could not be that death should keep him in its grip
(Acts 2:24).

Ant. Arise above the heavens, O Lord,
may your glory shine on earth.

My heart is ready, O God;
I will sing, sing your praise.
Awake, my soul;
awake, lyre and harp.
I will awake the dawn.

I will thank you, Lord, among the peoples,
praise you among the nations;
for your love reaches to the heavens
and your truth to the skies.
O God, arise above the heavens;
may your glory shine on earth!

O come and deliver your friends;
help with your right hand and reply.

Give us help against the foe:
for the help of man is vain.

Ant. Arise above the heavens, O Lord,
may your glory shine on earth.

Word of God Ex 24:3–8

Moses came down from the mountain and told the people
all the words of the Lord, all his laws. The whole people
answered with one voice and said, 'We will do all that the
Lord has told us.' Moses wrote down all the words of the
Lord. He rose early in the morning and built an altar at
the foot of the mountain, and put up twelve sacred pillars, one
for each of the twelve tribes of Israel. He then sent the young
men of Israel and they sacrificed bulls to the Lord as whole-
offerings and shared-offerings. Moses took half the blood
and put it in basins and the other half he flung against the
altar. Then he took the book of the covenant and read it
aloud for all the people to hear. They said, 'We will obey,
and do all that the Lord has said.' Moses then took the
210

blood and flung it over the people, saying, 'This is the
blood of the covenant which the Lord has made with you on
the terms of this book.'

Song of Zechariah

Ant. This is my blood, the blood of the covenant,
     shed for many for the forgiveness of sins.

Or as follows:

Old Testament Song   Jer 31:31–34

*Had that first covenant been faultless, there would have been
no need to look for a second in its place* (Heb 8:7).

Ant. I will remember their sin no more, says the Lord.

The time is coming, says the Lord,
when I will make a new covenant with Israel and Judah.
It will not be like the covenant I made with their
     forefathers,
when I took them by the hand and led them out of Egypt.

Although they broke my covenant,
I was patient with them, says the Lord.
But this is the covenant which I will make with Israel
after those days, says the Lord;
I will set my law within them
and write it on their hearts;
I will become their God
and they shall become my people.

No longer need they teach one another
to know the Lord;
all of them, high and low alike, shall know me,
says the Lord,
for I will forgive their wrongdoing
and remember their sin no more.

Ant. I will remember their sin no more, says the Lord.

Prayers

God, our Father, we praise you unceasingly for your great
gifts to men, and most of all for sending your Son to save us
from sin and death.

211

Strengthen those who give their energy and skill
to healing the sick in body and in mind,
doctors and nurses, surgeons and specialists,
and all who seek new ways of relieving suffering.

Created things exist only as seen by you,
only as known by you.
We praise you, Lord God, for your glory
displayed in all the creatures of the earth.

Lord Jesus Christ, may our penance bear fruit
by teaching us to be generous in caring for others.

Further prayers . . . Our Father . . .

Almighty and everliving God, in your love for man who sent
your Son our Saviour Jesus Christ to take our nature and to
die on the cross; mercifully grant that, following the example
of his great humility, we may share with him in the glory
of the resurrection, through the same Jesus Christ our
Lord. Amen.

May the Lord bless us,
may he keep us from all evil
and lead us to life everlasting. Amen.

EVENING PRAYER
Lord, open my lips . . .
Glory to the Father . . .

The Invitation
Lord, what unvalued pleasures crowned
   The times of old!
When thou wert so familiar found,
   Those days were gold.

When Abram wished, thou couldst afford
   With him to feast;
When Lot but said, 'Turn in, my Lord',
   Thou wert his guest.

But, ah, this heart of mine doth pant
   And beat for thee;

212

Yet thou art strange, and wilt not grant
   Thyself to me.

What, shall thy people be so dear
   To thee no more?
Or is not heaven to earth as near
   As heretofore?

The famished raven's hoarser cry
   Finds out thine ear;
My soul is famished, and I die
   Unless thou hear.

O thou great ALPHA, King of Kings,
   Or bow to me.
Or lend my soul seraphic wings
   To get to thee.

Nathaniel Wanley

Prayer of a man deserted by his friends   Ps 141(142)

By God's grace he had to experience death for all mankind
   (Heb 2:9).

Ant. The Lord is all that I have;
   therefore I will wait for him patiently.

With all my voice I cry to the Lord,
with all my voice I entreat the Lord.
I pour out my troubles before him;
I tell him all my distress
while my spirit faints within me.
But you, O Lord, know my path.

On the way where I shall walk
they have hidden a snare to entrap me.
Look on my right and see:
there is not one who takes my part.
I have no means of escape,
not one who cares for my soul.

I cry to you, O Lord.
I have said: 'You are my refuge,
all I have left in the land of the living.'

Listen then to my cry
for I am in the depths of distress.

Rescue me from those who pursue me
for they are stronger than I.
Bring my soul out of this prison
and then I shall praise your name.
Around me the just will assemble
because of your goodness to me.

Ant. The Lord is all that I have;
therefore I will wait for him patiently.

Invincible trust in God   Ps 22(23)

*O Death, where is your victory? O Death, where is your
sting?* (1 Cor 15:55).

Ant. Even in the valley of darkness, no evil would I fear.

The Lord is my shepherd;
there is nothing I shall want.
Fresh and green are the pastures
where he gives me repose.
Near restful waters he leads me,
to revive my drooping spirit.

He guides me along the right path;
he is true to his name.
If I should walk in the valley of darkness
no evil would I fear.
You are there with your crook and your staff;
with these you give me comfort.

You have prepared a banquet for me
in the sight of my foes.
My head you have anointed with oil;
my cup is overflowing.

Surely goodness and kindness shall follow me
all the days of my life.
In the Lord's own house shall I dwell
for ever and ever.

Ant. Even in the valley of darkness, no evil would I fear.

Word of God   Heb 9:18–20, 13–15

We find that the former covenant itself was not inaugurated
without blood. For when, as the Law directed, Moses had
recited all the commandments to the people, he took the
blood of the calves, with water, scarlet wool, and marjoram,
and sprinkled the law-book itself and all the people, saying,
'This is the blood of the covenant which God has enjoined
upon you.'

If the blood of goats and bulls and the sprinkled ashes of a
heifer have power to hallow those who have been defiled
and restore their external purity, how much greater is the
power of the blood of Christ; he offered himself without
blemish to God, a spiritual and eternal sacrifice; and his
blood will cleanse our conscience from the deadness of our
former ways and fit us for the service of the living God. And
therefore he is the mediator of a new covenant.

Song of the Virgin Mary

Ant. You have been chosen of old in the purpose of God
the Father,
   hallowed to his service by the Spirit,
   and consecrated with the sprinkled blood of Jesus
      Christ.

Or as follows:

New Testament Song   Phil 2:6–11

Ant. He humbled himself, and in obedience accepted even
death – death on a cross.

The divine nature was Christ's from the first;
yet he did not think to snatch at equality with God,
but made himself nothing,
assuming the nature of a slave.

Bearing the human likeness,
revealed in human shape,
he humbled himself,
and in obedience accepted even death –
death on a cross.

Therefore God raised him to the heights
and bestowed on him the name above all names,
that at the name of Jesus every knee should bow –
in heaven, on earth, and in the depths –
and every tongue confess, 'Jesus Christ is Lord',
to the glory of God the Father.

Ant. He humbled himself, and in obedience accepted even
   death – death on a cross.

Prayers

We should pray to God at all times, and in this season of
Lent try to deepen our life of prayer; let us now pray to God
as his children, from the depths of our hearts.

May we receive the gift of conversion
and discover a new way of living
in deeper faith and greater love.

We pray for all men and women who are suffering
   persecution;
Lord, help them to be faithful to the end,
that their love may overcome hatred.

Lord Jesus, through the example of Mary your mother,
teach us to respond to all you ask of us,
in humility and thanksgiving.

Further prayers . . . Our Father . . .

As the passover of Christ draws near, we ask you, Father,
that all Christians may share more fully in the death and
resurrection of your Son, and be made one in his Spirit.
We ask this through the same Jesus Christ our Lord. Amen.

May the Lord bless us,
may he keep us from all evil
and lead us to life everlasting. Amen.

HOLY THURSDAY

Lord, open my lips . . .

Corpus Christi

Come, dear Heart!
The fields are white to harvest: come and see
As in a glass the timeless mystery
Of love, whereby we feed
On God, our bread indeed.
Torn by the sickles, see him share the smart
Of travailing Creation: maimed, despised,
Yet by his lovers the more dearly prized
Because for us he lays his beauty down –
Last toll paid by Perfection for our loss!
Trace on these fields his everlasting Cross,
And o'er the stricken sheaves the Immortal Victim's
   crown.

From far horizons came a Voice that said,
'Lo! from the hand of Death take thou thy daily bread.'
Then I, awakening, saw
A splendour burning in the heart of things:
The flame of living love which lights the law
Of mystic death that works the mystic birth.
I knew the patient passion of the earth,
Maternal, everlasting, whence there springs
The Bread of Angels and the life of man.
Now in each blade
I, blind no longer, see
The glory of God's growth: know it to be
An earnest of the Immemorial Plan.
Yea, I have understood
How all things are one great oblation made:
He on our altars, we on the world's rood.
Even as this corn,
Earth-born,

We are snatched from the sod,
Reaped, ground to grist,
Crushed and tormented in the Mills of God,
And offered at Life's hands, a living Eucharist.

Evelyn Underhill

Gratitude to God   Ps 33(34)

Be full of brotherly affection, kindly and humble-hearted
(1 Pt 3:8).

Ant. Jesus had always loved his own who were in the world,
and now he was to show the full extent of his love.

I will bless the Lord at all times,
his praise always on my lips;
in the Lord my soul shall make its boast.
The humble shall hear and be glad.

Glorify the Lord with me.
Together let us praise his name.
I sought the Lord and he answered me;
from all my terrors he set me free.

Look towards him and be radiant;
let your faces not be abashed.
Taste and see that the Lord is good.
He is happy who seeks refuge in him.

Revere the Lord, you his saints.
They lack nothing, those who revere him.
Strong lions suffer want and go hungry
but those who seek the Lord lack no blessing.

Come, children, and hear me
that I may teach you the fear of the Lord.
Who is he who longs for life
and many days, to enjoy his prosperity?

Then keep your tongue from evil
and your lips from speaking deceit.
Turn aside from evil and do good;
seek and strive after peace.

Ant. Jesus has always loved his own who were in the world,
    and now he was to show the full extent of his love.

The blessings of unity   Ps 132(133)

May they all be one (Jn 17:21).

Ant. If there is love among you,
    then all men will know that you are my disciples.

How good and how pleasant it is,
brothers dwelling in unity!

It is like precious oil upon the head
running down upon the beard,
running down upon Aaron's beard
upon the collar of his robes.

It is like the dew of Hermon which falls
on the heights of Zion.
For there the Lord gives his blessing,
life for ever.

Ant. If there is love among you,
    then all men will know that you are my disciples.

Word of God   Jn 13:3–9, 12–17

During supper, Jesus, well aware that the Father had entrusted everything to him, and that he had come from God and
was going back to God, rose from table, laid aside his garments, and taking a towel, tied it round him. Then he poured
water into a basin, and began to wash his disciples' feet and
to wipe them with the towel.
When it was Simon Peter's turn, Peter said to him, 'You,
Lord, washing my feet?' Jesus replied, 'You do not understand now what I am doing, but one day you will.' Peter
said, 'I will never let you wash my feet.' 'If I do not wash
you,' Jesus replied, 'you are not in fellowship with me.'
'Then, Lord,' said Simon Peter, 'not my feet only; wash my
hands and head as well!'
After washing their feet and taking his garments again, he
sat down. 'Do you understand what I have done for you?' he

219

asked. You call me "Master" and "Lord", and rightly so, for that is what I am. Then if I, your Lord and Master, have washed your feet, you also ought to wash one another's feet. I have set you an example: you are to do as I have done for you. In very truth I tell you, a servant is not greater than his master, nor a messenger than the one who sent him. If you know this, happy are you if you act upon it.'

Song of Zechariah

Ant. I give you a new commandment: love one another;
     as I have loved you, so you are to love one another.

Or as follows:

New Testament Song   Jn 15:4, 5, 9–10, 12–14

Ant. This is my commandment: love one another.

Dwell in me, as I in you.
He who dwells in me,
as I dwell in him,
bears much fruit.

As the Father has loved me,
so I have loved you.
Dwell in my love.

If you heed my commands,
you will dwell in my love,
as I have heeded the Father's commands
and dwell in his love.

This is my commandment:
love one another,
as I have loved you.

There is no greater love than this,
that a man lay down his life for his friends.
You are my friends,
if you do what I command you.

Ant. This is my commandment: love one another.

Prayers

God, we witness
unheard of things.
You, God, have given power
to Jesus of Nazareth,
whom we recognize as one of us,
to be merciful to others
and to forgive them.

We ask you, God,
for this power, this freedom
to be a healing grace
to all those who live with us
in this world,
as a sign that you are
the forgiveness of sins.

God,
we break bread for one another
and receive the body
of Jesus Christ, your Son.

We ask you
that, strengthened by him,
we may live in love and peace,
so that he may be present wherever we speak words,
and may become his body
in this world, for ever. Amen.
Omit the usual Conclusion during the Triduum.

EVENING PRAYER

Lord, open my lips ...

Verbum Supernum

The mighty Word of God came forth,
United to the Father still;
Came forth to do his earthly work,
Obedient to the Father's will.

221

The night that he was giv'n to death
He gave his Body to his friends;
In living and life-giving Bread
The Lord of all to man descends.

He gives to man in two-fold kind
His sacred Body and his Blood;
Man's two-fold self receives from him
The body and the spirit's food.

Our friend and brother he was born,
Whose death redeemed us on the tree;
He reigns for ever, God supreme,
Our prize for all eternity.

O Victim sacrificed for men,
Give strength against the foe within;
Throw open your eternal gates,
That all your own may enter in.

Blest Trinity, we give you praise,
Whose pow'r and might all things transcend;
Bring us to where your glory dwells,
And grant us life that never ends.

The Stanbrook Abbey Hymnal

God's care for his people   Ps 147

*When we break the bread, is it not a means of
sharing in the body of Christ?* (1 Cor 10:16).

Ant. He establishes peace on your borders,
    he feeds you with finest wheat.

O praise the Lord, Jerusalem!
Zion, praise your God!

He has strengthened the bars of your gates,
he has blessed the children within you.
He established peace on your borders,
he feeds you with finest wheat.

He sends out his word to the earth
and swiftly runs his command.

He showers down snow white as wool,
he scatters hoar-frost like ashes.

He hurls down hailstones like crumbs.
The waters are frozen at his touch;
he sends forth his word and it melts them:
at the breath of his mouth the waters flow.

He makes his word known to Jacob,
to Israel his laws and decrees.
He has not dealt thus with other nations;
he has not taught them his decrees.

Ant. He establishes peace on your borders,
   he feeds you with finest wheat.

Thanksgiving   Ps 115(116)

When we bless 'the cup of blessing', is it not a means
of sharing in the blood of Christ? (1 Cor 14:16).

Ant. The cup of salvation I will raise,
   I will call on the Lord's name.

I trusted, even when I said:
'I am sorely afflicted,'
and when I said in my alarm:
'No man can be trusted.'

How can I repay the Lord
for his goodness to me?
The cup of salvation I will raise;
I will call on the Lord's name.

My vows to the Lord I will fulfil
before all his people.
O precious in the eyes of the Lord
is the death of his faithful.

Your servant, Lord, your servant am I;
you have loosened my bonds.
A thanksgiving sacrifice I make:
I will call on the Lord's name.

My vows to the Lord I will fulfil
before all his people,
in the courts of the house of the Lord,
in your midst, O Jerusalem.

Ant. The cup of salvation I will raise,
 I will call on the Lord's name.

Word of God   1 Cor 11:23–29

The tradition which I handed on to you came to me from the
Lord himself: that the Lord Jesus, on the night of his arrest,
took bread and, after giving thanks to God, broke it and
said: 'This is my body, which is for you; do this as a memorial of me.' In the same way, he took the cup after supper,
and said: 'This cup is the new covenant sealed by my blood.
Whenever you drink it, do this as a memorial of me.' For
every time you eat this bread and drink the cup, you proclaim
the death of the Lord, until he comes.
It follows that anyone who eats the bread or drinks the cup
of the Lord unworthily will be guilty of desecrating the body
and blood of the Lord. A man must test himself before eating his share of the bread and drinking from the cup. For he
who eats and drinks eats and drinks judgment on himself if
he does not discern the Body.

Song of the Virgin Mary

Ant. O sacred banquet at which Christ is received!
 Here the memory of his passion is renewed,
 our minds are filled with grace,
 and a pledge of the glory to come is given to us.

Or as follows:

New Testament Song   Jn 6, passim

Ant. Whoever eats this bread shall live for ever.

The bread that God gives comes down from heaven
and gives life to the world.
I am the bread of life.
Whoever comes to me shall never be hungry,
and whoever believes in me shall never be thirsty.

I am the bread of life.
I am that living bread which has come down from heaven;
if anyone eats this bread he shall live for ever.
The bread which I will give is my own flesh;
I give it for the life of the world.

Unless you eat the flesh of the Son of Man and drink his
    blood
you can have no life in you.
Whoever eats my flesh and drinks my blood
possesses eternal life,
and I will raise him up on the last day.

My flesh is real food; my blood is real drink.
Whoever eats my flesh and drinks my blood
dwells continually in me and I dwell in him.
As the living Father sent me, and I live because of the Father
so he who eats me shall live because of me.

Ant. Whoever eats this bread shall live for ever.

Prayers

Lord our God,
you have sown in us your word,
given us your Son –
he, who was broken and died for us,
is bread and life
for the world.

We ask you
to let us find strength to tread his path,
to let us be for each other
as fertile as seed
and as nourishing as bread,
and thus lead a happy life.

We have heard your word, O God,
and have broken bread
for each other.
May this be a sign for us
that you are very near,
that we are your people,
nourished and loved by you.

225

Never forsake us;
be the light around us
and our firm ground
and even more,
be our future, our father.
Lord God,
we have received your word
and have tasted your truth –
Jesus Christ, the Son of your love,
delivered into the hands of men
and put to death.

We pray
that we may never be scandalised
by this man,
but take him as he is,
and that we may learn to see
that we owe our lives to him
today and for ever. Amen.

GOOD FRIDAY

MORNING PRAYER

Lord, open my lips ...

Still Falls the Rain

STILL falls the Rain –
Dark as the world of man, black as our loss –
Blind as the nineteen hundred and forty nails
Upon the Cross.

Still falls the Rain
With a sound like the pulse of the heart that is changed to
 the hammer-beat
In the Potter's Field, and the sound of the impious feet

On the Tomb:
           Still falls the Rain
In the Field of Blood where the small hopes breed and the
 human brain
Nurtures its greed, that worm with the brow of Cain.

226

Still falls the Rain
At the feet of the Starved Man hung upon the Cross.
Christ that each day, each night, nails there,

have mercy on us –

On Dives and on Lazarus:
Under the Rain the sore and the gold are as one.

Still falls the Rain –
Still falls the Blood from the Starved Man's wounded Side:
He bears in his Heart all wounds, – those of the light

that died,

The last faint spark
In the self-murdered heart, the wounds of the sad

uncomprehending dark,

The wounds of the baited bear, –
The blind and weeping bear whom the keepers beat
On his helpless flesh . . . the tears of the hunted hare.

Still falls the Rain –
Then – O Ile leape up to my God: who pulles me doune –
See, see where Christ's blood streames in the firmament:
It flows from the Brow we nailed upon the tree
Deep to the dying, to the thirsting heart
That holds the fires of the world, – dark-smirched with
   pain
As Caesar's laurel crown.

Then sounds the voice of One who like the heart of man
Was once a child who among beasts has lain –
'Still do I love, still shed my innocent light, my Blood,
   for thee.'

Edith Sitwell

Appeal for help   Ps 34(35)

He saved others: now let him save himself,
if this is God's Messiah, his Chosen (Lk 23:35).

Ant. Carrying his own cross, Jesus went out to the
Place of the Skull, where they crucified him.

GOOD FRIDAY: MORNING

O Lord, plead my cause against my foes;
fight those who fight me.
Take up your buckler and shield;
arise to help me.

Take up the javelin and the spear
against those who pursue me.
O Lord, say to my soul:
'I am your salvation.'

Lying witnesses arise
and accuse me unjustly.
They repay me evil for good:
my soul is forlorn.

When they were sick I went into mourning,
afflicted with fasting.
My prayer was ever on my lips,
as though for a brother, a friend.
I went as though mourning a mother,
bowed down with grief.

Now that I am in trouble they gather,
they gather and mock me.
They take me by surprise and strike me
and tear me to pieces.
They provoke me with mockery on mockery
and gnash their teeth.

O Lord, you have seen, do not be silent,
do not stand afar off!
Awake, stir to my defence,
to my cause, O God!

Vindicate me, Lord, in your justice,
do not let them rejoice.
Do not let them think: 'Yes! we have won,
we have brought him to an end!'

Let there be joy for those who love my cause.
Let them say without end:
'Great is the Lord who delights
in the peace of his servant.'

Then my tongue shall speak of your justice
and all the day long of your praise.

Ant. Carrying his own cross, Jesus went out to the
Place of the Skull, where they crucified him.

Word of God
Heb 2:10–11, 14—18

It was clearly fitting that God for whom and through whom
all things exist should, in bringing many sons to glory, make
the leader who delivers them perfect through sufferings. For
a consecrating priest and those whom he consecrates are all
of one stock. The children of a family share the same flesh
and blood; and so he too shared ours, so that through death
he might break the power of him who had death at his command, that is, the devil; and might liberate those who,
through fear of death, had all their lifetime been in servi-
tude. It is not angels, mark you, that he takes to himself, but
the sons of Abraham. And therefore he had to be made
like these brothers of his in every way, so that he might be
merciful and faithful as their high priest before God, to ex-
piate the sins of the people. For since he himself has passed
through the test of suffering, he is able to help those who are
meeting their test now.

Prayer of Saint Philip Howard

O Christ, my Lord, which for my sins didst hang upon a tree,
grant that thy grace in me, poor wretch, may still ingrafted
    be.

Grant that thy naked hanging there may kill in me all pride
and care of wealth, sith thou didst then in such poor state
    abide.

Grant that thy crown of pricking thorns, which thou for me
    didst wear,
may make me willing for thy sake all shame and pain to bear.

Grant that those scorns and taunts which thou didst on the
    cross endure
may humble me, and in my heart all patience still procure.

229

Grant that thy praying for thy foes may plant within my breast
such charity as from my heart I malice may detest.

Grant that thy pierced hands, which did of nothing all things frame,
may move me to lift up my hands and ever praise thy name.

Grant that thy wounded feet, whose steps were perfect evermore,
may learn my feet to tread those paths which thou hast gone before.

Grant that those drops of blood which ran out from thy heart amain
may meek my heart into salt tears to see thy grievous pain.

Grant that thy blessed grave, wherein thy body lay awhile,
may bury all such vain delights as may my mind defile.

Grant that thy going down to them which did thy sight desire
may keep my soul, when I am dead, clean from the purging fire.

Grant that thy rising up from death may raise my thoughts from sin;
grant that thy parting from this earth from earth my heart may win.

Grant, Lord, that thy ascending then may lift my mind to thee
that there my heart and joy may rest, though here in flesh I be. Amen.

EVENING PRAYER

Lord, open my lips ...

The Dream of the Rood

Listen, for I mean to tell   of a most marvellous dream,
which once I dreamed   in the deep night,
when every living soul   was sound asleep.

It seemed to me that I beheld   bright in the air
a wondrous cross of wood   speeding its way,
brightest of beams: and all that blessed sign,
glorious with gold,   glittered with jewels,
one on each earth-o'erstretching arm,   and yet a fifth,
glowing upon its heart.   The angelic hosts all gazed,
lovely as God decreed.   This was no loathsome gallows
which all the angels saw,   the holy souls,
the men of earth   and all things made by God.

Blessed was this triumphal sign   and I was stained with
     sins,
transfixed by my misdeeds.   To me the glorious tree
     appeared
decked in solemn vestments,   sumptuously shining,
radiant with rich gold   and royal jewels
adorning with glory   the Almighty's tree.
And still through all this splendour   I could see
its agonies of long ago,   as it began
to bleed from its right side.   At this strange, lovely sight
I was downcast with sorrows   and with dread.
It seemed to change,   this speeding sign,
both robes and hue;   sometimes all red with blood
running in torrents,   sometimes with treasure hung.
And so I lay and watched   for a long while
with rueful sorrow   the Redeemer's tree,
until I heard   how it began,
most blessed of all trees,   to talk to me.

'It was long years ago –   I can recall it yet –
that I was felled   in a place in the forest,
hauled away from my home.   Hostile hands seized me,
bade me lift miscreants up   for men to see their shame.
They heaved me on their shoulders,   set me up upon a
     hill,
crowded round to fix me fast.   Then far off I saw the Lord
     of men
hastening, hero-like   to mount upon me high.
How then could I dare   to disobey my Lord,
to bend or break   even though I beheld

all the earth quaking?   Quick though it would have been
to fell our foes,   I none the less stood fast.
He made ready, the young hero,   he, the Lord of hosts,
resolute and strong   upon his gallows rose aloft,
valiant for the crowd to see,   for he vouchsafed to set man
     free.
I shook as he, the Son of Man, enfolded me,   yet still I
     feared to bow to earth,
fall to the ground;   yet still I must stand firm.
I was set up, the Cross,   I lifted up a mighty King,
the heaven's Lord; and yet   I dared not yield.
They stabbed me with their nails of iron black –   my
     wounds can still be seen,
the gaping marks of malice.   Not one of them might I
     harm.
They mocked us both together;   I was suffused with
     blood
poured from the side of the Son of Man   when he had
     sent forth his spirit.

'Much did I suffer,   standing on the mount,
at many hostile hands,   as I watched the Lord of hosts
dolorously labour.   Clouds of darkness
covered in blackness   the body of the Lord,
his shining radiance,   as his shade departed,
wan beneath the heavens   and all creation wept,
proclaiming the King's death.   Christ was upon the
     Cross

'And yet there hastened   to the Hero's help
men from afar,   and I must watch it all.
Sorely I was downcast with sorrows,   yet I suffered these
     men's hands,
humble and brave as he.   Him they took, Almighty God,
bore him away from his cruel torment,   brave men who
     left me
to wait, wet with his blood,   pierced through and through
     with his wounds.
Weary in limb he was carried away,   and they stood and
     watched around his body,

looking upon the Lord of heaven   as he lay there at rest,
weary after much warfare.   They would make him a tomb
where I, his death, saw it,   cut from the shining rock;
in it they laid their victorious Lord   as they chanted
> his lament,
sorrowing as the night came down   and they made ready
> to depart,
wearily leaving the mighty Prince   who lay there deprived
> of guard.
Yet we stood there weeping   for a long while
where we were planted   as their wailing died away,
his valiant cohort.   His corpse grew cold,
the lovely casket of his soul.   Then cruelly men began
to fell us to the earth: that was our fearful fate!
They buried us in a deep pit,   and yet the servants of the
> Prince,
his friends, discovered where I lay . . .
they made me splendid   with silver and gold.'

> From the Old English, trans. E. Colledge

Prayer of the suffering servant   Ps 21(22)

He suffered death, so that, by God's gracious will,
in tasting death he should stand for us all (Heb 2:9).

Ant. My God, my God, why have you forsaken me?

My God, my God, why have you forsaken me?
You are far from my plea and the cry of my distress.
O my God, I call by day and you give no reply;
I call by night and I find no peace.

Yet you, O God, are holy,
enthroned on the praises of Israel.
In you our fathers put their trust;
they trusted and you set them free.
When they cried to you, they escaped.
In you they trusted and never in vain.

But I am a worm and no man,
the butt of men, laughing-stock of the people.
All who see me deride me.
They curl their lips, they toss their heads.

'He trusted in the Lord, let him save him;
let him release him if this is his friend.'

Yes, it was you who took me from the womb,
entrusted me to my mother's breast.
To you I was committed from my birth,
from my mother's womb you have been my God.
Do not leave me alone in my distress;
come close, there is none else to help.

Many bulls have surrounded me,
fierce bulls of Bashan close me in.
Against me they open wide their jaws,
like lions, rending and roaring.

Like water I am poured out,
disjointed are all my bones.
My heart has become like wax,
it is melted within my breast.

Parched as burnt clay is my throat,
my tongue cleaves to my jaws.

Many dogs have surrounded me,
a band of the wicked beset me.
They tear holes in my hands and my feet
and lay me in the dust of death.

I can count every one of my bones.
These people stare at me and gloat;
they divide my clothing among them.
They cast lots for my robe.

O Lord, do not leave me alone,
my strength, make haste to help me!
Rescue my soul from the sword,
my life from the grip of these dogs.
Save my life from the jaws of these lions,
my poor soul from the horns of these oxen.

I will tell of your name to my brethren
and praise you where they are assembled.
'You who fear the Lord give him praise;
all sons of Jacob, give him glory.
Revere him, Israel's sons.

For he has never despised
nor scorned the poverty of the poor.
From him he has not hidden his face,
but he heard the poor man when he cried.'

You are my praise in the great assembly.
My vows I will pay before those who fear him.
The poor shall eat and shall have their fill.
They shall praise the Lord, those who seek him.
May their hearts live for ever and ever!

All the earth shall remember and return to the Lord,
all families of the nations worship before him
for the kingdom is the Lord's; he is ruler of the nations.
They shall worship him, all the mighty of the earth;
before him shall bow all who go down to the dust.

And my soul shall live for him, my children serve him.
They shall tell of the Lord to generations yet to come,
declare his faithfulness to peoples yet unborn:
'These things the Lord has done.'

Ant My God, my God, why have you forsaken me?

Word of God Heb 5:1–5, 7–10
Every high priest is taken from among men and appointed
their representative before God, to offer gifts and sacrifices
for sins. He is able to bear patiently with the ignorant and
erring, since he too is beset by weakness; and because of
this he is bound to make sin-offerings for himself no less
than for the people. And nobody arrogates the honour to
himself: he is called by God, as indeed Aaron was. So it is
with Christ: he did not confer upon himself the glory of
becoming high priest; it was granted by God.
In the days of his earthly life he offered up prayers and
petitions, with loud cries and tears, to God who was able to
deliver him from the grave. Because of his humble sub-
mission his prayer was heard: son though he was, he learned
obedience in the school of suffering, and, once perfected,
became the source of eternal salvation for all who obey him,
named by God high priest in the succession of Melchizedek.

Prayers

Let us pray
for this world, which is sighing
and groaning for redemption,
for the whole of suffering mankind in the present age,
for all those who are the victims of war and racial conflict,
for those who are overwhelmed by natural disasters,
for all who meet with any kind of accident,
for those who are in any kind of danger,
let us pray:

> Lord God,
> you want the well-being of men
> and not their destruction.
> Take all violence from our midst.
> Extinguish hatred in our hearts.
> Curb the passion in us
> that makes us seek each others' lives.
> Give peace on earth
> to all mankind.
> We ask you this
> through Jesus Christ our Lord.

Let us pray
for those who are deprived and live in poverty,
for all who are despairing
and feel themselves to be beyond help,
for all whose minds are disturbed or who are mentally ill,
for those who suffer physically for years
and whose bodies are gradually broken down.
Let us pray
for all who must die alone
without the hope of life after death
and without faith in the resurrection of their bodies.

> Lord God,
> you have made us mortal
> and we must die.
> Do not, we beseech you,
> take our lives away for ever,

you who are
a God of the living.
We ask you this
for Jesus' sake,
today and every day
for ever and ever.

Let us pray
for all those who are in great difficulty –
for those who have lost their faith
in man and love, their faith in God,
for those who seek truth but cannot find it.
Let us pray for all married people
who have drifted apart from each other
and for all priests who have broken down
under the strain of their office.

Lord God,
you are the comfort of the sorrowful
and the strength of the tortured.
Hear the prayers
of all men in distress
and all who appeal to your mercy,
so that they may recognise with joy
that you have helped them
in every ordeal,
through Jesus Christ our Lord.

Let us pray
for the town we live and work in,
for all the people in it who are lonely,
for those whose voices are never heard
and those who find no friends.
Let us pray
for the homeless and those without shelter
and for all who are disheartened
and feel that they have been betrayed.

Lord God,
you have given us
a place to live in,

a town and space to build in
and people to live with.
Open our eyes to each other.
Make us humble enough
to help other people
and comfort them,
so that a little of your love
may be seen in this town,
through Jesus Christ our Lord.

Let us ask the Lord for forgiveness
for the suffering that we cause to others,
for our forgetfulness and neglect of others,
for our lack of understanding for each other,
for speaking ill of other people
and for the bitterness and spite
we so often feel toward our fellows,
for not being able to forgive.
Let us pray for forgiveness
of all the sins that men, in their helplessness,
commit against each other.

Lord God,
we behold you
in the broken body
of Jesus our brother
and know who you are
for this world.
In the broken bread
we receive the promise
that you are the forgiveness
of our sins.
We pray, for the sake of him
in whom everything is consummated;
let us enter into your peace,
whoever we are,
and send your Spirit upon us
so that we may be
open and receptive
to you and pray to you

with the words of the prayer
that he taught us –

(Prayers by Huub Oosterhuis)

Our Father, who art in heaven,
hallowed by thy name.
Thy kingdom come.
Thy will be done
on earth, as it is in heaven.
Give us this day our daily bread,
and forgive us our trespasses
as we forgive those who trespass against us;
and lead us not into temptation,
but deliver us from evil.
For thine is the kingdom
and the power and the glory,
for ever and ever. Amen.

HOLY SATURDAY

Morning Prayer

Lord, open my lips . . .

The Dream of the Rood

'Now you have heard the tale,   man dear to my heart,
of what I once endured   at the hands of wicked men,
of my cruel wrongs.   And so my time has come,
for far and wide   they worship me,
the men of earth   and all things made by God,
to this sign they address their prayers.   On me the
    Son of God
suffered for a season,   and so in splendour now
I soar up to the skies,   and I can save
each man who in his heart   has holy dread for me.
I whom they made to be   most hateful to all men,
most dreadful of all deaths,   do now make straight
the way of life   to every living man.
See how the King of glory   has greatly honoured me:
no tree in all the wood   is dearer to heaven's Lord;
me he has magnified   as was his mother, Mary,

239

chosen from all mankind   by him, Almighty God,
who made her richer far   than all the race of Eve.

'Now I command you,   man dear to my heart,
that you make this vision   known to men.
Tell with your words   that this is a tree of glory
on which Almighty God   suffered once
for the many sins   of all mankind
and for the ancient trespass   done by Adam.
There he tasted death,   yet the Lord of life did rise,
in all his majesty,   to help mankind.
Then he ascended to the heavens,   yet he will come again
upon this earth   each man to seek,
he, our very Lord,   on Judgment Day,
he, Almighty God,   and all his angels with him.
He who has power to judge   will judgment give
to every single man   as he has merited
here before,   during his fleeting life.
No man shall then   not fear to think
with what words   the Lord will speak to him.
He will ask of all that throng   where he may be, that man
who for sake of the Lord's name   shrank not from tasting
death's bitter cup,   as once he did upon the Cross.
But they shall tremble   as they seek in vain
for words with which   to answer Christ.
Yet there is none   who need despair
if in his heart he bore   that best of tokens;
but through the sacred Cross   each single soul
shall find its homeward way   from earth to heaven,
there where it longs to live   together with the Lord.'

So with a lightened heart   to that Tree of Life I prayed
with all devotion,   there, alone,
with no one near at hand;   now was my mind
eager to depart,   and I endured
much longing.   All that life holds for me
is to place all my trust   in the victorious Tree,
I who among all men   know most its might,
its honour due.   And this is the delight

great in my heart,   this is my hope
set all upon the Cross.
                I count on none,
on no one to protect me on this earth.   They are all gone,
severed from this world's joys,   they have sought the
    King of glory,
they now live in the heavens   with the Father on high,
they dwell in glory;   and, each single day,
I long for when   the Lord's own Cross
which once on earth below   I have beheld
shall bid me leave   this fleeting life,
and bring me there   to that great bliss,
to that heavenly joy   where his own people
sit at the banquet of the Lord   where there is everlasting
    bliss.
Let him but seat me there   and let me then
dwell in that glory,   and with the saints of God
partake of his own joy.
                May the Lord protect me with
    his love,
he who on earth   once suffered
upon a gallows tree   for guilty man.
He let us loose,   he gave us life again,
a heavenly home;   hope was renewed
with blessings and with bliss   for those who burned in
    purging fires.
He journeyed on in victory,   the vanquishing Son,
mighty, invincible;   and when he and all his main,
that company of spirits,   entered the kingdom of God,
he, the almighty Ruler,   then the angels rejoiced
and all the saints   who sat in heaven above,
dwelling in glory,   when their God returned,
the almighty Lord,   into his own native land.
            From the Old English, trans. E. Colledge

Rest in God

Ps 61(62)

*Taking the body of Jesus down from the cross, Joseph
wrapped it in a linen sheet, and laid it in a tomb* (Lk 23:53).

Ant. O my enemies, do not exult over me;
   I have fallen, but shall rise again;
   though I dwell in darkness, the Lord is my light.

In God alone is my soul at rest;
my help comes from him.
He alone is my rock, my stronghold,
my fortress: I stand firm.

How long will you all attack one man
to break him down,
as though he were a tottering wall,
or a tumbling fence?

Their plan is only to destroy:
they take pleasure in lies.
With their mouth they utter blessing
but in their heart they curse.

In God alone be at rest, my soul;
for my hope comes from him.
He alone is my rock, my stronghold,
my fortress: I stand firm.

Ant. O my enemies, do not exult over me;
   I have fallen, but shall rise again;
   though I dwell in darkness, the Lord is my light.

Song of serenity

Ps 130(131)

*Joseph laid the body of Jesus in a tomb cut out of the rock,
in which no one had been laid before* (Lk 23:53).

Ant. Without protection, without justice, he was taken away;
   and who gave a thought to his fate?

O Lord, my heart is not proud
nor haughty my eyes.
I have not gone after things too great
nor marvels beyond me.

Truly I have set my soul
in silence and peace.

A weaned child on its mother's breast,
even so is my soul.

O Israel, hope in the Lord
both now and for ever.

Ant. Without protection, without justice, he was taken away;
and who gave a thought to his fate?

Word of God   Heb 9:11–14

Now Christ has come, high priest of good things already in
being. The tent of his priesthood is a greater and more perfect one, not made by men's hands, that is, not belonging to
this created world; the blood of his sacrifice is his own
blood, not the blood of goats and calves; and thus he has
entered the sanctuary once and for all and secured an eternal
deliverance. For if the blood of goats and bulls and the
sprinkled ashes of a heifer have power to hallow those who
have been defiled and restore their external purity, how
much greater is the power of the blood of Christ; he offered
himself without blemish to God, a spiritual and eternal
sacrifice; and his blood will cleanse our conscience from the
deadness of our former ways and fit us for the service of the
living God.

Song of Zechariah

Ant. The women went home and prepared spices and per-
fumes, and on the Sabbath day they rested.

Or as follows:

Old Testament Song   Lam 3:52–57, 25–26

*Joseph rolled a large stone against the entrance, and went
away* (Mt 27:60).

Ant. I called on thy name, O Lord, from the depths of the pit.

Those who for no reason were my enemies
drove me cruelly like a bird;
they thrust me alive into the silent pit,
and they closed it over me with a stone;
the waters rose high above my head,
and I said, 'My end has come.'

But I called on thy name, O Lord,
from the depths of the pit;
thou heardest my voice; do not turn a deaf ear
when I cry, 'Come to my relief.'
Thou wast near when I called to thee;
thou didst say, 'Have no fear.'

The Lord is good to those who look for him,
to all who seek him;
it is good to wait in patience and sigh
for deliverance by the Lord.

Ant. I called on thy name, O Lord, from the depths of
the pit.

Prayer

Almighty and eternal God, your only-begotten Son went
down into the grave and came up from thence in glory;
grant that, through his resurrection, your faithful who have
been buried with him in baptism may journey safely to
everlasting life, through Christ our Lord. Amen.

EVENING PRAYER

Lord, open my lips ...

Sorrow

Sorrow is true for everyone – a word
That illiterate men may read
By divining in the heart
God's human name, and natural shroud.

Sorrow is deep and vast – we travel on
As far as pain can penetrate, to the end
Of power and possibility; to find
The contours of the world, with heaven aligned
Upon infinity; the shape of man!

Kathleen Raine

Release after pain Ps 4

The women took note of the tomb and observed how the body of Jesus was laid (Lk 23:55, 56).

Ant. He was assigned a grave with the wicked,
   though he had done no violence
   and spoken no word of treachery.

When I call, answer me, O God of justice;
from anguish you released me, have mercy and hear me!

O men, how long will your hearts be closed,
will you love what is futile and seek what is false?

It is the Lord who grants favours to those whom he loves;
the Lord hears me whenever I call him.

Fear him; do not sin: ponder on your bed and be still.
Make justice your sacrifice and trust in the Lord.

'What can bring us happiness?' many say.
Lift up the light of your face on us, O Lord.

You have put into my heart a greater joy
than they have from abundance of corn and new wine.

I will lie down in peace and sleep comes at once
for you alone, Lord, make me dwell in safety.

Ant. He was assigned a grave with the wicked,
   though he had done no violence
   and spoken no word of treachery.

Confidence in God Ps 3

The chief priests and the pharisees made the grave secure; they sealed the stone, and left the guard in charge (Mt 27:66).

Ant. The Lord took thought for his tortured servant
   and healed him who had made himself a sacrifice for sin.

How many are my foes, O Lord!
How many are rising up against me!
How many are saying about me:
'There is no help for him in God.'

But you, Lord, are a shield about me,
my glory, who lift up my head.
I cry aloud to the Lord.
He answers from his holy mountain.

I lie down to rest and I sleep.
I wake, for the Lord upholds me.
I will not fear even thousands of people
who are ranged on every side against me.

Arise, Lord; save me, my God.
O Lord of salvation, bless your people!

Ant. The Lord took thought for his tortured servant
and healed him who had made himself a sacrifice for sin.

Word of God   Heb 10:10–14, 19–23

It is by the will of God that we have been consecrated,
through the offering of the body of Jesus Christ once and for
all.
Every priest stands performing his service daily and offering
time after time the same sacrifices, which can never remove
sins. But Christ offered for all time one sacrifice for sins,
and took his seat at the right hand of God, where he waits
henceforth until his enemies are made his footstool. For
by one offering he has perfected for all time those who are
thus consecrated.

So now, my friends, the blood of Jesus makes us free to
enter boldly into the sanctuary by the new, living way which
he has opened for us through the curtain, the way of his
flesh. We have, moreover, a great priest set over the
household of God; so let us make our approach in sincerity
of heart and full assurance of faith, our guilty hearts
sprinkled clean, our bodies washed with pure water. Let us
be firm and unswerving in the confession of our hope, for
the Giver of the promise may be trusted.

Song of the Virgin Mary

Ant. When the Sabbath was over, the women brought

aromatic oils, intending to go and anoint the body of Jesus.

Or as follows:

New Testament Song Phil 2:6–11

Ant. Let every tongue confess, 'Jesus Christ is Lord!'

The divine nature was Christ's from the first;
yet he did not think to snatch at equality with God,
but made himself nothing,
assuming the nature of a slave.

Bearing the human likeness,
revealed in human shape,
he humbled himself,
and in obedience accepted even death –
death on a cross.

Therefore God raised him to the heights
and bestowed on him the name above all names,
that at the name of Jesus every knee should bow –
in heaven, on earth, and in the depths –
and every tongue confess, 'Jesus Christ is Lord',
to the glory of God the Father.

Ant. Let every tongue confess, 'Jesus Christ is Lord!'

Prayer

Almighty and eternal God, your only-begotten Son went down into the grave and came up from thence in glory; grant that, through his resurrection, your faithful who have been buried with him in baptism may journey safely to everlasting life, through Christ our Lord. Amen.

Eastertide

SUNDAY

MORNING PRAYER

Lord, open my lips, and my mouth shall proclaim your praise.
To you be glory in the Church and in Christ Jesus
from generation to generation evermore.
Amen, alleluia!

Easter day: From Sonnets LXVIII

Most glorious Lord of Life! that, on this day
Didst make thy triumph over death and sin,
And, having harrowed hell, didst bring away
Captivity thence captive, us to win:
This joyous day, dear Lord, with joy begin,
And grant that we, for whom thou didest die,
Being with dear blood clean washed from sin,
May live for ever in felicity!
And that thy love we weighing worthily,
May likewise love thee for the same again,
And for thy sake, that all like dear didst buy,
With love may one another entertain.
   So let us love, dear love like as we ought –
   Love is the lesson which the Lord us taught.

Edmund Spenser

Thanksgiving for deliverance   Ps 29(30)

God raised him to life again (Acts 2:24).

Ant. You have raised my soul from the dead, alleluia!

I will praise you, Lord, you have rescued me
and have not let my enemies rejoice over me.

O Lord, I cried to you for help
and you, my God, have healed me.
O Lord, you have raised my soul from the dead,
restored me to life from those who sink into the grave.

Sing psalms to the Lord, you who love him,
give thanks to his holy name.
His anger lasts but a moment; his favour through life.
At night there are tears, but joy comes with dawn.

I said to myself in my good fortune:
'Nothing will ever disturb me.'
Your favour had set me on a mountain fastness,
then you hid your face and I was put to confusion.

To you, Lord, I cried,
to my God I made appeal:
'What profit would my death be, my going to the grave?
Can dust give you praise or proclaim your truth?'

The Lord listened and had pity.
The Lord came to my help.
For me you have changed my mourning into dancing,
you removed my sackcloth and girdled me with joy.
So my soul sings psalms to you unceasingly.
O Lord my God, I will thank you for ever.

Ant. You have raised my soul from the dead, alleluia!

Acknowledgement of God's kingship   Ps 92(93)

*He was declared Son of God by a mighty act in that he rose
from the dead* (Rom 1:4)

Ant. The Lord has girded himself with power, alleluia!

The Lord is king, with majesty enrobed;
the Lord has robed himself with might,
he has girded himself with power.

The world you made firm, not to be moved;
your throne has stood firm from of old.
From all eternity, O Lord, you are.

The waters have lifted up, O Lord,
the waters have lifted up their voice,
the waters have lifted up their thunder.

Greater than the roar of mighty waters,
more glorious than the surgings of the sea,
the Lord is glorious on high.

Truly your decrees are to be trusted.
Holiness is fitting to your house,
O Lord, until the end of time.

Ant. The Lord has girded himself with power, alleluia!

Word of God
Col 3:1–4, 12–15

Were you not raised to life with Christ? Then aspire to the realm above, where Christ is, seated at the right hand of God, and let your thoughts dwell on that higher realm, not on this earthly life. I repeat, you died; and now your life lies hidden with Christ in God. When Christ, who is our life, is manifested, then you too will be manifested with him in glory.

Then put on the garments that suit God's chosen people, his own, his beloved: compassion, kindness, humility, gentleness, patience. Be forbearing with one another, and forgiving, where any of you has cause for complaint: you must forgive as the Lord forgave you. To crown all, there must be love, to bind all together and complete the whole. Let Christ's peace be arbiter in your hearts; to this peace you were called as members of a single body. And be filled with gratitude.

Song of Zechariah

Ant. It is true: the Lord has risen, alleluia!
He has appeared to Simon, alleluia, alleluia!
Or as follows:

New Testament Song
Phil 2:6–11

Ant. Let every tongue confess, 'Jesus Christ is Lord,' alleluia!

The divine nature was Christ's from the first;
yet he did not think to snatch at equality with God,
but made himself nothing,
assuming the nature of a slave.

Bearing the human likeness,
revealed in human shape,

he humbled himself,
and in obedience accepted even death –
death on a cross.

Therefore God raised him to the heights
and bestowed on him the name above all names,
that at the name of Jesus every knee should bow –
in heaven, on earth, and in the depths –
and every tongue confess, 'Jesus Christ is Lord,'
to the glory of God the Father.

Ant. Let every tongue confess, 'Jesus Christ is Lord,'
alleluia!

Prayers

God our Father, today your Son Jesus has overcome death
and opened for us the way to eternal life. As we celebrate
the mystery of his resurrection, may its power fill our lives
with love and peace.

This is the day the Lord has made,
let us rejoice and be glad!

Renew your Church on the day of resurrection,
and grant that all Christians may be alive with Christ.

Christ our Lord, you are the corner-stone rejected by
the builders;
build us as living stones into your Church.

Further prayers . . . Our Father . . .

Blessed be the God and Father of our Lord Jesus Christ.
In his mercy we have been born again to a living hope,
through the resurrection of Jesus Christ from the dead.

Almighty God, through the resurrection of Jesus Christ you
gave to every man the hope of eternal life. Renew us by the
gift of your Spirit and enable us to live in the new life of
Christ our Lord, who lives and reigns with you for ever.
Amen.

May the Lord bless us,
may he keep us from all evil
and lead us to life everlasting. Amen.

251

Evening Prayer

Lord, open my lips, and my mouth shall proclaim your praise.
Glory to the Father, and to the Son, and to the Holy Spirit:
as in the beginning, so now, and for ever. Amen, alleluia!

The Bee-Keeper

In the plain of the world's dust like a great Sea,
The golden thunders of the Lion and the Honey-Bee
In the Spirit, held with the Sun a colloquy

Where an old woman stood – thick Earthiness –
Half Sun, half Clod,
A plant alive from the root, still blind with earth
And all the weight of Death and Birth.

She, in her primitive dress
Of clay, bent to her hives
And heard her sisters of the barren lives

Begin to stir . . . the Priestesses of the Gold Comb
Shaped by Darkness, and the Prophetesses
Who, from a wingless pupa, spark of gold

In the Dark, rose with gold bodies bright as the Lion,
And the trace of the Hand of God on ephemeral wings
To sing the great Hymn of Being to the lost:

'This Earth is the honey of all Beings, and all Beings
Are the honey of this Earth . . . O bright immortal Lover
That is incarnate in the body's earth –
O bright immortal Lover Who is All!'

'This Water is the honey of all Beings, and all Beings
Are the honey of this Water . . . O the bright immortal
    Lover
That is in water and that is the seed
Of Life . . . O bright immortal Lover Who is All!'

'This Fire is the honey of all Beings, and all Beings
Are the honey of this Fire . . . O bright immortal Lover
That is in fire and shines in mortal speech –
O bright immortal Lover Who is All!'

'This Air is the honey of all Beings, and all Beings
Are the honey of this Air . . . O bright immortal Lover

That is in air and is our Being's breath –
O bright immortal Lover Who is All!'

'This Sun is the honey of all Beings, and all Beings
Are the honey of this Sun . . . O bright immortal Lover
That is in the sun and is our Being's sight –
O bright immortal Lover Who is All!'

'This Thunder is the honey of all Beings, and all Beings
Are the honey of this Thunder. . . O the bright immortal
   Lover,
That is in thunder and all voices – the beasts' roar –
Thunder of rising saps – the voice of Man!
O bright immortal Lover Who is All!'

This was the song that came from the small span
Of thin gold bodies shaped by the holy Dark . . .

And the old woman in her mortal dress of clay
(That plant alive from the root, still thick with earth)
Felt all the saps of Day.

And in the plain of dust like a great Sea
The Lion in the Spirit cried, 'Destroy – destroy
The old and wrinkled Darkness.' But the Sun
– That great gold simpleton – laughed like a boy,
And kissed the old woman's cheek and blessed her clay.

The great Sun laughed, and dancing over Chaos,
Shouts to the dust 'O mortal Lover! Think what wonders
May be born of our love – what golden heroes!'

The Bee in the Spirit said 'The gold combs lay
In the cold rock and the slain Lion, amid spent golden
   thunders.'

Edith Sitwell

The Messiah, king, priest and judge   Ps 109(110)

He must reign until he has put all his enemies under his feet
(1 Cor 15:25).

Ant. An angel of the Lord descended from heaven;
   he came to the stone and rolled it away,
   and sat himself down on it, alleluia!

The Lord's revelation to my Master:
'Sit on my right:
I will put your foes beneath your feet.'

The Lord will send from Zion
your sceptre of power:
rule in the midst of all your foes.

A prince from the day of your birth
on the holy mountains;
from the womb before the daybreak I begot you.

The Lord has sworn an oath he will not change.
'You are a priest for ever.
a priest like Melchizedek of old.'

The Master standing at your right hand
will shatter kings in the day of his great wrath.

He shall drink from the stream by the wayside
and therefore he shall lift up his head.

Ant. An angel of the Lord descended from heaven;
  he came to the stone and rolled it away,
  and sat himself down on it, alleluia!

The wonders of the Exodus   Ps 113A(114)
  All of us who have been baptized into Christ Jesus
  were baptized into his death (Rom 6:3).

Ant. Suddenly there was a violent earthquake;
  an angel of the Lord descended from heaven, alleluia!

When Israel came forth from Egypt,
Jacob's sons from an alien people,
Judah became the Lord's temple,
Israel became his kingdom.

The sea fled at the sight:
the Jordan turned back on its course,
the mountains leapt like rams
and the hills like yearling sheep.

Why was it, sea, that you fled,
that you turned back, Jordan, on your course?

Mountains, that you leapt like rams,
hills, like yearling sheep?

Tremble, O earth, before the Lord,
in the presence of the God of Jacob,
who turns the rock into a pool
and flint into a spring of water.

Ant. Suddenly there was a violent earthquake;
and angel of the Lord descended from heaven, alleluia!

Word of God   1 Cor 5:7–8

'A little leaven leavens all the dough.' The old leaven of
corruption is working among you. Purge it out, and then
you will be bread of a new baking. As Christians you are
unleavened Passover bread; for indeed our Passover has
begun; the sacrifice is offered – Christ himself. So we who
observe the festival must not use the old leaven, the leaven
of corruption and wickedness, but only the unleavened
bread which is sincerity and truth.

Song of the Virgin Mary

Ant. A flame burns within our hearts:
Jesus Christ abides with us, his mystery dwells in us.
Death opens out into glory, alleluia!

Or as follows:

New Testament Song   Rev 19:2, 5–8

Ant. Have nothing to fear.
I know you are looking for Jesus who was crucified.
He is not here; he has been raised again, alleluia!

Alleluia, alleluia!
Victory and glory and power
belong to our God, alleluia!
for true and just are his judgements.
Alleluia, alleluia!

Praise our God,
all you his servants, alleluia!
you that fear him,

both great and small.
Alleluia, alleluia!

The Lord our God,
sovereign over all, alleluia!
has entered on his reign.
Exult and shout for joy and do him homage.
Alleluia, alleluia!

For the wedding day of the Lamb
has come, alleluia!
His bride
has made herself ready.
Alleluia, alleluia!

For her dress
she has been given, alleluia!
fine linen,
clean and shining.
Alleluia, alleluia!

Ant. Have nothing to fear.
I know you are looking for Jesus who was crucified.
He is not here; he has been raised again, alleluia!

Prayers

Easter is the heart of our faith. Today Jesus, who was dead,
lives again.

May we always trust in him,
so that death may not sweep us away,
but be the meeting with the Lord we love.

We pray with great confidence today
for all who have died in the faith,
(especially N. and N.);
since they hoped in the resurrection,
may they now share its fruits.

Help us to make our Easter faith a reality in our lives.
In all moments of happiness, we will express the joy of
Easter;

in all difficulties, recall the victory of Christ
over suffering and death;
each day we will turn again to the Father in thanksgiving
and love.

Further prayers . . . Our Father . . .

Lord of all life, we praise you, that through Christs' resurrection, the old order of sin and death is overcome and all things made new in him: grant that being dead to sin and alive to you in union with Jesus Christ, we may live and reign for ever with him in glory, to whom with you and the Holy Spirit be praise and honour, glory and might now and in all eternity. Amen.

May the Lord bless us,
may he keep us from all evil
and lead us to life everlasting. Amen.

MONDAY

MORNING PRAYER

Lord, open my lips . . .
To you be glory . . .

The Windhover

To Christ our Lord

I caught this morning morning's minion, king-
    dom of daylight's dauphin, dapple-dawn-drawn Falcon,
    in his riding
    Of the rolling level underneath him steady air, and
    striding
High there, how he rung upon the rein of a wimpling wing
In his ecstasy! then off, off forth on swing,
    As a skate's heel sweeps smooth on a bow-bend: the
    hurl and gliding
Rebuffed the big wind. My heart in hiding
Stirred for a bird, the achieve of, the mastery of the
    thing!

Brute beauty and valour and act, oh, air, pride, plume here
    Buckle! AND the fire that breaks from thee then, a
    billion
Times told lovelier, more dangerous, O my chevalier!

No wonder of it: shéer plód makes plough down sillion
Shine, and blue-bleak embers, ah my dear,
Fall, gall themselves, and gash gold-vermilion.

Gerard Manley Hopkins

After victory Ps 20(21)

*You killed him who has led the way to life. But God raised
him from the dead* (Acts 3:15).

Ant. He asked you for life and this you have given, alleluia!

O Lord, your strength gives joy to the king;
how your saving help makes him glad!
You have granted him his heart's desire;
you have not refused the prayer of his lips.

You came to meet him with the blessings of success,
you have set on his head a crown of pure gold.
He asked you for life and this you have given,
days that will last from age to age.

Your saving help has given him glory.
You have laid upon him majesty and splendour,
you have granted your blessings to him for ever.
You have made him rejoice with the joy of your presence.

The king has put his trust in the Lord:
through the mercy of the Most High he shall stand firm.
O Lord, arise in your strength;
we shall sing and praise your power.

Ant. He asked you for life and this you have given, alleluia!

The universal reign of God Ps 95(96)

When the disciples saw the Lord, they were filled with joy
(Jn 20:20).

Ant. Let the heavens rejoice and earth be glad
at the presence of the Lord, for he comes, alleluia!

O sing a new song to the Lord,
sing to the Lord all the earth.
O sing to the Lord, bless his name.

Proclaim his help day by day,
tell among the nations his glory
and his wonders among all the peoples.

The Lord is great and worthy of praise,
to be feared above all gods;
the gods of the heathens are naught.

It was the Lord who made the heavens,
his are majesty and state and power
and splendour in his holy place.

Give the Lord, you families of peoples,
give the Lord glory and power,
give the Lord the glory of his name.

Bring an offering and enter his courts,
worship the Lord in his temple.
O earth, tremble before him.

Proclaim to the nations: 'God is king.'
The world he made firm in its place;
he will judge the peoples in fairness.

Let the heavens rejoice and earth be glad,
let the sea and all within it thunder praise,
let the land and all it bears rejoice,
all the trees of the wood shout for joy

at the presence of the Lord for he comes,
he comes to rule the earth.
With justice he will rule the world,
he will judge the peoples with his truth.

Ant. Let the heavens rejoice and earth be glad
at the presence of the Lord, for he comes, alleluia!

Word of God   1 Cor 15:20–26

Christ was raised to life – the firstfruits of the harvest of the
dead. For since it was a man who brought death into the
world, a man also brought resurrection of the dead. As in
Adam all men die, so in Christ all will be brought to life;
but each in his own proper place: Christ the firstfruits, and
afterwards, at his coming, those who belong to Christ. Then

comes the end, when he delivers up the kingdom to God the Father, after abolishing every kind of domination, authority, and power. For he is destined to reign until God has put all enemies under his feet; and the last enemy to be abolished is death.

Song of Zechariah

Ant. He has been raised from the dead
and is going on before you into Galilee;
there you will see him, alleluia!

Or as follows:

Old Testament Song   Ex 15:1–4, 8–13

And now, the Red Sea's channel past,
To Christ our Prince we sing at last (Ad coenam Agni,
tr. Neale).

Ant. In thy constant love thou hast led the people
whom thou didst ransom, alleluia!

I will sing to the Lord, for he has risen up in triumph;
the horse and his rider he has hurled into the sea.

The Lord is my refuge and my defence,
he has shown himself my deliverer.
He is my God, and I will glorify him;
he is my father's God, and I will exalt him.

The Lord is a warrior: the Lord is his name.
The chariots of Pharaoh and his army
he has cast into the sea;
the flower of his officers
are engulfed in the Red Sea.

Thou didst blow with thy blast; the sea covered them.
They sank like lead in the swelling waves.

Who is like thee, O Lord, among the gods?
Who is like thee, majestic in holiness,
worthy of awe and praise, who work wonders?
Thou didst stretch out thy right hand,
earth engulfed them.

In thy constant love thou hast led the people
whom thou didst ransom:
thou hast guided them by thy strength
to thy holy dwelling-place.

Ant. In thy constant love thou hast led the people
whom thou didst ransom, alleluia!

Prayers

Almighty God, by glorifying your Son Jesus, you have
raised our human nature to life with you. Give us joy and
hope as we follow our Lord.

We pray for the world in which your Son
lived, died, and was raised;
may the whole world be made new in him,
to your praise and glory.

We pray that the power of his resurrection
may be seen among men:
in compassion, kindness and patience,
in the love that binds us together,
in the courage to forgive and be forgiven.

Bless all those who contribute to the welfare of man
by working for justice and peace.

Further prayers ... Our Father ...

Father in heaven, we praise you
because Christ took upon himself all the evil of the
world
and has overcome it.
He is our life and our hope!

Heavenly Father, you raised Jesus your Son from the humili-
ation of the cross to the glory of the resurrection. May our
faith in the risen Lord bring new meaning to the routine of
daily life, through the same Christ our Lord. Amen.

May the Lord bless us,
may he keep us from all evil
and lead us to life everlasting. Amen.

EVENING PRAYER

Lord, open my lips . . .
Glory to the Father . . .

An Arundel Tomb

Side by side, their faces blurred,
The earl and countess lie in stone,
Their proper habits vaguely shown
As jointed armour, stiffened pleat,
And that faint hint of the absurd –
The little dogs under their feet.

Such plainness of the pre-baroque
Hardly involves the eye, until
It meets his left-hand gauntlet, still
Clasped empty in the other; and
One sees, with a sharp tender shock,
His hand withdrawn, holding her hand.

They would not think to lie so long.
Such faithfulness in effigy
Was just a detail friends would see:
A sculptor's sweet commissioned grace
Thrown off in helping to prolong
The Latin names around the base.

They would not guess how early in
Their supine stationary voyage
The air would change to soundless damage,
Turn the old tenantry away;
How soon succeeding eyes begin
To look, not read. Rigidly they

Persisted, linked, through lengths and breadths
Of time. Snow fell, undated. Light
Each summer thronged the glass. A bright
Litter of birdcalls strewed the same
Bone-riddled ground. And up the paths
The endless altered people came,

Washing at their identity.
Now, helpless in the hollow of

An unarmorial age, a trough
Of smoke in slow suspended skeins
Above their scrap of history,
Only an attitude remains:

Time has transfigured them into
Untruth. The stone fidelity
They hardly meant has come to be
Their final blazon, and to prove
Our almost-instinct almost true:
What will survive of us is love.

Philip Larkin

Litany of praises

Ps 135(136)I

*God loved the world so much that he gave his only Son,
that everyone who has faith in him may have eternal life*
(Jn 3:16).

Ant. He alone has wrought marvellous works,
    for his great love is without end, alleluia!

O give thanks to the Lord for he is good,
for his great love is without end.
Give thanks to the God of gods,
for his great love is without end.
Give thanks to the Lord of lords,
for his great love is without end;

who alone has wrought marvellous works,
for his great love is without end;
whose wisdom it was made the skies,
for his great love is without end;
who fixed the earth firmly on the seas,
for his great love is without end.

It was he who made the great lights,
for his great love is without end,
the sun to rule in the day,
for his great love is without end,
the moon and stars in the night,
for his great love is without end.

Ps 135(136)II

He divided the Red Sea in two,
for his great love is without end;
he made Israel pass through the midst,
for his great love is without end;
he flung Pharaoh and his force in the sea,
for his great love is without end.

Through the desert his people he led,
for his great love is without end.
Nations in their greatness he struck,
for his great love is without end.
He let Israel inherit their land,
for his great love is without end.

He remembered us in our distress,
for his great love is without end.
He gives food to all living things,
for his great love is without end.
To the God of heaven give thanks,
for his great love is without end.

Ant. He alone has wrought marvellous works,
for his great love is without end, alleluia!

Word of God   Rom 6:4–11

By baptism we were buried with him, and lay dead, in order
that, as Christ was raised from the dead in the splendour of
the Father, so also we might set our feet upon the new path
of life.
For if we have become incorporate with him in a death like
his, we shall also be one with him in a resurrection like his.
We know that the man we once were has been crucified
with Christ, for the destruction of the sinful self, so that
we may no longer be the slaves of sin, since a dead man is
no longer answerable for his sin. But if we thus died with
Christ, we believe that we shall also come to life with him.
We know that Christ, once raised from the dead, is never
to die again; he is no longer under the dominion of death.
For in dying as he died, he died to sin, once for all, and in
living as he lives, he lives to God. In the same way you must

regard yourselves as dead to sin and alive to God, in union
with Christ Jesus.

Song of the Virgin Mary

Ant. Fear nothing; you are looking for Jesus of Nazareth.
He has been raised again; he is not here, alleluia!
Or as follows:

New Testament Song   1 Pt 1:3–4, 18–21

Ant. The price was paid in precious blood, the blood of
Christ, alleluia!

Praise be to the God and Father of our Lord Jesus Christ,
who in his great mercy gave us new birth into a living hope
by the resurrection of Jesus Christ from the dead!
Nothing can destroy or spoil or wither
the inheritance to which we are born, alleluia!

It was no perishable stuff, like gold or silver,
that bought your freedom from the folly of your ways.
The price was paid in precious blood,
as it were of a lamb without mark or blemish –
the blood of Christ, alleluia!

Predestined before the foundation of the world,
he was made manifest in this last period of time
for your sake, alleluia!
Through him you have come to trust in God,
who raised him from the dead and gave him glory,
alleluia!

Ant. The price was paid in precious blood, the blood of
Christ, alleluia!

Prayers

God our Father, may the whole world join in a hymn of
thanksgiving
for the great love you have shown us in Jesus Christ
our Lord.

265

We thank you for the obedience of your Son
in accepting the cross.
May his example inspire us always to do your will.

We thank you for the Church:
for all Christians trying to manifest Christ in their lives,
and for those who minister to them
in their life of dedication to your people.

We thank you for the goodness of men:
founded on the power of resurrection,
may it be stronger than the forces of evil.

Further prayers . . . Our Father . . .

Almighty God of peace, whose son Jesus Christ gave himself
In sacrifice for sin on the cross and by his resurrection from
the dead was declared to be your Son, the great shepherd of
the sheep. By the blood of his eternal covenant make us
perfect in all goodness that we may do your will, through
Jesus Christ our Lord. Amen.

May the Lord bless us,
may he keep us from all evil
and lead us to life everlasting. Amen.

TUESDAY

Morning Prayer

Lord, open my lips . . .
To you be glory . . .

Easter Day
Rise, Heire of Fresh Eternity,
From thy Virgin Tombe:
Rise, mighty Man of wonders, and thy World with thee
Thy Tombe, the universall East,
Natures new Wombe,
Thy Tombe, fair Immortalities perfumed Nest.

Of all the Gloryes Make Noone gay
This is the Morne.
This rocke buds forth the fountaine of the streames of
Day.

In joyes white Annals live this houre,
When life was borne,
No cloud scoule on his radiant lids no tempest lowre.

Life, by this light's Nativity
All creatures have.
Death onely by this Dayes just Doome is forc't to Dye;
Nor is Death forc't; for may hee ly
Thron'd in thy Grave;
Death will on this condition be content to Dy.

Richard Crashaw

Song of the redeemed   Ps 125(126)

I shall see you again, and then you shall be joyful (Jn 16:22).

Ant. Your grief shall be turned to joy,
   and no one shall rob you of it, alleluia!

When the Lord delivered Zion from bondage,
It seemed like a dream.
Then was our mouth filled with laughter,
on our lips there were songs.

The heathens themselves said: 'What marvels
the Lord worked for them!'
What marvels the Lord worked for us!
Indeed we were glad.

Deliver us, O Lord, from our bondage
as streams in dry land.
Those who are sowing in tears
will sing when they reap.

They go out, they go out, full of tears,
carrying seed for the sowing:
they come back, they come back, full of song,
carrying their sheaves.

Ant. Your grief shall be turned to joy,
   and no one shall rob you of it, alleluia!

Earth rejoices in its king   Ps 96(97)

I desire that these men may be with me where I am,
so that they may look upon my glory (Jn 17:24).

Ant. All peoples see his glory, alleluia!

The Lord is king, let earth rejoice,
the many coastlands be glad.
Cloud and darkness are his raiment;
his throne, justice and right.

A fire prepares his path;
it burns up his foes on every side.
His lightnings light up the world,
the earth trembles at the sight.

The mountains melt like wax
before the Lord of all the earth.
The skies proclaim his justice;
all peoples see his glory.

Zion hears and is glad;
the people of Judah rejoice
because of your judgments O Lord.

For you indeed are the Lord
most high above all the earth
exalted far above all spirits.

The Lord loves those who hate evil:
he guards the souls of his saints;
he sets them free from the wicked.

Light shines forth for the just
and joy for the upright of heart.
Rejoice, you just, in the Lord;
give glory to his holy name.

Ant. All peoples see his glory, alleluia!

Word of God   Acts 13:27–33, 38

The people of Jerusalem and their rulers did not recognize
Jesus, or understand the words of the prophets which are
read Sabbath by Sabbath; indeed they fulfilled them by

268

condemning him. Though they failed to find grounds for the sentence of death, they asked Pilate to have him executed. And when they had carried out all that the scriptures said about him, they took him down from the gibbet and laid him in a tomb. But God raised him from the dead; and there was a period of many days during which he appeared to those who had come up with him from Galilee to Jerusalem. They are now his witnesses before our nation; and we are here to give you the good news that God, who made the promise to the fathers, has fulfilled it for the children by raising Jesus from the dead; and you must understand, my brothers, that it is through him that forgiveness of sins is now being proclaimed to you.

Song of Zechariah

Ant. Look, here is the place where they laid him, alleluia!
Or as follows:

Easter Song

Ant. Alleluia! Christ is risen, alleluia!

I will sing to the Lord, for he has risen up in triumph;
the horse and his rider he has hurled into the sea.
O Lord, you are great and glorious,
you are marvellous in your strength, invincible.
God has arisen, and his foes are scattered.
Those who hate him have fled before him.

He has burst the gates of bronze
and shattered the iron bars.
This God of ours is a God who saves;
the Lord our God holds the keys of death.
This is the day which the Lord has made;
let us rejoice and be glad.

Awake, sleeper, rise from the dead
and Christ will shine upon you;
for he has been raised from the dead,
never to die again.
God has not left his soul among the dead
nor let his beloved know decay.

The Lord is risen from the tomb
who hung for us upon the tree.
Be not afraid, you cattle in the field,
for the pastures shall be green,
the trees shall bear fruit,
the fig and the vine yield their harvest.

Ant. Alleluia! Christ is risen, alleluia!

Prayers

God our Father, in this great mystery of Easter you have
made a new covenant of love with us; may the love which
we profess with our lips be a reality in our lives.

We pray that we may learn to love each other
as Jesus loved us;
only then will we be his true disciples.

We pray that we may be faithful to our mission
as members of your Church;
may all men see in our lives a sign that you have saved
mankind
through the work of your Son.

We pray that today we may be filled with the Spirit of
your love:
free us from all jealousy and hatred,
that we may live as children of God.

Further prayers ... Our Father ...

To the God of all grace,
who has called us into his eternal glory in Christ,
belong glory and power for ever and ever.

Lord God, you have restored us to eternal life in the resurrection of Christ. Grant us such constancy in faith and hope
that we may never doubt that the promises you have made
will be fulfilled, through Christ our Lord. Amen.

May the Lord bless us,
may he keep us from all evil
and lead us to life everlasting. Amen.

Evening Prayer

Lord, open my lips . . .
Glory to the Father . . .

Ruler of the World

O thou, whose all-creating hands sustain
The radiant Heav'ns, and Earth, and ambient main!
Eternal Reason! whose presiding soul
Informs great nature and directs the whole!
Who wert, e're time his rapid race began,
And badst the years in long procession run:
Who fix't thy self amidst the rowling frame,
Gav'st all things to be chang'd, yet ever art the same!
Oh teach the mind t'aetherial heights to rise,
And view familiar, in its native skies,
The source of good; thy splendour to descry,
And on thy self, undazzled, fix her eye.

Oh quicken this dull mass of mortal clay;
Shine through the soul, and drive its clouds away!
For thou art Light. In thee the righteous find
Calm rest, and soft serenity of mind;
Thee they regard alone; to thee they tend;
At once our great original and end,
At once our means, our end, our guide, our way,
Our utmost bound, and our eternal stay!

Boethius, translated by Alexander Pope

Processional song of praise　　　　　Ps 117(118)I

*This Jesus is the stone rejected by the builders
which has become the keystone (Acts 4:11).*

Ant. This day was made by the Lord;
　　we rejoice and are glad, alleluia!

Give thanks to the Lord for he is good,
for his love has no end.

Let the sons of Israel say:
'His love has no end.'
Let the sons of Aaron say:

'His love has no end.'
Let those who fear the Lord say:
'His love has no end.'

I called to the Lord in my distress;
he answered and freed me.
The Lord is at my side; I do not fear.
What can man do against me?
It is better to take refuge in the Lord
than to trust in men:

I was thrust, thrust down and falling
but the Lord was my helper.
The Lord is my strength and my song;
he was my savour.
There are shouts of joy and victory
in the tents of the just.

Ps 117(118)II

The Lord's right hand has triumphed;
his right hand raised me up.
I shall not die, I shall live
and recount his deeds.
I was punished, I was punished by the Lord,
but not doomed to die.

Open to me the gates of holiness:
I will enter and give thanks.
This is the Lord's own gate
where the just may enter.
I will thank you for you have given answer
and you are my saviour.

The stone which the builders rejected
has become the corner stone.
This is the work of the Lord,
a marvel in our eyes.
This day was made by the Lord;
we rejoice and are glad.

O Lord, grant us salvation;
O Lord, grant success.

Blessed in the name of the Lord
is he who comes.
We bless you from the house of the Lord;
the Lord God is our light.

Go forward in procession with branches
even to the altar.
You are my God, I thank you.
My God, I praise you.
Give thanks to the Lord for he is good;
for his love has no end.

Ant. This day was made by the Lord;
we rejoice and are glad, alleluia!

Word of God
1 Pt 1:14–21

As obedient children, do not let your characters be shaped
any longer by the desires you cherished in your days of
ignorance. The One who called you is holy; like him, be holy
in all your behaviour, because Scripture says, 'You shall be
holy, for I am holy.'
If you say 'our Father' to the One who judges every man
impartially on the record of his deeds, you must stand in
awe of him while you live out your time on earth. Well you
know that it was no perishable stuff, like gold or silver, that
bought your freedom from the empty folly of your traditional ways. The price was paid in precious blood, as it
were of a lamb without mark or blemish – the blood of
Christ. Predestined before the foundation of the world, he
was made manifest in this last period of time for your sake.
Through him you have come to trust in God who raised him
from the dead and gave him glory, and so your faith and
hope are fixed on God.

Song of the Virgin Mary

Ant. Why search among the dead for one who lives?
Alleluia!
Or as follows:

Easter Song

Ant. Alleluia! Christ is risen, alleluia!

I have trodden the winepress alone;
no man, no nation was with me.
I have laid down my life of my own free will,
and by my own power I have taken it up anew.
Do not be afraid, I am the first and the last,
and I am the living one.

Was the Messiah not bound to suffer thus
before entering upon his glory?
The chastisement he bore is health for us
and by his scourging we are healed.
The Lord took thought for his tortured servant
and healed him who had made himself a sacrifice for sin.

By his holy and glorious wounds
May Christ the Lord guard us and keep us.
If we die with him, we shall live with him.
If we endure, we shall reign with him.
Christ yesterday and today,
the beginning of all things and their end.
Alpha and Omega,
all time belongs to him and all the ages.

Ant. Alleluia! Christ is risen, alleluia!

Prayers

Great God and Father of our Lord Jesus Christ, we praise
you with greater joy than ever at this Easter time. May the
joy and faith we experience now penetrate every moment of
our lives.

We thank you, Father, for the joy that children bring
us:
in them life is fresh and full of promise;
may we learn from them innocence and trust.

May all nations live together in peace.
May human rights be everywhere respected.
May the resources of the world be shared justly among
all men.

Lord Jesus, by your death and resurrection
you proclaimed peace and victory;
set free all who are bound by fear or despair.

Further prayers . . . Our Father . . .

God our Father, we thank you for your Son our Lord
Jesus Christ: he is the first one risen from the sleep of death,
who died once and now lives for ever. Amen.

May the Lord bless us,
may he keep us from all evil
and lead us to life everlasting. Amen.

WEDNESDAY

MORNING PRAYER

Lord, open my lips . . .
To you be glory . . .

On a Drop of Dew

See how the Orient dew,
Shed from the bosom of the morn
Into the blowing roses,
Yet careless of its mansion new;
For the clear region where 'twas born
Round in its self incloses:
And in its little globe's extent,
Frames as it can its native element.
How it the purple flow'r does slight,
Scarce touching where it lies,
But gazing back upon the skies,
Shines with a mournful light;
Like its own tear,
Because so long divided from the sphere.
Restless it rolls and unsecure,
Trembling lest it grow impure:
Till the warm sun pity its pain,
And to the skies exhale it back again.

So the soul, that drop, that ray
Of the clear fountain of eternal day,
Could it within the human flow'r be seen,
Rememb'ring still its former height,
Shuns the sweet leaves and blossoms green;
And, recollecting its own light,
Does, in its pure and circling thoughts, express
The greater heaven in an heaven less.
In how coy a figure wound,
Every way it turns away:
So the world excluding round,
Yet receiving in the day.
Dark beneath, but bright above:
Here disdaining, there in love,
How loose and easy hence to go:
How girt and ready to ascend.
Moving but on a point below,
It all about does upwards bend.
Such did the manna's sacred dew distil;
White, and entire, though congeal'd and chill.
Congeal'd on earth: but does, dissolving, run
Into the glories of th'almighty sun.

Andrew Marvell

Thanksgiving for God's saving action Ps 15(16)
*David spoke with foreknowledge of the resurrection of the
Messiah* (Acts 2:31).

Ant. You will not leave my soul among the dead,
nor let your beloved know decay, alleluia!

Preserve me, God, I take refuge in you.
I say to the Lord: 'You are my God.
My happiness lies in you alone.'

He has put into my heart a marvellous love
for the faithful ones who dwell in his land.
Those who choose other gods increase their sorrows.
Never will I offer their offerings of blood.
Never will I take their name upon my lips.

O Lord, it is you who are my portion and cup;

it is you yourself who are my prize.
The lot marked out for me is my delight:
welcome indeed the heritage that falls to me!

I will bless the Lord who gives me counsel,
who even at night directs my heart.
I keep the Lord ever in my sight:
since he is at my right hand, I shall stand firm.

And so my heart rejoices, my soul is glad;
even my body shall rest in safety.
For you will not leave my soul among the dead,
nor let your beloved know decay.

You will show me the path of life,
the fullness of joy in your presence,
at your right hand happiness for ever.

Ant. You will not leave my soul among the dead,
nor let your beloved know decay, alleluia!

Thanksgiving for help given in distress   Ps 39(40)

*God raised him to life again, setting him free from the
pangs of death* (Acts 2:24).

Ant. He heard my cry. He drew me from the deadly pit,
from the miry clay, alleluia!

I waited, I waited for the Lord
and he stooped down to me;
he heard my cry.

He drew me from the deadly pit,
from the miry clay.
He set my feet upon a rock
and made my footsteps firm.

He put a new song into my mouth,
praise of our God.
Many shall see and fear
and shall trust in the Lord.

Happy the man who has placed
his trust in the Lord
and has not gone over to the rebels
who follow false gods.

How many, O Lord my God,
are the wonders and designs
that you have worked for us;
you have no equal.
Should I proclaim and speak of them,
they are more than I can tell!

O let there be rejoicing and gladness
for all who seek you.
Let them ever say: 'The Lord is great,'
who love your saving help.

Ant. He heard my cry. He drew me from the deadly pit,
from the miry clay, alleluia!

Word of God   Col 2:9–10, 12-13

It is in Christ that the complete being of the Godhead
dwells embodied, and in him you have been brought to
completion. Every power and authority in the universe is
subject to him as Head. In baptism you were buried with
him, in baptism also you were raised to life with him through
your faith in the active power of God who raised him from
the dead.

Song of Zechariah

Ant. I have seen the Lord, alleluia, alleluia!

Or as follows:

New Testament Song

                    1 Cor 5:7–8; Rom 6:9–11; 1 Cor 15:20–22

Ant. Alleluia, alleluia, alleluia!

Our Passover has begun;
the sacrifice is offered – Christ himself.
So we who observe the festival
must not use the old leaven,
the leaven of corruption and wickedness,
but only the unleavened bread
which is sincerity and truth.

278

Christ, once raised from the dead,
is never to die again:
he is no longer under the dominion of death.
For in dying as he died, he died to sin, once for all,
and in living as he lives, he lives to God.
In the same way you must regard yourselves
as dead to sin and alive to God,
in union with Christ Jesus.

Christ was raised to life –
the firstfruits of the harvest of the dead.
For since it was a man who brought death into the world,
a man also brought resurrection of the dead.
As in Adam all men die,
so in Christ all will be brought to life.

Ant. Alleluia, alleluia, alleluia!

Prayers

Father in heaven, unite all your children in one heart and
one mind: teach us to love to do your will, so that our
hearts may always be fixed where true joy is to be found.

Lord Jesus Christ, teach us to be humble as you were
humble,
to serve others, not to be served,
so that we, too, may share in your glory.

We pray for all who are suffering:
be close to them, Lord,
and bring them through their pain to joy with you.

Jesus Christ, whose strength is gentleness,
whose power is tender love,
help all men to find your way to the Father.

Further prayers . . . Our Father . . .

Lord Jesus Christ, you are the lamb that was slain,
worthy to receive power and wisdom and might,
honour and glory and blessing.

Year by year we recall the mysteries through which mankind
was restored to the likeness of God and granted the hope of

resurrection. We ask you, Lord, through Jesus Christ your
Son, that we may hold fast to these realities which we now
celebrate in faith. Amen.

May the Lord bless us,
may he keep us from all evil
and lead us to life everlasting. Amen.

EVENING PRAYER

Lord, open my lips . . .
Glory to the Father . . .

That Nature is a Heraclitean Fire
and
of the Comfort of the Resurrection

Cloud-puffball, torn tufts, tossed pillows ' flaunt forth, then
    chevy on an air –
built thoroughfare: heaven-roysterers, in gay-gangs ' they
    throng; they glitter in marches.
Down roughcast, down dazzling whitewash, ' wherever an
    elm arches,
Shivelights and shadowtackle in long ' lashes, lace, lance,
    and pair.
Delightfully the bright wind boisterous ' ropes, wrestles,
    beats earth bare
Of yestertempest's creases;' in pool and rut peel parches
Squandering ooze to squeezed ' dough, crust, dust;
    stanches, starches
Squadroned masks and manmarks ' treadmire toil there
Footfretted in it. Million-fuelèd, ' nature's bonfire burns
    on.
But quench her bonniest, dearest ' to her, her clearest-
    selvèd spark
Man, how fast his firedint, ' his mark on mind, is gone!
Both are in an unfathomable, all is in an enormous dark
Drowned. O pity and indig ' nation! Manshape, that
    shone
Sheer off, disseveral, a star, ' death blots black out; nor
    mark

Is any of him at all so stark
But vastness blurs and time ' beats level. Enough! the
    Resurrection,
A heart's-clarion! Away grief's gasping, ' joyless days,
    dejection.
        Across my foundering deck shone
A beacon, an eternal beam. ' Flesh fade, and mortal trash
Fall to the residuary worm; ' world's wildfire, leave but
    ash:
        In a flash, at a trumpet crash,
I am all at once what Christ is, ' since he was what I am,
    and
This Jack, joke, poor potsherd, ' patch, matchwood,
    immortal diamond,
        Is immortal diamond.

                        Gerard Manley Hopkins

A people's thanksgiving   Ps 65(66)I

It was God's will that we, who were the first to set our hope
on Christ, should cause his glory to be praised (Eph 1:11).

Ant. O sing to the glory of his name, alleluia!
   O render him glorious praise, alleluia, alleluia!

Cry out with joy to God all the earth,
O sing to the glory of his name.
O render him glorious praise.
Say to God: 'How tremendous your deeds!

Because of the greatness of your strength
your enemies cringe before you.
Before you all the earth shall bow;
shall sing to you, sing to your name!'

Come and see the works of God,
tremendous his deeds among men.
He turned the sea into dry land,
they passed through the river dry-shod.

Let our joy then be in him;
he rules for ever by his might.
His eyes keep watch over the nations:
let rebels not rise against him.

Ps 65(66)II

O peoples, bless our God
let the voice of his praise resound,
of the God who gave life to our souls
and kept our feet from stumbling.

For you, O God, have tested us,
you have tried us as silver is tried:
you led us, God, into the snare;
you laid a heavy burden on our backs.

You let men ride over our heads;
we went through fire and through water
but then you brought us relief.

Burnt offering I bring to your house;
to you I will pay my vows,
the vows which my lips have uttered,
which my mouth spoke in my distress.

Come and hear, all who fear God.
I will tell what he did for my soul:
to him I cried aloud,
with high praise ready on my tongue.

Blessed be God who did not reject my prayer
nor withhold his love from me.

Ant. O sing to the glory of his name, alleluia!
    O render him glorious praise, alleluia, alleluia!

Word of God

Heb 7:24–28

The priesthood which Jesus holds is perpetual, because he
remains for ever. That is why he is also able to save abso-
lutely those who approach God through him; he is always
living to plead on their behalf.
Such a high priest does indeed fit our condition – devout,
guileless, undefiled, separated from sinners, raised high
above the heavens. He has no need to offer sacrifices daily
as the high priests do, first for his own sins and then for
those of the people; for this he did once and for all when he
offered up himself. The high priests made by the Law are

men in all their frailty; but the priest appointed by the words
of the oath which supersedes the Law is the Son, made
perfect now for ever.

Song of the Virgin Mary

Ant. Lord, stay with us, for evening draws on,
  and the day is almost over, alleluia!

Or as follows:

New Testament Song   2 Cor 4:10–11, 14
                                          1 Cor 15:20–27, 55

Ant. He is destined to reign, alleluia, alleluia!

Wherever we go we carry death with us in our body,
the death that Jesus died,
that in this body also life may reveal itself,
the life that Jesus lives, alleluia!
He who raised the Lord Jesus to life
will, with Jesus, raise us too,
and bring us into his presence, alleluia!

Christ was raised to life –
the first-fruits of the harvest of the dead.
For since it was a man who brought death into the world,
a man also brought resurrection of the dead.
As in Adam all men die, so in Christ all will be brought
  to life:
Christ the first-fruits, and afterwards, at his coming,
those who belong to Christ, alleluia!

Then comes the end, alleluia,
when he delivers up the kingdom to God the Father
after abolishing every kind of domination and power.
For he is destined to reign, alleluia,
until God has put all enemies under his feet;
and the last enemy to be abolished is death.
O Death, where is your victory? O Death, where is your
  sting? Alleluia!

Ant. He is destined to reign, alleluia, alleluia!

Prayers

Father, we share in the mystery of Easter by our baptism in
Jesus Christ; may all Christians be reunited in faith, to
show to the world the power of your love.

We thank you, Father, for the holiness of so many
Christians;
may your light shine out among men.

We thank you for the beauty of creation:
may the achievements of men not disfigure it,
but enhance it to your greater glory.

We pray for all those who do not believe;
bring them to full knowledge and love of you.

Further prayers ... Our Father ...

Almighty and eternal God, as Jesus Christ your Son died and
was raised in glory, may all of us who have been baptized
in him to new life be one day united with him in glory.
We ask you this through him whom we believe lives and
reigns with you for ever. Amen.

May the Lord bless us,
may he keep us from all evil
and lead us to life everlasting. Amen.

THURSDAY

MORNING PRAYER

Lord, open my lips ...
To you be glory ...

Cantico del Sole (Canticle of the Sun)

Most high Lord,
Yours are the praises,
The glory and the honors,
And to you alone must be accorded
All graciousness; and no man there is
Who is worthy to name you.
Be praisèd, O God, and be exalted,

My Lord of all creatures,
And in especial of the most high Sun
Which is your creature, O Lord, that makes clear
The day and illumines it,
Whence by its fairness and its splendor
It is become thy face;
And of the white moon (be praised, O Lord)
And of the wandering stars,
Created by you in the heaven
So brilliant and so fair.
Praisèd be my Lord, by the flame
Whereby night groweth illumined
In the midst of its darkness,
For it is resplendent,
Is joyous, fair, eager; is mighty.
Praisèd be my Lord, of the air,
Of the winds, of the clear sky,
And of the cloudy, praisèd
Of all seasons whereby
Live all these creatures
Of lower order.
Praisèd be my Lord
By our sister the water,
Element meetest for man,
Humble and chaste in its clearness.
Praised be the Lord by our mother
The Earth that sustaineth,
That feeds, that produceth
Multitudinous grasses
And flowers and fruitage.
Praisèd be my Lord, by those
Who grant pardons through his love,
Enduring their travail in patience
And their infirmity with joy of the spirit.
Praisèd be my Lord by death corporal
Whence escapes no one living.
Woe to those that die in mutual transgression
And blessed are they who shall
Find in death's hour thy grace that comes

From obedience to thy holy will,
Wherethrough they shall never see
The pain of the death eternal.
Praise and give grace to my Lord,
Be grateful and serve him
In humbleness e'en as ye are,
Praisè him all creatures!

Francis of Assissi, trans. Ezra Pound

The ruler of the universe enters his   Ps 23(24)
chosen dwelling place

*He who descended is no other than he who ascended far
above all heavens, so that he might fill the universe* (Eph
4:10).

Ant. Alleluia! Let him enter, the king of glory!

O gates, lift high your heads;
grow higher, ancient doors.
Let him enter, the king of glory!

Who is the king of glory?
The Lord, the mighty, the valiant,
the Lord, the valiant in war.

O gates, lift high your heads;
grow higher, ancient doors.
Let him enter, the king of glory!

Who is he, the king of glory?
He, the Lord of armies,
he is the king of glory.

Ant. Alleluia! Let him enter, the king of glory!

To God, king of the world   Ps 46(47)

*When he had brought about the purgation of sins, he took
his seat at the right hand of Majesty on high* (Heb 1:3).

Ant. God goes up with shouts of joy;
the Lord goes up with trumpet blast, alleluia!

All peoples, clap your hands,
cry to God with shouts of joy!
For the Lord, the Most High, we must fear,
great king over all the earth.

He subdues peoples under us
and nations under our feet.
Our inheritance, our glory, is from him,
given to Jacob out of love.

God goes up with shouts of joy;
the Lord goes up with trumpet blast.
Sing praise for God, sing praise,
sing praise to our king, sing praise.

God is king of all the earth.
Sing praise with all your skill.
God is king over the nations;
God reigns on his holy throne.

The princes of the peoples are assembled
with the people of Abraham's God.
The rulers of the earth belong to God,
to God who reigns over all.

Ant. God goes up with shouts of joy;
the Lord goes up with trumpet blast, alleluia!

Word of God   Eph 2:4–10

God, rich in mercy, for the great love he bore us, brought
us to life with Christ even when we were dead in our sins;
it is by his grace you are saved. And in union with Christ
Jesus he raised us up and enthroned us with him in the
heavenly realms, so that he might display in the ages to
come how immense are the resources of his grace, and how
great his kindness to us in Christ Jesus. For it is by his grace
you are saved, through trusting him; it is not your own
doing. It is God's gift, not a reward for work done. There
is nothing for anyone to boast of. For we are God's handiwork, created in Christ Jesus to devote ourselves to the good
deeds for which God has designed us.

Song of Zechariah

Ant. Go to my brothers, and tell them
that I am now ascending to my Father and your Father,
my God and your God, alleluia!

Or as follows:

287

Old Testament Song Hos 6:1–3

God raised him to life on the third day (Acts 10:40).

Ant. On the third day he will restore us,
that in his presence we may live, alleluia!

Come, let us return to the Lord;
for he has torn us and will heal us,
he has struck us and he will bind up our wounds;
after two days he will revive us,
on the third day he will restore us,
that in his presence we may live.

Let us humble ourselves, let us strive to know the Lord,
whose justice dawns like morning light,
and its dawning is as sure as the sunrise.
It will come to us like a shower,
like spring rains that water the earth.

Ant. On the third day he will restore us,
that in his presence we may live, alleluia!

Prayers

Accept us, Father, as we offer ourselves to you today. Make all that we do or say, at home or at work, worthy to be offered to you.

Father, you loved the world so much
that you sent your Son to live and die for us;
make us remember your love for the people
whom we shall see and meet today.

Lord, lead us in the way you want us to go,
and give us joy on the way.

We think of brothers and sisters and relatives.
May all families live in harmony:
where there have been jealousies,
let them be forgotten and new understanding be found.

Further prayers . . . Our Father . . .

Lord God, no flash of beauty, no enchantment of goodness, no element of force, but finds in you the ultimate refinement and consummation of itself.

Eternal Father, who through Jesus Christ, our ascending Lord, sent your Holy Spirit to be the bond of fellowship in the Church: unify the whole created order in Christ; who reigns supreme over all things with you and the same Spirit, one God, for ever and ever. Amen.

May the Lord bless us,
may he keep us from all evil
and lead us to life everlasting. Amen.

EVENING PRAYER

Lord, open my lips ...
Glory to the Father ...

Easter Hymn (based on Is 63:1–7)

Who is this who comes to us in triumph,
Clothed in royal garments dyed with blood,
Walking in the greatness of his glory,
Bearing in his hand the holy rood?

This is Christ the risen Lord, the Strong One,
He who trod the wine-press all alone;
Out of death he comes with life unending,
Seeking those he purchased for his own.

Great and wonderful is our Redeemer,
Christ the Living One, the just and true,
Praise him with the Father and the Spirit,
Ever with us, making all things new.

The Stanbrook Abbey Hymnal

To the God of glory and compassion   Ps 112(113)

He is now at the right hand of God (1 Pt 3:22).
Ant. Who is like the Lord our God,
    who has risen on high to his throne? Alleluia!
Praise, O servants of the Lord,
praise the name of the Lord!
May the name of the Lord be blessed
both now and for evermore!
From the rising of the sun to its setting
praised be the name of the Lord!

High above all nations is the Lord,
above the heavens his glory.
Who is like the Lord, our God,
who has risen on high to his throne
yet stoops from the heights to look down,
to look down upon heaven and earth?

From the dust he lifts up the lowly,
from the dungheap he raises the poor
to set him in the company of princes,
yes, with the princes of his people.
To the childless wife he gives a home
and gladdens her heart with children.

Ant. Who is like the Lord our God,
who has risen on high to his throne? Alleluia!

Man the viceroy of God Ps 8

*In Jesus we see one who for a short while was made lower
than the angels, crowned now with glory and honour
because he suffered death* (Heb 2:9).

Ant. With glory and honour you crowned him, alleluia!

How great is your name, O Lord our God,
through all the earth!

Your majesty is praised above the heavens;
on the lips of children and of babes
you have found praise to foil your enemy,
to silence the foe and the rebel.

When I see the heavens, the work of your hands,
the moon and the stars which you arranged,
what is man that you should keep him in mind,
mortal man that you care for him?

Yet you have made him little less than a god;
with glory and honour you crowned him,
gave him power over the works of your hand,
put all things under his feet.

All of them, sheep and cattle,
yes, even the savage beasts,

birds of the air, and fish
that make their way through the waters

How great is your name, O Lord our God,
through all the earth!

Ant. With glory and honour you crowned him alleluia!

Word of God   1 Pet 3:18–22

Christ died for our sins once and for all. He, the just,
suffered for the unjust, to bring us to God.
In the body he was put to death; in the spirit he was brought
to life. And in the spirit he went and made his proclamation
to the imprisoned spirits. They had refused obedience long
ago, while God waited patiently in the days of Noah and
the building of the ark, and in the ark a few persons, eight
in all, were brought to safety through the water. This water
prefigured the water of baptism through which you are
now brought to safety. Baptism is not the washing away of
bodily pollution, but the appeal made to God by a good
conscience; and it brings salvation through the resurrection
of Jesus Christ, who entered heaven after receiving the sub-
mission of angelic authorities and powers, and is now at
the right hand of God.

Song of the Virgin Mary

Ant. When I am lifted up from the earth,
    I shall draw all men to myself, alleluia, alleluia!
Or as follows:

Old Testament Song   Is 63:1–5

*He was robed in a garment drenched in blood. He was
called the Word of God* (Rev 19:13).

Ant. The year for ransoming my own had come, alleluia!

Who is this coming from Edom,
coming from Bozrah, his garments stained red?
Under his clothes his muscles stand out,
and he strides, stooping in his might.

It is I, who announce that right has won the day,
I, who am strong to save.

Why is your clothing all red,
like the garments of one who treads grapes in the va⁺ ͡

I have trodden the winepress alone;
no man, no nation was with me.
I trod them down in my rage,
I trampled them in my fury;
and their life-blood spurted over my garments
and stained all my clothing.

For I resolved on a day of vengeance;
the year for ransoming my own had come.
I looked for a helper but found no one,
I was amazed that there was no one to support me;
yet my own arm brought me victory,
alone my anger supported me.

Ant. The year for ransoming my own had come, alleluia!

Prayers

As night falls, let us give thanks to the Father:

> We thank you, Lord, for the things we tend to take for granted,
> or to expect as of right;
> teach us gratitude for everything we have.

> We thank you, Father, that Jesus Christ died, trusting fully in you;
> may all Christians have the same confidence in the hour of death
> and may all men know that the Lord Jesus has conquered death for them.

> We thank you for giving us one another;
> may we become one family in your love.

Further prayers . . . Our Father . . .

Father, we trust that, through the mystery of the resurrection, you will preserve in the hearts of those reborn in baptism the gifts of your everlasting grace and blessing, through our risen Lord Jesus Christ, who lives and reigns with you for ever. Amen.

May the Lord bless us,
may he keep us from all evil
and lead us to life everlasting. Amen.

FRIDAY

MORNING PRAYER

Lord, open my lips . . .
To you be glory . . .

Glorificamus Te
I offer thee
Every flower that ever grew,
Every bird that ever flew,
Every wind that ever blew.

> Good God!

Every thunder rolling,
Every church bell tolling,
Every leaf and sod.

> *Laudamus Te!*

I offer thee
Every wave that ever moved,
Every heart that ever loved,
Thee, thy Father's Well-Beloved.

> Dear Lord.

Every river dashing,
Every lightning flashing,
Like an angel's sword.

> *Benedicimus Te!*

I offer thee
Every cloud that ever swept
O'er the skies, and broke and wept
In rain, and with the flowerets slept.

> My King!

Each communicant praying,
Every angel staying
Before thy throne to sing.

> *Adoramus Te!*

I offer thee
Every flake of virgin snow,
Every spring of earth below,
Every human joy and woe,
>   My Love!

O Lord! And all thy glorious
Self o'er death victorious,
Throned in heaven above.
>   *Glorificamus Te!*
>   An ancient Irish Prayer

A pilgrim song   Ps 83(84)

> *He died on the cross in weakness, but he lives by the power of God* (2 Cor 13:4).

Ant. My heart and my soul ring out their joy
to God, the living God, alleluia!

How lovely is your dwelling place,
Lord, God of hosts.

My soul is longing and yearning,
is yearning for the courts of the Lord.
My heart and my soul ring out their joy
to God, the living God.

The sparrow herself finds a home
and the swallow a nest for her brood;
she lays her young by your altars,
Lord of hosts, my king and my God.

They are happy, who dwell in your house,
for ever singing your praise.
They are happy, whose strength is in you,
in whose hearts are the roads to Zion.

Lord, God of hosts,
happy the man who trusts in you!

Ant. My heart and my soul ring out their joy
to God, the living God, alleluia!

Praise to God, king of the world   Ps 97(98)

*Let all Israel accept as certain that God has made this
Jesus, whom you crucified, both Lord and Messiah* (Acts
2:36).

Ant. With trumpets and the sound of the horn
  acclaim the King, the Lord, alleluia!

Sing a new song to the Lord
for he has worked wonders.
His right hand and his holy arm
have brought salvation.

The Lord has made known his salvation;
has shown his justice to the nations.
He has remembered his truth and love
for the house of Israel.

All the ends of the earth have seen
the salvation of our God.
Shout to the Lord all the earth,
ring out your joy.

Sing psalms to the Lord with the harp
with the sound of music.
With trumpets and the sound of the horn
acclaim the King, the Lord.

Let the sea and all within it, thunder;
the world, and all its peoples.
Let the rivers clap their hands
and the hills ring out their joy

at the presence of the Lord: for he comes,
he comes to rule the earth.
He will rule the world with justice
and the peoples with fairness.

Ant. With trumpets and the sound of the horn
  acclaim the King, the Lord, alleluia!

Word of God   Heb 10:19–23;13:20–21

My friends, the blood of Jesus makes us free to enter boldly
into the sanctuary by the new, living way which he has
opened for us through the curtain, the way of his flesh.

295

We have, moreover, a great priest set over the household of
God; so let us make our approach in sincerity of heart and
full assurance of faith, our guilty hearts sprinkled clean,
our bodies washed with pure water. Let us be firm and
unswerving in the confession of our hope, for the Giver of
the promise may be trusted.

May the God of peace, who brought up from the dead
our Lord Jesus, the great Shepherd of the sheep, by the
blood of the eternal covenant, make you perfect in all
goodness so that you may do his will; and may he make of
us what he would have us be through Jesus Christ, to whom
be glory for ever and ever! Amen.

Song of Zechariah

Ant. Look at my hands and feet.
It is I myself, alleluia, alleluia!

Or as follows:

Old Testament Song   Is 63:7–9

*The children of a family share the same flesh and blood,
and so he too shared ours, so that through death he might
break the power of the devil* (Heb 2:14, 15).

Ant. He himself ransomed them by his love and pity, alleluia!

I will recount the Lord's acts of unfailing love
and the Lord's praises as High God,
all that the Lord has done for us
and his great goodness to the house of Israel,
all that he has done for them in his tenderness
and by his many acts of love.

He said, 'Surely they are my people,
my sons who will not play me false;'
and he became their deliverer in all their troubles.

It was no envoy, no angel, but he himself that delivered
    them;
he himself ransomed them by his love and pity,
lifted them up and carried them
through all the years gone by.

Ant. He himself ransomed them by his love and pity, alleluia!

Prayers

Loving Father, you have restored us to life through your risen Son; increase in us the strength of this new life, to overcome the sin that still holds us back.

Teach us to know how much we need you:
we offer you now all that we do today.

Teach us to hunger and thirst for what is right:
may we not look the other way when we see someone wronged.

Teach us to care for others:
for the old and the dying, for those who are sick,
for those who grieve.

Further prayers . . . Our Father . . .

Praise without limit, glory without end,
be yours for ever, God our Father,
because you raised Jesus to new life.

Almighty God, we have come to know your love in the resurrection of our Lord; grant that we, too, may rise to newness of life through the love of your Spirit. Amen.

May the Lord bless us,
may he keep us from all evil
and lead us to life everlasting. Amen.

EVENING PRAYER

Lord, open my lips . . .
Glory to the Father . . .

Love

Love bade me welcome: yet my soul drew back,
        Guiltie of dust and sinne.
But quick-ey'd Love, observing me grow slack
        From my first entrance in,
Drew nearer to me, sweetly questioning,
        If I lack'd any thing.

A guest, I answer'd, worthy to be here:
        Love said, you shall be he.

I the unkinde, ungrateful? Ah my deare,
        I cannot look on thee.
Love took my hand, and smiling did reply,
        Who made the eyes but I?

Truth Lord, but I have marr'd them: let my shame
        Go where it doth deserve.
And know you not, sayes Love, who bore the blame?
        My deare, then I will serve.
You must sit down, sayes Love, and taste my meat:
        So I did sit and eat.

                      George Herbert

The just man advances towards the city of God   Ps 14(15)

We must run with resolution the race for which we are entered, our eyes fixed on Jesus, on whom faith depends from start to finish (Heb 12:2).

Ant. Let the hearts that seek the Lord, rejoice, alleluia!

Lord, who shall be admitted to your tent
and dwell on your holy mountain?

He who walks without fault;
he who acts with justice
and speaks the truth from his heart;
he who does not slander with his tongue;

he who does no wrong to his brother,
who casts no slur on his neighbour,
who holds the godless in disdain,
but honours those who fear the Lord;

he who keeps his pledge come what may;
who takes no interest on a loan
and accepts no bribes against the innocent.
Such a man will stand firm for ever.

Ant. Let the hearts that seek the Lord rejoice, alleluia!

Triumphant trust in God   Ps 26(27)

I am the resurrection and I am life (Jn 11:25).

Ant. I shall see the Lord's goodness
in the land of the living, alleluia!

The Lord is my light and my help;
whom shall I fear?
The Lord is the stronghold of my life;
before whom shall I shrink?

When evil-doers draw near
to devour my flesh,
it is they, my enemies and foes,
who stumble and fall.

Though an army encamp against me
my heart would not fear.
Though war break out against me
even then would I trust.

There is one thing I ask of the Lord,
for this I long,
to live in the house of the Lord,
all the days of my life,
to savour the sweetness of the Lord,
to behold his temple.

O Lord, hear my voice when I call;
have mercy and answer.
Of you my heart has spoken:
'Seek his face.'

I am sure I shall see the Lord's goodness
in the land of the living.
Hope in him, hold firm and take heart.
Hope in the Lord!

Ant. I shall see the Lord's goodness
  in the land of the living, alleluia!

Word of God   Acts 10:34–43

Peter said to Cornelius, 'I now see how true it is that God
has no favourites, but that in every nation the man who is
godfearing and does what is right is acceptable to him. He
sent his word to the Israelites and gave the good news of
peace through Jesus Christ, who is Lord of all. I need not
tell you what happened lately all over the land of the Jews,
starting from Galilee after the baptism proclaimed by

John. You know about Jesus of Nazareth, how God anointed him with the Holy Spirit and with power. He went about doing good and healing all who were oppressed by the devil, for God was with him. And we can bear witness to all that he did in the Jewish country-side and in Jerusalem. He was put to death by hanging on a gibbet; but God raised him to life on the third day, and allowed him to appear, not to the whole people but to witnesses whom God had chosen in advance – to us, who ate and drank with him after he rose from the dead. He commanded us to proclaim him to the people, and affirm that he is the one who has been designated by God as judge of the living and the dead. It is to him that all the prophets testify, declaring that everyone who trusts in him receives forgiveness of sins through his name.

Song of the Virgin Mary

Ant. Touch me and see; no ghost has flesh and bones
as you can see that I have, alleluia!

Or as follows:

New Testament Song   1 Pt 3 & 4, passim

Ant. In the spirit he was brought to life, alleluia!

Christ died for our sins once and for all.
He, the just, suffered for the unjust,
to bring us to God, alleluia!

In the body he was put to death,
in the spirit he was brought to life,
and is now at the right hand of God, alleluia!

Remembering that Christ endured bodily suffering,
arm yourselves with a temper of mind like his;
when his glory is revealed, your joy will be triumphant,
    alleluia!

The end of all things is upon us;
do not be bewildered by the fiery ordeal that is upon you,
for the Spirit of God is resting upon you, alleluia!

Ant. In the spirit he was brought to life, alleluia!

300

Prayers

Father, in the death and resurrection of Jesus Christ you have given us new life; may our share in this mystery grow strong within us, and be expressed in the Christian dedication of our lives.

Father, from you all true peace comes:
fill the hearts of those who rule nations
with a love of peace and justice.

Merciful Lord, you are the source of all justice:
give to all judges and magistrates
and all officers of the law
your gifts of wisdom and integrity.

Lord, inspire us with hope in you:
grant us courage and perseverence.

Further prayers . . . Our Father . . .

Almighty God, your prophets promised us a day when young men would see visions, old men would dream dreams, and when your Spirit would fill all men with joy. Easter is that day; may its light fill our whole life, through Christ our Lord, who lives and reigns with you for ever. Amen.

May the Lord bless us,
may he keep us from all evil
and lead us to life everlasting. Amen.

SATURDAY

MORNING PRAYER

Lord, open my lips . . .
To you be glory . . .

Morning Hymn of Adam and Eve
from Paradise Lost, Bk V

These are thy glorious works, Parent of good,
Almighty, thine this universal frame,
Thus wondrous fair; thyself how wondrous then!
Unspeakable, who sitst above these Heavens

To us invisible or dimly seen
In these thy lowest works, yet these declare
Thy goodness beyond thought, and Power Divine:
Speak ye who best can tell, ye sons of light,
Angels, for ye behold him, and with songs
And choral symphonies, day without night,
Circle his throne rejoicing, ye in Heav'n,
On earth join all ye creatures to extol
Him first, him last, him midst, and without end.

Join voices all ye living souls, ye birds,
That singing up to Heaven gate ascend,
Bear on your wings and in your notes his praise;
Ye that in waters glide, and ye that walk
The earth, and stately tread, or lowly creep;
Witness if I be silent, morn or even,
To hill, or valley, fountain, or fresh shade
Made vocal by my song, and taught his praise.
Hail universal Lord, be bounteous still
To give us only good; and if the night
Have gathered aught of evil or concealed,
Disperse it, as now light dispels the dark.

John Milton

Praise and fear of God

Ps 33(34)

Surely you have tasted that the Lord is good. So come to him, our living Stone (1 Pt 2:3).

Ant. Taste and see that the Lord is good, alleluia!

I will bless the Lord at all times,
his praise always on my lips;
in the Lord my soul shall make its boast.
The humble shall hear and be glad.

Glorify the Lord with me.
Together let us praise his name.
I sought the Lord and he answered me;
from all my terrors he set me free.

Look towards him and be radiant;
let your faces not be abashed.

This poor man called; the Lord heard him
and rescued him from all his distress.

The angel of the Lord is encamped
around those who revere him, to rescue them.
Taste and see that the Lord is good.
He is happy who seeks refuge in him.

Revere the Lord, you his saints.
They lack nothing, those who revere him.
Strong lions suffer want and go hungry
but those who seek the Lord lack no blessing.

Come, children, and hear me
that I may teach you the fear of the Lord.
Who is he who longs for life
and many days, to enjoy his prosperity?

Then keep your tongue from evil
and your lips from speaking deceit.
Turn aside from evil and do good;
seek and strive after peace.

Ant. Taste and see that the Lord is good, alleluia!

The power and holiness of God   Ps 98(99)

The One who called you is holy; like him be holy in all your behaviour (1 Pet 2:15)

Ant. The Lord our God, he is holy and full of power, alleluia!

The Lord is king; the peoples tremble.
He is throned on the cherubim; earth quakes.
The Lord is great in Zion.

He is supreme over all the peoples.
Let them praise his name, so terrible and great.
He is holy, full of power.

You are a king who loves what is right;
you have established equity, justice and right;
you have established them in Jacob.

Exalt the Lord our God;
bow down before Zion, his footstool.
He the Lord is holy.

Among his priests were Aaron and Moses,
among those who invoked his name was Samuel.
They invoked the Lord and he answered.

To them he spoke in the pillar of cloud.
They did his will; they kept the law,
which he, the Lord, had given.

O Lord our God, you answered them.
For them you were a God who forgives;
yet you punished all their offences.

Exalt the Lord our God;
bow down before his holy mountain
for the Lord our God is holy.

Ant. The Lord our God, he is holy and full of power,
alleluia!

Word of God   1 Pt 2:4–10

Come to him, our living Stone – the stone rejected by men
but choice and precious in the sight of God. Come, and let
yourselves be built, as living stones, into a spiritual temple;
become a holy priesthood, to offer spiritual sacrifices
acceptable to God through Jesus Christ. For it stands
written:

'I lay in Zion a choice corner-stone of great worth.
The man who has faith in it will not be put to shame.'

The great worth of which it speaks is for you who have
faith. For those who have no faith, the stone which the
builders rejected has become not only the corner-stone, but
also 'a stone to trip over, a rock to stumble against'. They
fall when they disbelieve the Word. Such was their appointed
lot!

But you are a chosen race, a royal priesthood, a dedicated
nation, and a people claimed by God for his own, to proclaim the triumphs of him who has called you out of
darkness into his marvellous light. You are now the people

of God, who once were not his people; outside his mercy once, you have now received his mercy.

Song of Zechariah

Ant. Jesus came and stood among his disciples and said, 'Peace be with you, alleluia!'

Or as follows:

Song of the Spirit

Ant. Come, Holy Spirit, renew the face of the earth, alleluia!

Things beyond our seeing, things beyond our hearing,
things beyond our imagining,
all prepared by God for those who love him –
these it is that God has revealed to us through the Spirit.
It is God also who has set his seal upon us,
and has given the Spirit to dwell in our hearts:
Father of the poor and light of our hearts,
our comfort in sorrow, our strength in tribulation.

Here is the proof that we dwell in him and he dwells in
  us:
he has imparted his Spirit to us,
the fountain of life, wisdom and holiness,
sevenfold gift of the Father.
We are no longer under the law,
but under the grace of God.
He has set his law within us
and written it in our hearts.

No longer need we teach one another to know the Lord;
all of us shall know him, high and low alike.
Now at last God has his dwelling among men!
They shall be his people and God himself will be with
  them.
He shall wipe away every tear from their eyes;
there shall be an end to death, and to mourning and pain.
For the old order has passed away;
all things are new.

Ant. Come, Holy Spirit, renew the face of the earth, alleluia!

Prayers

Father, open our hearts to the mystery of your Son's
  resurrection.
Enable us to proclaim it in everything we do.

Lord, set us free from faith and hope in lesser things.
Set us free for faith and hope in you.
Set us free to live and work and serve, building your
  future.
Set us free to be your children.

We pray for cheerfulness and a joyful heart,
in our homes, at work, and with all whom we meet.

We pray for those who are mentally ill:
teach us to love them, for we are all children of God.

Further prayers ... Our Father ...

We praise you, Lord, and we bless you,
because by your cross you have redeemed the world.

Almighty and eternal God, you gave us new life in baptism:
we ask you to bring the Easter mystery to perfection in our
lives, through Christ our risen Lord, who lives and reigns
with you for ever. Amen.

May the Lord bless us,
may he keep us from all evil
and lead us to life everlasting. Amen.

EVENING PRAYER

Lord, open my lips ...
Glory to the Father ...

Night Music

At one the wind rose,
And with it the noise
Of the black poplars.

Long since had the living
By a thin twine
Been led into their dreams
Where lanterns shine

Under a still veil
Of falling streams;
Long since had the dead
Become untroubled
In the light soil.
There were no mouths
To drink of the wind,
Nor any eyes
To sharpen on the stars'
Wide heaven-holding,
Only the sound
Long sibilant-muscled trees
Were lifting up, the black poplars.

And in their blazing solitude
The stars sang in their sockets through the night:
'Blow bright, blow bright
The coal of this unquickened world.'

Philip Larkin

Longing for God's dwelling place   Pss 41 & 42 (42 & 43)

> *You stand before Mount Zion and the city of the living God* (Heb 12:22).

Ant. Bring me to your holy mountain,
    to the place where you dwell, alleluia!

Like the deer that yearns
for running streams
so my soul is yearning
for you, my God.

My soul is thirsting for God,
the God of my life;
when can I enter and see
the face of God?

O send forth your light and your truth;
let these be my guide.
Let them bring me to your holy mountain
to the place where you dwell.

307

And I will come to the altar of God,
the God of my joy.
My redeemer, I will thank you on the harp,
O God, my God.

Why are you cast down, my soul,
why groan within me?
Hope in God; I will praise him still,
my saviour and my God.

Ant. Bring me to your holy mountain,
to the place where you dwell, alleluia!

Song of peace   Ps 130(131)

A sabbath rest still awaits the people of God (Heb 4:10)

Ant. Hope in the Lord, hope in him,
now and for ever, alleluia!

O Lord, my heart is not proud
nor haughty my eyes.
I have not gone after things too great
nor marvels beyond me.

Truly I have set my soul
in silence and peace.
A weaned child on its mother's breast,
even so is my soul.

O Israel, hope in the Lord
both now and for ever.

Ant. Hope in the Lord, hope in him,
now and for ever, alleluia!

Word of God   Titus 3:3–8

At one time we ourselves in our folly and obstinacy were all
astray. We were slaves to passions and pleasures of every
kind. Our days were passed in malice and envy; we were
odious ourselves and we hated one another. But when the
kindness and generosity of God our Saviour dawned upon
the world, then, not for any good deeds of our own, but
because he was merciful, he saved us through the water of
rebirth and the renewing power of the Holy Spirit. For

he sent down the Spirit upon us plentifully through Jesus
Christ our Saviour, so that, justified by his grace, we might
in hope become heirs to eternal life.

Song of the Virgin Mary

Ant. Happy are they who never saw me
and yet have found faith, alleluia, alleluia!

Or as follows:

Song of the Spirit

Ant. Come, Holy Spirit, enkindle in us the fire of your love.

He who inspires us
is greater than he who inspires the godless world.
The Spirit of God is the seal
with which we are marked for the day of liberation.
The Spirit that God gave us is no craven spirit,
but one to inspire strength and love,
the Spirit of his Son in our hearts,
crying, 'Abba! Father!'

The harvest of the Spirit is love,
joy, peace, patience, kindness and goodness.
There is nothing love cannot face,
no limit to its faith, its hope and its endurance.
A man reaps what he sows:
if we sow in the field of the Spirit,
the Spirit will bring us a harvest of eternal life.

Hear, you who have ears to hear,
what the Spirit says to the Churches.
'Come!' say the Spirit and the bride.
'Come!' let each hearer reply.
Come forward, you who are thirsty,
accept the water of life, a free gift to all who desire it.
O give thanks to the Lord for he is good,
for his love endures for ever.

Ant. Come, Holy Spirit, enkindle in us the fire of your love.

309

Prayers

Holy Spirit of God, give us the sure hope that the love of God in Christ Jesus is stronger than the forces of evil.

We pray for an end to war and hatred,
that mankind may be truly the one family of God in Christ.

May all families be united in love and harmony.

We pray for those who are suffering,
for the sick and the dying, for those who are homeless;
we pray for the young, we pray for the old.

Further prayers ... Our Father ...

Father in heaven, unite us in joy and hope through the resurrection of your Son; send your Spirit upon us to fill the whole universe with your love. Amen.

May the Lord bless us,
may he keep us from all evil
and lead us to life everlasting. Amen.

PENTECOST SUNDAY

MORNING PRAYER

Lord, open my lips ...
To you be glory ...

Fire in the earth

It is done.
Once again the Fire has penetrated the earth.
Not with the sudden crash of thunderbolt,
riving the mountain tops:
does the Master break down doors to enter his own home?
Without earthquake, or thunderclap:
the flame has lit up the whole world from within.

All things individually and collectively
are penetrated and flooded by it,
from the inmost core of the tiniest atom
to the mighty sweep of the most universal laws of being:
so naturally has it flooded every element, every energy,
every connecting link in the unity of our cosmos,
that one might suppose the cosmos to have burst
  spontaneously into flame.

Pierre Teilhard de Chardin

God's power seen in a storm
Ps 28(29)

*There appeared to them tongues like flames of fire,
dispersed among them and resting on each one* (Acts 2:3).

Ant. The Lord's voice flashes flames of fire, alleluia!

O give the Lord you sons of God,
give the Lord glory and power;
give the Lord the glory of his name.
Adore the Lord in his holy court.

The Lord's voice resounding on the waters,
the Lord on the immensity of waters;
the voice of the Lord, full of power,
the voice of the Lord, full of splendour.

The Lord's voice shattering the cedars,
the Lord shatters the cedars of Lebanon;
he makes Lebanon leap like a calf
and Sirion like a young wild-ox.

The Lord's voice flashes flames of fire.
The Lord's voice shaking the wilderness,
the Lord shakes the wilderness of Kadesh;
the Lord's voice rending the oak tree
and stripping the forest bare.

The God of glory thunders.
In his temple they all cry: 'Glory!'
The Lord sat enthroned over the flood;
the Lord sits as king for ever.

311

The Lord will give strength to his people,
the Lord will bless his people with peace.

Ant. The Lord's voice flashes flames of fire, alle uia!

Summons to praise   Ps 150

*You will receive power when the Holy Spirit comes upon
you, and you will bear witness for me to the ends of the
earth* (Acts 1:8).

Ant. The Spirit of the Lord fills the whole world, alleluia!

Praise God in his holy place,
praise him in his mighty heavens.
Praise him for his powerful deeds,
praise his surpassing greatness.

O praise him with sound of trumpet,
praise him with lute and harp.
Praise him with timbrel and dance,
praise him with strings and pipes.

O praise him with resounding cymbals,
praise him with clashing of cymbals.
Let everything that lives and that breathes
give praise to the Lord.

Ant. The Spirit of the Lord fills the whole world, alleluia!

Word of God   Rom 8:5-11

Those who live on the level of our lower nature have their
outlook formed by it, and that spells death; but those who
live on the level of the spirit have the spiritual outlook, and
that is life and peace. For the outlook of the lower nature
is enmity with God; it is not subject to the law of God;
indeed it cannot be: those who live on such a level cannot
possibly please God.

But that is not how you live. You are on the spiritual level,
if only God's Spirit dwells within you; and if a man does
not possess the Spirit of Christ, he is no Christian. But if
Christ is dwelling within you, then although the body is a
dead thing because you sinned, yet the spirit is life
itself because you have been justified. Moreover, if the
Spirit of him who raised Jesus from the dead dwells within

you, then the God who raised Christ Jesus from the dead will also give new life to your mortal bodies through his indwelling Spirit.

Song of Zechariah

Ant. Receive the Holy Spirit!
 If you forgive any man's sins, they stand forgiven, alleluia!
Or as follows:

Old Testament Song   Ez 36:23–28

No one can enter the kingdom of God without being born from water and spirit (Jn 3:5).

Ant. The day shall come when I will pour out my spirit
 on all mankind, alleluia, alleluia!

When they see that I reveal my holiness through you,
the nations will know that I am the Lord.
I will take you out of the nations
and gather you from every land
and bring you to your own soil, alleluia!

I will sprinkle clean water over you,
and you shall be cleansed from all that defiles you;
I will cleanse you from the taint of all your idols.
I will give you a new heart
and put a new spirit within you, alleluia!

I will take the heart of stone from your body
and give you a heart of flesh.
I will put my spirit into you and make you conform to
 my statutes.
You shall become my people
and I will become your God, alleluia!

Ant. The day shall come when I will pour out my spirit
 on all mankind, alleluia, alleluia!

Prayers

Spirit of God, you came suddenly to the waiting Church at Pentecost. The eyes of those who walked in darkness were gladdened with the glorious light of your presence, and their faint hearts were filled with your strength.

Father, now you are finally with us.
No one can flee from your Spirit.
Help us so to transform ourselves
that our lives may reveal your presence to others.

Father, you are with all men.
No one is cut off from your Spirit.
Help us so to transform our lives
that we who are united by a common birth
may live as brothers.

Father, you have given yourself to us completely.
No one is poor who has your love.
Help us to change our hearts
until we are able to give ourselves generously
to you and to our brothers.

Further prayers . . . Our Father . . .

Lord Spirit, you have made a darkened world alive with the fullness of light and love; lead us forward out of solitude to open the eyes of the blind, to proclaim the Word of light, to reap together the harvest of life.

May the Lord bless us,
may he keep us from all evil
and lead us to life everlasting. Amen.

EVENING PRAYER

Lord, open my lips . . .
Glory to the Father . . .

Veni, Creator Spiritus

Come, O Creator Spirit, come,
And make within our hearts thy home;
To us thy grace celestial give,
Who of thy breathing move and live.

O Comforter, that name is thine,
Of God most high the gift divine;
The well of fire, the fire of love,
Our souls' anointing from above.

Thou dost appear in sevenfold dower
The sign of God's almighty power;
The Father's promise, making rich
With saving truth our earthly speech.

Our senses with thy light inflame,
Our hearts to heavenly love reclaim;
Our bodies' poor infirmity
With strength perpetual fortify.

Our mortal foe afar repel,
Grant us henceforth in peace to dwell;
And so to us, with thee for guide,
No ill shall come, no harm betide.

May we by thee the Father learn,
And know the Son, and thee discern,
Who art of both; and thus adore
In perfect faith for evermore. Amen.

Translated by Robert Bridges

The Messiah, King, Priest and Judge   Ps 109(110)

*He is destined to reign until God has put all enemies under
his feet* (1 Cor 15:25).

Ant. When the Spirit of truth is given to you,
he will glorify me, alleluia!

The Lord's revelation to my Master:
'Sit on my right:
I will put your foes beneath your feet.'

The Lord will send from Zion
your sceptre of power:
rule in the midst of all your foes.

A prince from the day of your birth
on the holy mountains;
from the womb before the daybreak I begot you.

The Lord has sworn an oath he will not change.
'You are a priest for ever,
a priest like Melchizedek of old.'

The Master standing at your right hand
will shatter kings in the day of his great wrath.

He shall drink from the stream by the wayside
and therefore he shall lift up his head.

Ant. When the Spirit of truth is given to you,
   he will glorify me, alleluia!

The wonders of the Exodus   Ps 113A(114)

*We were all brought into one body by baptism, in the one
Spirit, and that one Holy Spirit was poured out for all of
us to drink* (1 Cor 12:13).

Ant. Suddenly there came from the sky
   a noise like that of a strong driving wind, alleluia!

When Israel came forth from Egypt,
Jacob's sons from an alien people,
Judah became the Lord's temple,
Israel became his kingdom.

The sea fled at the sight:
the Jordan turned back on its course,
the mountains leapt like rams
and the hills like yearling sheep.

Why was it, sea, that you fled,
that you turned back, Jordan, on your course?
Mountains, that you leapt like rams,
hills, like yearling sheep?

Tremble, O earth, before the Lord,
in the presence of the God of Jacob,
who turns the rock into a pool
and flint into a spring of water.

Ant. Suddenly there came from the sky
   a noise like that of a strong driving wind, alleluia!

Word of God   Eph 4:1–7, 11–13

I entreat you – I, a prisoner for the Lord's sake: as God has
called you, live up to your calling. Be humble always and
gentle, and patient too. Be forbearing with one another and
charitable. Spare no effort to make fast with bonds of peace

the unity which the Spirit gives. There is one body and one Spirit, as there is also one hope held out in God's call to you; one Lord, one faith, one baptism; one God and Father of all, who is over all and through all and in all.

But each of us has been given his gift, his due portion of Christ's bounty. And these were his gifts: some to be apostles, some prophets, some evangelists, some pastors and teachers, to equip God's people for work in his service, to the building up of the body of Christ.

Song of the Virgin Mary

Ant. That glorious Spirit which is the Spirit of God
is resting upon you, alleluia, alleluia!

Or as follows:

New Testament Song   Rev 19:2, 6–8

Ant. Filled with the joy of the Spirit,
let us exult and do him homage, alleluia!

Alleluia, alleluia!
Victory and glory and power
belong to our God, alleluia!
for true and just are his judgments.
Alleluia, alleluia!

Praise our God,
all you his servants, alleluia!
You that fear him,
both great and small.
Alleluia, alleluia!

The Lord our God,
sovereign over all, alleluia!
has entered on his reign.
Exult and shout for joy and do him homage.
Alleluia, alleluia!

For the wedding day of the Lamb
has come, alleluia!
His bride
has made herself ready.
Alleluia, alleluia!

For her dress
she has been given, alleluia!
fine linen,
clean and shining,
Alleluia, alleluia!

Ant. Filled with the joy of the Spirit,
let us exult and do him homage, alleluia!

Prayers

Father, may our minds and hearts be made whole and filled
with grace by your Spirit; may we praise you with full
hearts as brothers of your only Son.

Enable us to live in love:
let our lives be at one in praise
with the Church, with all mankind,
and with the hymn of the universe.

Father, send down on us the Spirit, the Comforter;
give us the Holy Spirit of wisdom and understanding,
of courage and love.

Let our striving for God's kingdom not fall short
through selfishness or fear;
may the universe be alive with the Spirit,
and our own homes pledges of a world redeemed.

Further prayers . . . Our Father . . .

Heavenly Father, tonight we offer ourselves freely to you.
Take our lives up into the reign of your Spirit, so that we
may serve you well, through your Son Jesus Christ. Amen.

May the Lord bless us,
may he keep us from all evil
and bring us to life everlasting. Amen.

FEAST OF THE HOLY TRINITY

Morning Prayer
Lord, open my lips . . .
To you be glory . . .

To God the Father
Great God: within whose simple essence, we
   nothing but that which is Thy Self can find;
   when on Thyself thou didst reflect thy mind,
    Thy Thought was God, which took the form of Thee:
And when this God, thus born, Thou lov'st, and He
   lov'd Thee again, with passion of like kind,
   as lovers' sighs which meet become one mind,
    both breath'd one Spirit of equal deity.
Eternal Father, whence these two do come
   and wil'st the title of my father have,
   an heavenly knowledge in my mind engrave,
That it thy Son's true Image may become:
   incense my heart with sighs of holy Love,
   that it the temple of the Spirit may prove.

Henry Constable

Joyful song to the Creator
Ps 32(33) I

*The Word was with God at the beginning, and through him
all things came to be* (Jn 1:2, 3).

Ant. Yours the glory before all ages;
   yours be the glory now and for ever,
    Three equal persons, one only Godhead.

Ring out your joy to the Lord, O you just;
for praise is fitting for loyal hearts.

Give thanks to the Lord upon the harp,
with a ten-stringed lute sing him songs.
O sing him a song that is new,
play loudly, with all your skill.

For the word of the Lord is faithful
and all his works to be trusted.

The Lord loves justice and right
and fills the earth with his love.

By his word the heavens were made,
by the breath of his mouth all the stars.
He collects the waves of the ocean;
he stores up the depths of the sea.

Let all the earth fear the Lord,
all who live in the world revere him.
He spoke; and it came to be.
He commanded; it sprang into being.

Ps 32(33) II

He frustrates the designs of the nations,
he defeats the plans of the peoples.
His own designs shall stand for ever,
the plans of his heart from age to age.

They are happy, whose God is the Lord,
the people he has chosen as his own.
From the heavens the Lord looks forth,
he sees all the children of men.

From the place where he dwells he gazes
on all the dwellers on the earth,
he who shapes the hearts of them all
and considers all their deeds.

A king is not saved by his army,
nor a warrior preserved by his strength.
A vain hope for safety is the horse;
despite its power it cannot save.

The Lord looks on those who revere him,
on those who hope in his love,
to rescue their souls from death,
to keep them alive in famine.

Our soul is waiting for the Lord.
The Lord is our help and our shield.
In him do our hearts find joy.
We trust in his holy name.

May your love be upon us, O Lord,
as we place all our hope in you.

Ant. Yours the glory before all ages;
   yours be the glory, now and for ever,
    Three equal persons, one only Godhead.

Word of God   Jn 14:8–17

Philip said to Jesus, 'Lord, show us the Father and we ask
no more.' Jesus answered, 'Have I been all this time with
you, Philip, and you still do not know me? Anyone who has
seen me has seen the Father. Then how can you say, "Show
us the Father"? Do you not believe that I am in the Father,
and the Father in me, or else accept the evidence of the
deeds themselves. In truth, in very truth, I tell you, he who
has faith in me will do what I am doing; and he will do
greater things still because I am going to the Father. Indeed
anything you ask in my name I will do, so that the Father
may be glorified in the Son. If you ask anything in my name
I will do it.
'If you love me you will obey my commands; and I will ask
the Father, and he will give you another to be your Advocate, who will be with you for ever – the Spirit of truth. The
world cannot receive him, because the world neither sees
nor knows him; but you know him, because he dwells with
you and is in you.'

Song of Zechariah

Ant. Blessed be the holy and undivided Trinity,
   Creator and Ruler of all things,
    now and for ever, through ages unending.

Or as follows:

New Testament Song   Eph 1:3–10

Ant. You are the true and only Trinity,
   the sole and highest Godhead,
    Unity holy and undivided.

Praise be to the God and Father
of our Lord Jesus Christ,
who has bestowed on us in Christ
every spiritual blessing in the heavenly realms.

In Christ he chose us
before the world was founded,
to be dedicated, to be without blemish in his sight,
to be full of love.

He destined us – such was his will and pleasure –
to be accepted as his sons through Jesus Christ,
in order that the glory of his gracious gift,
so graciously bestowed on us in his Beloved,
might redound to his praise.

For in Christ our release is secured
and our sins are forgiven
through the shedding of his blood.
Therein lies the richness of God's grave lavished upon us,
imparting full wisdom and insight.

He has made known to us his hidden purpose
to be put into effect when the time was ripe:
that the universe, all in heaven and on earth,
might be brought into a unity in Christ.

Ant. You are the true and only Trinity,
the sole and highest Godhead,
Unity, holy and undivided.

Prayers

Father, your Son who came to bring life to all men was
conceived by the power of the Holy Spirit. Praise to you,
Father, through the Son and in the Holy Spirit!

    Father, almighty and eternal God, in the name of your
       Son
    send the Spirit to your Church
    to unite all believers in love and truth.

    Lord, send labourers into the harvest to teach all
       nations,
    to baptize them in the name of the Father,
    and of the Son and of the Holy Spirit.

    Father, strengthen all those who are persecuted
    for your name's sake.

Send your Spirit of truth to speak for them
as Christ promised.

Further prayers . . . Our Father . .

Lord of all time and space, by whose inspiration we have
been led to acknowledge the glory of the eternal Trinity and
in the power of your divine majesty to worship the Unity.
Keep us steadfast in this faith, that we may be united in your
boundless love through Jesus Christ your Son our Lord,
who with you and the Holy Spirit lives and reigns in the
unity of perfect love, supreme over all things, God, for
ever and ever. Amen.

May the Lord bless us,
may he keep us from all evil
and lead us to life everlasting. Amen.

EVENING PRAYER

Lord, open my lips . . .
Glory to the Father . . .

Trinity in Unity
from The Divine Comedy

Within the clear profound Light's aureole
    Three circles from its substance now appeared,
    Of three colours, and each an equal whole.
One its reflection on the next conferred
    As rainbow upon rainbow, and the two
    Breathed equally the fire that was the third.
To my conception O how frail and few
    My words! and that, to what I looked upon,
    Is such that 'little' is more than is its due.
O Light Eternal, who in thyself alone
    Dwell'st and thyself know'st, and self-understood,
    Self-understanding, smilest on thine own!
That circle which, as I conceived it, glowed
    Within thee like reflection of a flame,
    Being by mine eyes a little longer wooed,
Deep in itself, with colour still the same,
    Seemed with our human effigy to fill,

Wherefore absorbed in it my sight became.
As the geometer who bends all his will
  To measure the circle, and howsoe'er he try
  Fails, for the principle escapes him still,
Such at this mystery new-disclosed was I,
  Fain to understand how the image doth alight
  Upon the circle, and with its form comply.
But these my wings were fledged not for that flight,
  Save that my mind a sudden glory assailed
  And its wish came revealed to it in that light.
To the high imagination force now failed;
  But like to a wheel whose circling nothing jars
  Already on my desire and will prevailed
The Love that moves the sun and the other stars.

Dante, trans. Laurence Binyon

A psalm of worship   Ps 112(113)

*Through Christ we have access to the Father in the one
Spirit* (Eph 2:18).

Ant. Everlasting glory and praise to God the Father,
  to the Son, and to the blessed Advocate,
  unto all ages!

Praise, O servants of the Lord,
praise the name of the Lord!
May the name of the Lord be blessed
both now and for evermore!
From the rising of the sun to its setting
praised be the name of the Lord!

High above all nations is the Lord,
above the heavens his glory.
Who is like the Lord, our God,
who has risen on high to his throne
yet stoops from the heights to look down,
to look down upon heaven and earth?

From the dust he lifts up the lowly,
from the dungheap he raises the poor
to set him in the company of princes,

yes, with the princes of his people.
To the childless wife he gives a home
and gladdens her heart with children.

Ant. Everlasting glory and praise to God the Father,
to the Son, and to the blessed Advocate,
unto all ages!

God's care for his people   Ps 147

When all things began, the Word already was (Jn 1:1).

Ant. From him and through him and to him are all things.
To him be glory for ever!

O praise the Lord, Jerusalem!
Zion, praise your God!

He has strengthened the bars of your gates,
he has blessed the children within you.
He established peace on your borders,
he feeds you with finest wheat.

He sends out his word to the earth
and swifty runs his command.
He showers down snow white as wool,
he scatters hoar-frost like ashes.

He hurls down hailstones like crumbs.
The waters are frozen at his touch;
he sends forth his word and it melts them:
at the breath of his mouth the waters flow.

He makes his word known to Jacob,
to Israel his laws and decrees.
He has not dealt thus with other nations;
he has not taught them his decrees.

Ant. From him and through him and to him are all things.
To him be glory for ever!

Word of God   Mt 28:16–20

The eleven disciples made their way to Galilee, to the
mountain where Jesus had told them to meet him. When they

saw him, they fell prostrate before him, though some were doubtful. Jesus then came up and spoke to them. He said: 'Full authority in heaven and on earth has been committed to me. Go forth therefore and make all nations my disciples; baptize men everywhere in the name of the Father and the Son and the Holy Spirit, and teach them to observe all that I have commanded you. And be assured, I am with you always, to the end of time.'

Song of the Virgin Mary

Ant. With our whole heart and tongue we acclaim you,
O God;
we praise and bless you, the unbegotten Father,
the only-begotten Son,
the Holy Spirit, the Advocate:
holy and undivided Trinity.
To you be glory for ever and ever!

Or as follows:

New Testament Song   Rev 5:11, 12; 4:8; 19:2, 6, 7

Ant. Give glory to the Father,
and to the Son he has begotten;
to the Holy Spirit likewise give unending praise.

Voices of countless angels praise him,
myriads upon myriads, thousands upon thousands
sing to him without ceasing:
Holy, holy, holy is God, the sovereign Lord of all,
who was and is, and is to come.
Alleluia, alleluia!

Victory and glory and power
belong to our God, alleluia!
for true and just are his judgments.
Alleluia, alleluia!

Praise our God,
all you his servants, alleluia!
you that fear him,
both great and small.
Alleluia, alleluia!

The Lord our God
is sovereign over all, alleluia!
Exult and shout for joy and do him homage.
Alleluia, alleluia!

Ant. Give glory to the Father,
    and to the Son he has begotten;
    to the Holy Spirit likewise give unending praise.

Prayers

Let us give praise to the Father who has made us his sons,
to the Son who has brought us new life,
and to the Spirit who abides with us.

> Lord God Almighty, your Spirit enables us to call you
>   Father;
> may we become your true sons.

> Christ, son of the Father,
> you promised to send the Spirit to your apostles.
> May the same Spirit always be with your Church.

> Come, Holy Spirit, fill us with your gifts,
> especially those of patience, joy and faith.

Further prayers . . . Our Father . . .

Holy God, Holy Strong One, Holy Immortal One, have
    mercy on us.
To you be praise, to you be glory, to you be thanksgiving
through endless ages, O blessed Trinity! Amen.

May the Lord bless us,
may he keep us from all evil
and lead us to life everlasting. Amen.

FEASTS OF OUR LADY

Morning Prayer

Lord, open my lips . . .
To you be glory . . .

I sing of a maiden

I sing of a maiden
That is matchless;
King of all kings
For her son she chose.

He came all so still
Where his mother was,
As dew in April
That falleth on the grass.

He came all so still
To his mother's bowr,
As dew in April
That falleth on the flower.

He came all so still
where his mother lay,
As dew in April
That falleth on the spray.

Mother and maiden
Was never none but she;
Well may such a lady
Godes mother be.

Anonymous

Royal wedding song   Ps 44(45)

Happy are those who are invited to the wedding-supper of the Lamb (Rev 19:9).

Ant. All generations will count me blessed.

Listen, O daughter, give ear to my words:
forget your own people and your father's house.

So will the king desire your beauty:
He is your lord, pay homage to him.

And the people of Tyre shall come with gifts,
the richest of the people shall seek your favour.
The daughter of the king is clothed with splendour
her robes embroidered with pearls set in gold.

She is led to the king with her maiden companions.
They are escorted amid gladness and joy;
they pass within the palace of the king.

Sons shall be yours in place of your fathers:
you will make them princes over all the earth.
May this song make your name for ever remembered.
May the peoples praise you from age to age.

Ant. All generations will count me blessed.

God, the succour and strength of his people   Ps 45(46)
   You shall conceive and bear a son (Lk 1:31).

Ant. God is within her, she cannot be shaken.

God is for us a refuge and strength,
a helper close at hand, in time of distress:
so we shall not fear though the earth should rock,
though the mountains fall into the depths of the sea,
even though its waters rage and foam,
even though the mountains be shaken by its waves.

The Lord of hosts is with us:
the God of Jacob is our stronghold.

The waters of a river give joy to God's city,
the holy place where the Most High dwells.
God is within, it cannot be shaken;
God will help it at the dawning of the day.
Nations are in tumult, kingdoms are shaken:
he lifts his voice, the earth shrinks away.

The Lord of hosts is with us:
the God of Jacob is our stronghold.
Come, consider the works of the Lord
the redoubtable deeds he has done on the earth.

He puts an end to wars over all the earth;
the bow he breaks, the spear he snaps.
He burns the shields with fire.
"Be still and know that I am God,
supreme among the nations, supreme on the earth!"

The Lord of hosts is with us:
the God of Jacob is our stronghold.

Ant. God is within her, she cannot be shaken.

Word of God   Gen 3:9–15

The Lord God called to the man and said to him, 'Where
are you?' He replied, 'I heard the sound as you were walking
in the garden, and I was afraid because I was naked, and
I hid myself.' God answered, 'Who told you that you were
naked? Have you eaten from the tree which I forbade you?'
The man said, 'The woman you gave me for a companion,
she gave me fruit from the tree and I ate it.' Then the Lord
God said to the woman, 'What is this that you have done?'
The woman said, 'The serpent tricked me, and I ate.'
Then the Lord God said to the serpent:

'Because you have done this you are accursed
more than all cattle and all wild creatures.
On your belly you shall crawl, and dust you shall eat
all the days of your life.
I will put enmity between you and the woman,
between your brood and hers.
They shall strike at your head,
and you shall strike at their heel.'

Song of Zechariah

Ant. Blessed are you, holy Virgin Mary,
    for the sun of justice, Christ our God, was born of you.
Or as follows:

New Testament Song   Eph 1:3–10

Ant. Praise to you, God our Father, who have bestowed on
us in Christ every spiritual blessing.

Praise be to the God and Father
of our Lord Jesus Christ,
who has bestowed on us in Christ
every spiritual blessing in the heavenly realms.

In Christ he chose us
before the world was founded,
to be dedicated, to be without blemish, in his sight,
to be full of love.

He destined us – such was his will and pleasure –
to be accepted as his sons through Jesus Christ,
in order that the glory of his gracious gift,
so graciously bestowed on us in his Beloved,
might redound to his praise.

For in Christ our release is secured
and our sins are forgiven
through the shedding of his blood.
Therein lies the richness of God's grace lavished upon us,
imparting full wisdom and insight.

He has made known to us his hidden purpose
to be put into effect when the time was ripe:
that the universe, all in heaven and on earth,
might be brought into a unity in Christ.

Ant. Praise to you, God our Father, who have bestowed on
us in Christ every spiritual blessing.

Prayers

Lord God, may we always be attentive to your will and
respond to it with Mary: As you have spoken, so be it.

Father, by whom Mary was filled with grace, give us a share
in your life, so that we may be worthy followers of her Son.

As Mary was the loving mother of the household at
Nazareth, help all mothers to imitate her in their love and
care of their families.

Lord, help us to imitate Mary's humility by our kindness
and compassion towards those whom we meet.

Further prayers . . . Our Father . . .

331

We thank you, Lord our God, for the example of trust and love that you have given us in Mary. Help us always to be like her in our service of all men, through Christ our Lord. Amen.

May the Lord bless us,
may he keep us from all evil
and lead us to life everlasting. Amen.

EVENING PRAYER

Lord, open my lips . . .
Glory to the Father . . .

St Bernard's Prayer to the Virgin Mary
from The Divine Comedy

Maiden and Mother, daughter of thine own Son,
    Beyond all creatures lowly and lifted high,
    Of the Eternal Design the corner-stone!
Thou art she who did man's substance glorify
    So that its own Maker did not eschew
    Even to be made of its mortality.
Within thy womb the Love was kindled new
    By generation of whose warmth supreme
    This flower to bloom in peace eternal grew.
Here thou to us art the full noonday beam
    Of love revealed: below, to mortal sight,
    Hope, that for ever springs in living stream.
Lady, thou art so great and hast such might
    That whoso crave grace, nor to thee repair,
    Their longing even without wing seeketh flight.
Thy charity doth not only him up-bear
    Who prays, but in thy bounty's large excess
    Thou oftentimes dost even forerun the prayer.
In thee is pity, in thee tenderness,
    In thee magnificence, in thee the sum
    Of all that in creation most can bless.
                    Dante, trans. Laurence Binyon

The coming age of peace and justice   Ps 84(85)

Happy the womb that carried you and the breasts that suckled you! (Lk 11:27).

Ant. Our earth shall yield its fruit.

I will hear what the Lord God has to say,
a voice that speaks of peace,
peace for his people and his friends
and those who turn to him in their hearts.
His help is near for those who fear him
and his glory will dwell in our land.

Mercy and faithfulness have met;
justice and peace have embraced.
Faithfulness shall spring from the earth
and justice look down from heaven.

The Lord will make us prosper
and our earth shall yield its fruit.
Justice shall march before him
and peace shall follows his steps.

Ant. Our earth shall yield its fruit.

To the God of glory and compassion   Ps 112(113)

He casts the mighty from their thrones and raises the lowly (Lk 1:52).

Ant. He raises the poor, he lifts up the lowly.

Praise, O servants of the Lord,
praise the name of the Lord!
May the name of the Lord be blessed
both now and for evermore!
From the rising of the sun to its setting
praised be the name of the Lord!

High above all nations is the Lord,
above the heavens his glory.
Who is like the Lord, our God,
who has risen on high to his throne
yet stoops from the heights to look down,
to look down upon heaven and earth?

From the dust he lifts up the lowly,
from the dungheap he raises the poor
to set him in the company of princes,
yes, with the princes of his people.
To the childless wife he gives a home
and gladdens her heart with children.

Ant. He raises the poor, he lifts up the lowly.

Word of God   Acts 1:12–14

The apostles returned to Jerusalem from the hill called
Olivet, which is near Jerusalem, no farther than a Sabbath
day's journey. Entering the city they went to the room up-
stairs where they were lodging: Peter and John and James
and Andrew, Philip and Thomas, Bartholomew and
Matthew, James son of Alphaeus and Simon the Zealot,
and Judas son of James. All these were constantly at
prayer together, and with them a group of women, including
Mary the mother of Jesus, and his brothers.

Song of the Virgin Mary

Ant. There appeared a great portent in heaven,
   a woman robed with the sun,
   beneath her feet the moon,
   and on her head a crown of twelve stars.

Prayers

God our Father, we offer you our praise because you chose
Mary from among all women to become the Mother of our
Saviour, Jesus Christ.

   Lord Jesus, from the cross you gave Mary, your mother,
   to the beloved disciple, John. May she help us to be your
   disciples in spirit and truth.

   Christ Jesus, your Mother stood close to the cross.
   Through her prayers may we gladly accept suffering
   as a means of sharing in your passion.

   Father, you have given us Mary as our mother. Through
   her prayers, give rest to the weary, comfort to those who
   mourn, pardon to the sinner, and peace and salvation to
   all men.

Further prayers ... Our Father ...

Almighty God, Mary gave birth to a Son who offers salvation to the whole world. May we, like Mary, both treasure him in our hearts and bring him to all men.

May the Lord bless us,
may he keep us from all evil
and lead us to life everlasting. Amen.

FEASTS OF SAINTS

MORNING PRAYER

Lord, open my lips ...
To you be glory ...

Chorus of Angels

Praise to the holiest in the height,
And in the depth be praise:
In all his words most wonderful;
Most sure in all his ways!

O loving wisdom of our God!
When all was sin and shame,
A second Adam to the fight
And to the rescue came.

O wisest love! that flesh and blood
Which did in Adam fail,
Should strive afresh against the foe,
Should strive and should prevail.

And that a higher gift than grace
Should flesh and blood refine,
God's presence and his very self,
And essence all divine.

O generous love! that he who smote
In man for man the foe,
The double agony in man
For man should undergo;
And in the garden secretly,
And on the cross on high,
Should teach his brethren and inspire
To suffer and to die.   John Henry Newman

335

Two ways of living

He showed me the river of the water of life, flowing from the throne of God and of the Lamb (Rev 22:1).

Ant. No follower of mine shall wander in the dark;
he shall have the light of life.

Happy indeed is the man
who follows not the counsel of the wicked;
nor lingers in the way of sinners
nor sits in the company of scorners,
but whose delight is the law of the Lord
and who ponders his law day and night.

He is like a tree that is planted
beside the flowing waters,
that yields its fruit in due season
and whose leaves shall never fade;
and all that he does shall prosper.
Not so are the wicked, not so!

For they like winnowed chaff
shall be driven away by the wind.
When the wicked are judged they shall not stand,
nor find room among those who are just;
for the Lord guards the way of the just
but the way of the wicked leads to doom.

Ant. No follower of mine shall wander in the dark;
he shall have the light of life.

The man of integrity

*How blest are those whose hearts are pure;
they shall see God* (Mt 5:8).

Ant. Well done, my good and trusty servant!
Come and share your master's delight.

The Lord's is the earth and its fullness,
the world and all its peoples.
It is he who set it on the seas;
on the waters he made it firm.

Who shall climb the mountain of the Lord?
Who shall stand in his holy place?
The man with clean hands and pure heart,
who desires not worthless things,
who has not sworn so as to deceive his neighbour.

He shall receive blessings from the Lord
and reward from the God who saves him.
Such are the men who seek him,
seek the face of the God of Jacob.

Ant. Well done, my good and trusty servant!
Come and share your master's delight.

Word of God

1 Pt 3:8–18

Be one in thought and feeling, all of you; be full of brotherly
affection, kindly and humble minded. Do not repay wrong
with wrong, or abuse with abuse; on the contrary, retaliate
with blessing, for a blessing is the inheritance to which you
yourselves have been called.

'Whoever loves life and would see good days
must restrain his tongue from evil
and his lips from deceit;
must turn from wrong and do good,
seek peace and pursue it.
For the Lord's eyes are turned towards the righteous,
his ears are open to their prayers;
but the Lord's face is set against wrong-doers.'

Who is going to do you wrong if you are devoted to what is
good? And yet if you should suffer for your virtues, you may
count yourselves happy. Have no fear of them: do not be
perturbed, but hold the Lord Christ in reverence in your
hearts. Be always ready with your defence whenever you are
called to account for the hope that is in you, but make that
defence with modesty and respect. Keep your conscience
clear, so that when you are abused, those who malign your
Christian conduct may be put to shame. It is better to
suffer for well-doing, if such should be the will of God,

337

than for doing wrong. For Christ also died for our sins once and for all. He, the just, suffered for the unjust, to bring us to God.

Song of Zechariah

Ant. There must be no limit to your goodness,
as your heavenly Father's goodness knows no bounds

Or as follows:

New Testament Song   Rev 1:8, 18; 2 Tim 2:11–13; Rom 8:17

Ant. To him who loves us
and freed us from our sins with his life's blood,
to him be glory and dominion for ever and ever!

I am the Alpha and the Omega,
who is and who was and who is to come,
the sovereign Lord of all, alleluia!
I am the First and the Last,
and I am the living one, alleluia!

I was dead,
and now I am alive for evermore;
I am the faithful witness, alleluia!
the first born from the dead
and ruler of the kings of the earth, alleluia!

If you die with me, you shall live with me;
if you endure, you shall reign with me, alleluia!
You are the heirs of my God, and my fellow heirs;
if you share my sufferings now,
you shall share my splendour hereafter, alleluia!

Ant. To him who loves us
and freed us from our sins with his life's blood,
to him be glory and dominion for ever and ever!

In Lent, the following Song is used:
New Testament Song   1 Pt 2:21–25

Ant. By his wounds you have been healed.

Christ suffered on your behalf,
and thereby left you an example;
it is for you to follow in his steps.

He committed no sin,
he was convicted of no falsehood;
when he was abused he did not retort with abuse,
when he suffered he uttered no threats,
but committed his cause to the One who judges justly

In his own person he carried our sins to the gibbet,
so that we might cease to live for sin
and begin to live for righteousness.

By his wounds you have been healed.
You were straying like sheep,
but now you have turned
towards the Shepherd and Guardian of your souls.

Ant. By his wounds you have been healed.

Prayers

Father, you are the source of all holiness. Through the prayers and example of your saints, lead us to live holy lives.

As you have called us to be perfect in love,
so make us perfect in your service.

Lord Jesus Christ, you came to serve, not to be served.
Make us truly humble in your service and that of our
brothers.

The saints bore your cross willingly throughout their
lives;
enable us to bear any suffering in this life for your sake.

Further prayers . . . Our Father . . .

We thank you, Lord, for those who have chosen poverty or solitude for your sake, for men of prayer, for saints in every walk of life, and for all who in purity of life have endured pain with patience in the strength of Jesus Christ our Lord. Amen.

May the Lord bless us,
may he keep us from all evil
and lead us to life everlasting. Amen.

Evening Prayer

Lord, open my lips . . .
Glory to the Father . . .

Choruses from *The Rock VI*

It is hard for those who have never known persecution,
And who have never known a Christian,
To believe these tales of Christian persecution.
It is hard for those who live near a Bank
To doubt the security of their money.
It is hard for those who live near a Police Station
To believe in the triumph of violence.
Do you think that the Faith has conquered the World
And that lions no longer need keepers?
Do you need to be told that whatever has been, can still be?
Do you need to be told that even such modest attainments
As you can boast in the way of polite society
Will hardly survive the Faith to which they owe their
      significance?
Men! polish your teeth on rising and retiring;
Women! polish your fingernails:
You polish the tooth of the dog and the talon of the cat.
Why should men love the Church? Why should they love
      her laws?
She tells them of Life and Death, and of all that they would
      forget.
She is tender where they would be hard, and hard where they
      like to be soft.
She tells them of Evil and Sin, and other unpleasant facts.
They constantly try to escape
From the darkness outside and within
By dreaming of systems so perfect that no one will need to be
      good.
But the man that is will shadow
The man that pretends to be.
And the Son of Man was not crucified once for all,
The blood of the martyrs not shed once for all,
The lives of the Saints not given once for all:

340

Song of Mary

(MAGNIFICAT)

My soul proclaims the greatness of the Lord,
my spirit rejoices in God my Saviour;
for he has looked with favour on his lowly servant,
and from this day all generations will call me blessed.
The Almighty has done great things for me:
holy is his Name.
He has mercy on those who fear him
in every generation.
He has shown the strength of his arm,
he has scattered the proud in their conceit.
He has cast down the mighty from their thrones,
and has lifted up the lowly.
He has filled the hungry with good things,
and has sent the rich away empty.
He has come to the help of his servant Israel
for he has remembered his promise of mercy,
the promise he made to our fathers,
to Abraham and his children for ever.

Song of Zechariah

(BENEDICTUS)

Blessed be the Lord, the God of Israel;
he has come to his people and set them free.
He has raised up for us a mighty saviour,
born of the house of his servant David.
Through his holy prophets he promised of old
   that he would save us from our enemies,
   from the hands of all who hate us.
He promised to show mercy to our fathers
and to remember his holy covenant.
This was the oath he swore to our father Abraham:
to set us free from the hand of our enemies,
free to worship him without fear,
holy and righteous in his sight
   all the days of our life.

You, my child, shall be called the prophet of the Most High
for you will go before the Lord to prepare his way,
to give his people knowledge of salvation
by forgiving them their sins.
In the tender compassion of our God
the dawn from on high shall break upon us,
to shine on those who dwell in darkness and the shadow of
   death.
and to guide our feet on the road of peace.

But the Son of Man is crucified always
And there shall be Martyrs and Saints.

T. S. Eliot

The great works of God Ps 110(111)

*Have no fear, little flock; for your Father has chosen to
give you the Kingdom* (Lk 12:32).

Ant. Happy are those servants
whom the Master finds on the alert when he comes.

I will thank the Lord with all my heart
in the meeting of the just and their assembly.
Great are the works of the Lord;
to be pondered by all who love them.

Majestic and glorious his work,
his justice stands firm for ever.
He makes us remember his wonders.

The Lord is compassion and love.
He gives food to those who fear him;
keeps his covenant ever in mind.
He has shown his might to his people
by giving them the lands of the nations.

His works are justice and truth:
his precepts are all of them sure,
standing firm for ever and ever:
they are made in uprightness and truth.

He has sent deliverance to his people
and established his covenant for ever.
Holy his name, to be feared.

To fear the Lord is the beginning of wisdom;
all who do so prove themselves wise.
His praise shall last for ever!

Ant. Happy are those servants
whom the Master finds on the alert when he comes.

The generous and upright man Ps 111(112)

Sell your possessions and give in charity. Provide for yourselves never-failing treasure in heaven (Lk 12:33).

Ant. Where your treasure is, there will your heart be also.

Happy the man who fears the Lord,
who takes delight in his commands.
His sons will be powerful on earth;
the children of the upright are blessed.

Riches and wealth are in his house;
his justice stands firm for ever.
He is a light in the darkness for the upright:
he is generous, merciful and just.

The good man takes pity and lends,
he conducts his affairs with honour.
The just man will never waver:
he will be remembered for ever.

He has no fear of evil news;
with a firm heart he trusts in the Lord.
With a steadfast heart he will not fear;
he will see the downfall of his foes.

Open-handed, he gives to the poor;
his justice stands firm for ever.
His head will be raised in glory.

The wicked man sees and is angry,
gnashes his teeth and pines away;
the desire of the wicked leads to doom.

Ant. Where your treasure is, there will your heart be also.

Word of God 1 Jn 4:7–12

Dear friends, let us love one another, because love is from God. Everyone who loves is a child of God and knows God, but the unloving know nothing of God. For God is love; and his love was disclosed to us in this, that he sent his only Son into the world to bring us life. The love I speak of is not our love for God, but the love he showed to us in sending his Son as the remedy for the defilement of our sins. If God thus loved us, dear friends, we in turn are bound to love one another. Though God has never been seen by any man, God himself dwells in us if we love one another; his love is brought to perfection within us.

Song of the Virgin Mary

Ant. There is no greater love than this,
that a man should lay down his life for his friends.
Or as follows:

New Testament Song   Rev 2:7, 8, 17, 26; 3:5, 7, 12, 21

Ant. The Lamb is the Lord of lords and King of kings,
and his victory will be shared by his followers,
called and chosen and faithful, alleluia!

These are the words of the First and Last,
who was dead and came to life again:
To him who is victorious
I will give the right to eat from the tree of life
that stands in the Garden of God, alleluia!
Be faithful unto death
and I will give you the crown of life, alleluia!

To him who is victorious
I will give some of the hidden manna.
I will give him also a white stone, alleluia!
and on the stone will be written a new name,
known to none but him that receives it, alleluia!

To him who is victorious,
to him who perseveres in doing my will to the end,
I will give authority over the nations, alleluia!
that same authority which I received from my Father,
and I will give him also the star of dawn, alleluia!

He who is victorious shall be robed all in white;
his name I will never strike off the roll of the living,
for in the presence of my Father and his angels
I will acknowledge him as mine, alleluia!

These are the words of the holy one, the true one,
who holds the key of David, alleluia!

He who is victorious –
I will make him a pillar in the temple of my God;
he shall never leave it, alleluia!
And I will write the name of my God upon him,
and the name of the city of my God,
and my own new name, alleluia!

To him who is victorious
I will grant a place on my throne,
as I myself was victorious, alleluia!
and sat down with my Father on his throne.
These are the words of the Amen,
the faithful and true witness, alleluia!

Ant. The Lamb is the Lord of lords and King of kings,
and his victory will be shared by his followers,
called and chosen and faithful, alleluia!

*In Lent the alternative Song is that given above at the Morning Prayer,
p. 338*

Prayers

Lord God almighty, you alone are holy, and we see your
holiness reflected in the lives of your saints. Let us live,
serving you in holiness and justice.

Lord our God, we proclaim your greatness at all times.
May we be worthy sons, living lives of true service.

Lord, you filled your saints with the Holy Spirit,
so that they might lead your people with prudence and
love.
Give all leaders a share in that Spirit,
so that they may bring your people to you.

Lord Jesus, you called brother, sister and mother
those who do the will of your Father.
We pray that we may always do what pleases the Father.

Further prayers . . . Our Father . . .

Lord, may your peace and tranquillity, your love, grace and divine mercy be with us as long as we live, now and for ever, age after age. Amen.

May the Lord bless us,
may he keep us from all evil
and lead us to life everlasting. Amen.

PRAYER FOR THE DEPARTED

Morning Prayer

Lord, open my lips ...
To you be glory ...

The Angel of the Agony speaks

from The Dream of Gerontius

Jesu! by that shuddering dread which fell on thee;
Jesu! by that cold dismay which sicken'd thee;
Jesu! by that pang of heart which thrill'd in thee;
Jesu! by that mount of sins which crippled thee;
Jesu! by that sense of guilt which stifled thee;
Jesu! by that innocence which girdled thee;
Jesu! by that sanctity which reign'd in thee;
Jesu! by that Godhead which was one with thee;
Jesu! spare these souls which are so dear to thee,
Who in prison, calm and patient, wait for thee;
Hasten, Lord, their hour, and bid them come to thee,
To that glorious home, where they shall ever gaze on thee.

John Henry Newman

Longing for God Ps 41(42)I

We would rather leave our home in the body and go to live with the Lord (2 Cor 5:8).

Ant. My soul is thirsting for God;
when shall I see him face to face,
the God of my life?

Like the deer that yearns
for running streams,

so my soul is yearning
for you, my God.

My soul is thirsting for God,
the God of my life;
when can I enter and see
the face of God?

My tears have become my bread,
by night, by day,
as I hear it said all the day long:
'Where is your God?'

These things will I remember
as I pour out my soul:
how I would lead the rejoicing crowd
into the house of God,
amid cries of gladness and thanksgiving,
the throng wild with joy.

Why are you cast down, my soul,
why groan within me?
Hope in God; I will praise him still,
my saviour and my God.

My soul is cast down within me
as I think of you,
from the country of Jordan and Mount Hermon,
from the Hill of Mizar.

Deep is calling on deep,
in the roar of waters:
your torrents and all your waves
swept over me.

Ps 41(42)II

By day the Lord will send
his loving kindness;
by night I will sing to him,
praise the God of my life.

I will say to God, my rock:
'Why have you forgotten me?
Why do I go mourning
oppressed by the foe?'

With cries that pierce me to the heart,
my enemies revile me,
saying to me all the day long:
'Where is your God?'

Why are you cast down, my soul,
why groan within me?
Hope in God; I will praise him still,
my saviour and my God.

Ant. My soul is thirsting for God;
when shall I see him face to face,
the God of my life.

Word of God   I Cor 15:51–57

Listen! I will unfold a mystery: we shall not all die, but we
shall all be changed in a flash, in the twinkling of an eye,
at the last trumpet-call. For the trumpet will sound, and the
dead will rise immortal, and we shall be changed. This
perishable being must be clothed with the imperishable,
and what is mortal must be clothed with immortality.
And when our mortality has been clothed with immortality,
then the saying of Scripture will come true: 'Death is swallowed up; victory is won!' 'O Death, where is your victory?
O Death, where is your sting?' The sting of death is sin,
and sin gains its power from the law; but, God be praised,
he gives us the victory through our Lord Jesus Christ.

Song of Zechariah

Ant. I am the resurrection and I am life. If a man has faith
in me, even though he die, he shall come to life.

Or as follows:

New Testament Song   2 Cor 4:10–11, 14;
                                             1 Cor 15:20–27, 55

Ant. The last enemy to be destroyed is death.

Wherever we go we carry death with us in our body,
the death that Jesus died,
that in this body also life may reveal itself,
the life that Jesus lives.

He who raised the Lord Jesus to life
will, with Jesus, raise us too,
and bring us into his presence.

Christ was raised to life –
the first-fruits of the harvest of the dead.
For since it was a man who brought death into the world,
a man also brought resurrection of the dead.
As in Adam all men die, so in Christ all will be brought to
    life;
Christ the first-fruits, and afterwards, at his coming,
those who belong to Christ.

Then comes the end.
when he delivers up the kingdom to God the Father
after abolishing every kind of domination and power.
For he is destined to reign, alleluia,
until God has put all enemies under his feet;
and the last enemy to be abolished is death.
O Death, where is your victory? O Death, where is your
    sting?

Ant. The last enemy to be destroyed is death.

Prayers

Lord God almighty, you raised Christ from the dead;
bring all men to a new life in Christ.

    Father, through baptism we died and rose again with
      Christ.
    May our lives in this world make us worthy to share
      eternal life with him.

    Christ, son of the living God,
    as you raised your friend Lazarus from the dead,
    so bring all the dead (especially N.),
    who have been redeemed by your blood,
    to the glory of a new life with you.

    Christ, you comforted the widow of Naim and the family
      of Lazarus;
    give comfort now to all who mourn and are sorrowful.

Further prayers ... Our Father ...

Lord God, Creator of all men, you have made us creatures of this earth, but have also promised us a share in eternal life. May all who have died share this eternal life with your saints in heaven, where there is neither sorrow nor pain, but life everlasting. We ask you this through Christ our Lord. Amen.

May the Lord bless us,
may he keep us from all evil
and lead us to life everlasting. Amen.

EVENING PRAYER

Lord, open my lips ...
Glory to the Father ...

Hymne to God my God, in my Sicknesse

Since I am comming to that Holy roome,
    Where, with thy Quire of Saints for evermore,
I shall be made thy Musique; As I come
    I tune the Instrument here at the dore,
    And what I must doe then, thinke here before.

Whilst my Physitians by their love are growne
    Cosmographers, and I their Mapp, who lie
Flat on this bed, that by them may be showne
    That this is my South-west discoverie
    Per fretum febris, by these streights to die,

I joy, that in these straits, I see my West;
    For, though theire currants yeeld returne to none,
What shall my West hurt me? As West and East
    In all flatt Maps (and I am one) are one,
    So death doth touch the Resurrection.

Is the Pacifique Sea my home? Or are
    The Easterne riches? Is Jerusalem?
Anyan, and Magellan, and Gibraltare,
    All streights, and none but streights, are wayes to them,
    Whether where Japhet dwelt, or Cham, or Sem.

We thinke that Paradise and Calvarie,
  Christs Crosse, and Adams tree, stood in one place;
Looke, Lord, and finde both Adams met in me;
  As the first Adams sweat surrounds my face,
  May the Last Adams blood my soule embrace.

So, in his purple wrapp'd receive mee Lord,
  By these his thornes give me his other Crowne;
And as to others soules I preach'd thy word,
  Be this my Text, my Sermon to mine owne,
  Therefore that he may raise the Lord throws down.

John Donne

A psalm of confidence   Ps 22(23)
  I have come that men may have life, and may have it in all
  its fullness (Jn 10:10).

Ant. If I should walk in the valley of darkness,
  no evil would I fear.

The Lord is my shepherd;
there is nothing I shall want.
Fresh and green are the pastures
where he gives me repose.
Near restful waters he leads me,
to revive my drooping spirit.
He guides me along the right path;
he is true to his name.
If I should walk in the valley of darkness
no evil would I fear.

You are there with your crook and your staff;
with these you give me comfort.
You have prepared a banquet for me
in the sight of my foes.

My head you have anointed with oil;
my cup is overflowing.
Surely goodness and kindness shall follow me
all the days of my life.
In the Lord's own house shall I dwell
for ever and ever.

Ant. If I should walk in the valley of darkness,
  no evil would I fear.

Prayer of repentance and trust Ps 129(130)

He will save his people from their sins (Mt 1:21).

Ant. With the Lord there is mercy
and fullness of redemption.

Out of the depths I cry to you, O Lord,
Lord, hear my voice!
O let your ears be attentive
to the voice of my pleading.

If you, O Lord, should mark our guilt,
Lord, who would survive?
But with you is found forgiveness:
for this we revere you.

My soul is waiting for the Lord,
I count on his word.
My soul is longing for the Lord
more than watchman for daybreak.
Let the watchman count on daybreak
and Israel on the Lord.

Because with the Lord there is mercy
and fullness of redemption,
Israel indeed he will redeem
from all its iniquity.

Ant. With the Lord there is mercy
and fullness of redemption.

Word of God 1 Cor 15:12–21

If this is what we proclaim, that Christ was raised from the
dead, how can some of you say there is no resurrection
of the dead? If there be no resurrection, then Christ was not
raised; and if Christ was not raised, then our gospel is null
and void, and so is your faith; and we turn out to be lying
witnesses for God, because we bore witness that he raised
Christ to life, whereas, if the dead are not raised, he did not
raise him. For if the dead are not raised, it follows that
Christ was not raised; and if Christ was not raised, your
faith has nothing in it and you are still in your old state of
sin. It follows also that those who have died within Christ's

fellowship are utterly lost. If it is for this life only that Christ has given us hope, we of all men are most to be pitied. But the truth is, Christ was raised to life – the first fruits of the harvest of the dead.

Song of the Virgin Mary

Ant. All that the Father gives to me will come to me,
   and the man who comes to me I will never turn away.

Or as follows:

New Testament Song   Phil 2:6–11

Ant. As the Father raises the dead and gives them life,
   so the Son gives life to men.

The divine nature was Christ's from the first;
yet he did not think to snatch at equality with God,
but made himself nothing,
assuming the nature of a slave.

Bearing the human likeness,
revealed in human shape,
he humbled himself,
and in obedience accepted even death –
death on a cross.

Therefore God raised him to the heights
and bestowed on him the name above all names,
that at the name of Jesus every knee should bow –
in heaven, on earth, and in the depths –
and every tongue confess, 'Jesus Christ is Lord,'
to the glory of God the Father.

Ant. As the Father raises the dead and gives them life,
   so the Son gives life to men.

Prayers

Christ Jesus, you are the Resurrection and Life. We pray that we may be brought to the glory of your resurrection.

   Christ our Saviour,
   destroy all that is sinful in our lives,
   so that we may follow you to eternal life.

Lord, you have told us that, one day, this earth will pass
away;
when that happens, bring all men to your kingdom.

Christ our Redeemer, we pray for all who do not believe
and who have no hope in you.
May they come to believe in you
and in the promise of the life to come.

Further prayers . . . Our Father . . .

Lord God, the giver of all good things, give a place of life
and peace to all who have died. May we share in the glory
of Jesus Christ, who died to save us all. Amen.

May the Lord bless us,
may he keep us from all evil
and lead us to life everlasting. Amen.

MIDDAY PRAYER

Lord, open my lips . . .
Glory to the Father . . .

The Lake of Beauty

Let your mind be quiet, realising the beauty of the world,
and the immense the boundless treasures that it holds in
store.

All that you have within you, all that your heart desires, all
that your Nature so specially fits you for – that or the
counterpart of it waits embedded in the great Whole, for
you. It will surely come to you.

Yet equally surely not one moment before its appointed time
will it come. All your crying and fever and reaching out of
hands will make no difference.

Therefore do not begin that game at all.

Do not recklessly spill the waters of your mind in this direc-
tion and in that, lest you become like a spring lost and
dissipated in the desert.

But draw them together into a little compass, and hold them
still, so still;

And let them become clear, so clear – so limpid, so mirror-
   like;
At last the mountains and the sky shall glass themselves in
   peaceful beauty,
And the antelope shall descend to drink, and to gaze at his
   reflected image, and the lion to quench his thirst,
And Love himself shall come and bend over, and catch his
   own likeness in you   Edward Carpenter

God the protector   Ps 120(121)

*They shall never again feel hunger or thirst, the sun shall
not beat on them nor any scorching heat* (Rev 7:16).

Ant. My help shall come from the Lord
   who made heaven and earth.

I lift up my eyes to the mountains:
from where shall come my help?
My help shall come from the Lord
who made heaven and earth.

May he never allow you to stumble!
Let him sleep not, your guard.
No, he sleeps not nor slumbers,
Israel's guard.

The Lord is your guard and your shade;
at your right side he stands.
By day the sun shall not smite you
nor the moon in the night.

The Lord will guard you from evil,
he will guard your soul.
The Lord will guard your going and coming
both now and for ever.

Song of the returned exiles   Ps 125(126)

*If you have part in the suffering, you have part also in the
divine consolation* (1 Cor 1:7).

When the Lord delivered Zion from bondage,
It seemed like a dream.
Then was our mouth filled with laughter,
on our lips there were songs.

The heathens themselves said: 'What marvels
the Lord worked for them!'
What marvels the Lord worked for us!
Indeed we were glad.

Deliver us, O Lord, from our bondage
as streams in dry land.
Those who are sowing in tears
will sing when they reap.

They go out, they go out, full of tears,
carrying seed for the sowing:
they come back, they come back, full of song,
carrying their sheaves.

Ant. My help shall come from the Lord
who made heaven and earth.

Word of God   1 Jn 3:16–24

It is by this that we know what love is: that Christ laid
down his life for us. And we in our turn are bound to lay
down our lives for our brothers. But if a man has enough
to live on, and yet when he sees his brother in need shuts
up his heart against him, how can it be said that the divine
love dwells in him?
My children, love must not be a matter of words or talk,
it must be genuine, and show itself in action. This is how
we may know that we belong to the realm of truth, and
convince ourselves in his sight that even if our conscience
condemns us, God is greater than our conscience and
knows all.
Dear friends, if our conscience does not condemn us,
then we can approach God with confidence, and obtain
from him whatever we ask, because we are keeping his
commands and doing what he approves. This is his command: to give our allegiance to his son Jesus Christ and
love one another as he commanded. When we keep his
commands we dwell in him and he dwells in us. And this

355

is how we can make sure that he dwells within us: we know it from the Spirit he has given us.

Prayer

Our Father . . .

Lord, fire of everlasting love, give us through Christ our Lord the fervour to love you above all things, and our brother for your sake. Amen.

Let us bless the Lord.
Thanks be to God.

NIGHT PRAYER

Lord, open my lips . . .
Glory to the Father . . .

Phós Hilaron (*O Gladsome Light*)

O gladsome light, O grace
Of God the Father's face,
The eternal splendour wearing;
Celestial, holy, blest,
Our Saviour Jesus Christ,
Joyful in thine appearing.

Now, ere day fadeth quite,
We see the evening light,
Our wonted hymn outpouring;
Father of might unknown,
Thee, his incarnate Son,
And Holy Spirit adoring.

To thee of right belongs
All praise of holy songs,
O Son of God, Lifegiver;
Thee, therefore, O Most High,
The world doth glorify,
And shall exalt for ever.

Anonymous, translated by Robert Bridges

Under the wing of God's protection

Set your troubled hearts at rest (Jn 14:1).

Ant. Under the shadow of his wings,
we shall not fear the night.

He who dwells in the shelter of the Most High
and abides in the shade of the Almighty
says to the Lord: 'My refuge,
my stronghold, my God in whom I trust!'

It is he who will free you from the snare
of the fowler who seeks to destroy you;
he will conceal you with his pinions
and under his wings you will find refuge.

You will not fear the terror of the night
nor the arrow that flies by day,
nor the plague that prowls in the darkness
nor the scourge that lays waste at noon.

A thousand may fall at your side,
ten thousand fall at your right,
you, it will never approach;
his faithfulness is buckler and shield.

Your eyes have only to look
to see how the wicked are repaid,
you who have said: 'Lord, my refuge!'
and have made the Most High your dwelling.

Upon you no evil shall fall,
no plague approach where you dwell.
For you has he commanded his angels,
to keep you in all your ways.

They shall bear you upon their hands
lest you strike your foot against a stone.
On the lion and the viper you will tread
and trample the young lion and the dragon.

His love he set on me, so I will rescue him;
protect him for he knows my name.
When he calls I shall answer: 'I am with you.'
I will save him in distress and give him glory.

NIGHT PRAYER

With length of life I will content him;
I shall let him see my saving power.

Ant. Under the shadow of his wings,
we shall not fear the night.

Word of God   1 Thess 5:9-10

God has not destined us to the terrors of judgment, but to
the full attainment of salvation through our Lord Jesus
Christ. He died for us so that we, awake or asleep, might
live in company with him.

Song of Simeon

Ant. Lord, save us while we are awake;
protect us while we sleep:
and Christ, with whom we keep our watch,
will guard our souls in peace.

Now, Lord, you have kept your word:
let your servant go in peace.

With my own eyes I have seen the salvation
which you have prepared in the sight of every people:

a light to reveal you to the nations
and the glory of your people Israel.

Ant. Lord, save us while we are awake;
protect us while we sleep:
and Christ, with whom we keep our watch,
will guard our souls in peace.

Prayer

Our Father...

Lord Jesus Christ, gentle and lowly of heart, you lay upon
your followers an easy yoke and a light burden. Receive our
prayers and works of this day, and grant us rest so that we
may serve you with renewed fervour. Who live and reign
for ever and ever. Amen.

Marian Antiphons

Hail, holy Queen, mother of mercy,
hail, our life, our sweetness and our hope!
To you do we cry, poor banished children of Eve,
to you do we send up our sighs, mourning and weeping
   in this valley of tears.

Turn, then, most gracious advocate, your eyes of mercy
towards us;
and after this, our exile, show unto us
the blessed fruit of your womb, Jesus.
O clement, O loving, O sweet Virgin Mary!

Pray for us, O holy mother of God,
that we may be made worthy of the promises of Christ.

Almighty, eternal God, through the work of the Holy Spirit,
you prepared the body and soul of the Virgin Mary to be a
worthy dwelling for your Son; grant that we who remember
her with joy may, by her intercession, be freed from the
evils in this world and from everlasting death. Through
Christ our Lord. Amen.

In Paschaltide

Queen of heaven, rejoice, alleluia!
for he whom you were worthy to bear, alleluia!
has risen as he said, alleluia!

Rejoice and be glad, Virgin Mary, alleluia!
for the Lord is risen indeed, alleluia!

O God, you have given joy to the whole world through the
resurrection of your Son, our Lord Jesus Christ. Through
the prayers of his virgin mother, Mary, grant that we may
attain the joys of eternal life. Amen.

Let us bless the Lord.
Thanks be to God.

May the Almighty and merciful God,
Father, Son and Holy Spirit,
bless and preserve us. Amen.

359

Prayers
for Special Occasions

Prayer of St Thomas Aquinas
Before Holy Communion

Almighty, everlasting God,
I draw near to the sacrament of your only-begotten Son,
our Lord Jesus Christ.
I who am sick approach the physician of life.
I who am unclean come to the fountain of mercy;
blind, to the light of eternal brightness;
poor and needy to the Lord of heaven and earth.
Therefore, I impore you, in your boundless mercy,
to heal my sickness, cleanse my defilement,
enlighten my blindness, enrich my poverty,
and clothe my nakedness.
Then shall I dare to receive the bread of angels,
the King of kings and Lord of lords,
with reverence and humility,
contrition and love,
purity and faith,
with the purpose and intention necessary
for the good of my soul.
Grant, I beseech you, that I may receive
not only the Body and Blood of the Lord,
but also the grace and power of the sacrament.
Most merciful God,
enable me so to receive the Body of your only-begotten Son,
our Lord Jesus Christ, which he took from the Virgin Mary,
that I may be found worthy to be incorporated
into his mystical Body, and counted among his members.
Most loving Father, grant that
I may one day see face to face
your beloved Son, whom I now intend to receive
under the veil of the sacrament,

and who with you and the Holy Spirit,
lives and reigns for ever,
one God, world without end. Amen.

PRAYER OF ST THOMAS AQUINAS
AFTER HOLY COMMUNION

I give you thanks,
Lord, holy Father, everlasting God.
In your great mercy,
and not because of my own merits,
you have fed me, a sinner and your unworthy servant,
with the precious Body and Blood of your Son,
our Lord Jesus Christ.
I pray that this holy communion
may not serve as my judgment and condemnation,
but as my forgiveness and salvation.
May it be my armour of faith
and shield of good purpose.
May it root out in me all vice and evil desires,
increase my love and patience,
humility and obedience,
and every virtue.
Make it a firm defence
against the wiles of all my enemies, seen and unseen,
while restraining all evil impulses of flesh and spirit.
May it help me to cleave to you, the one true God,
and bring me a blessed death when you call.
I beseech you to bring me, a sinner,
to that ineffable feast where,
with your Son and the Holy Spirit,
you are the true light of your holy ones,
their flawless blessedness,
everlasting joy,
and perfect happiness.
Through Christ our Lord. Amen.

Anima Christi

Soul of Christ, sanctify me,
Body of Christ, save me,
Blood of Christ, inebriate me.
Water from the side of Christ, wash me.
Passion of Christ, strengthen me.
O good Jesus, hear me.
Hide me within your wounds
and never let me be separated from you.
From the wicked enemy defend me.
In the hour of my death, call me
and bid me come to you,
so that with your saints I may praise you
for ever and ever. Amen.

A General Intercession

O God, the creator and preserver of all mankind,
we humbly pray for all men of every race and in every
   kind of need
Make your ways known to them,
and reveal your salvation to all nations
(Especially we pray for . . .)
     Lord, in your mercy,
     hear our prayer.

We pray for the whole Church,
that it may be so guided and governed by your Holy Spirit
that all who profess and call themselves Christians
may be led into the way of truth,
and hold the faith in unity of spirit.
in the bond of peace, and in righteousness of life.
(Especially we pray for . . .)
     Lord, in your mercy,
     hear our prayer.

We commend to your fatherly goodness all those who are
in any way afflicted or distressed in mind or body or estate.
(especially we pray for . . .)

comfort and relieve them according to their needs, giving them patience under their sufferings, and a happy issue out of all their afflictions.

Lord, in your mercy,
hear our prayer.
All this we ask for the sake of your Son, Jesus Christ.
Amen.

A GENERAL THANKSGIVING

Almighty God, of all mercies Father,
we, your unworthy servants, give you most humble and
hearty thanks for all your goodness and loving kindness
to us and to all men.
We bless you for our creation, preservation,
and all the blessings of this life.
But, above all, we thank you for your infinite love in the
redemption of the world by our Lord Jesus Christ, for the
means of grace and the hope of glory.
And, we pray, give us a due sense of all your mercies,
that our hearts may be truly thankful,
and that we may declare your praise
not only with our lips but in our lives,
by giving ourselves to your service
and by walking before you in holiness and righteousness
all our days;
through Jesus Christ our Lord,
to whom, with you and the Holy Spirit,
be all honour and glory world without end. Amen.

THE ROSARY

The Rosary is a prayer that has been in use among Christians for centuries. Based on biblical themes, it records the whole history of salvation from the first announcement of Christ's birth to Mary, until Mary herself, redeemed by her Son, is united with him in his kingdom.

The Rosary consists of three groups of five 'mysteries', each of which has its own subject for meditation. Each mystery is comprised of the Our Father, followed by ten Hail Marys, and concluding with the Glory to the Father.

To help us appreciate this prayer we could hardly do better than quote from the book, written in 1971, *Five for Sorrow, Ten for Joy*, by the well-known Methodist Writer J. Neville Ward. He says:

'People unused to the Rosary may hesitate over its most frequently repeated prayer –

Hail Mary, full of grace, the Lord is with thee. Blessed art thou among women, and blessed is the fruit of thy womb, Jesus. Holy Mary, Mother of God, pray for us, sinners, now and at the hour of our death. Amen.

The first part of this prayer, from Luke 1:28 and 42, is a way of bringing to mind our belief that the Incarnation of the Son of God is the most wonderful thing that has ever happened in history, and therefore, of restoring the mind to the *joy* which is at the foundation of the Christian life. It seems to me to be also particularly inspired in that our joy that God has revealed himself to us is associated with his favouring and blessing another human being, so that a basis is laid in our regular prayer for our training in that happiness at God's blessing of other people which is such an important part of loving.

'The second part of the prayer is a reminder that Christ has abolished our loneliness, that we pray (even if alone at home or in an empty church) within the fabulous community of faith, live within it, owe more than we know to it, and particularly rely on the prayer of others, the whole communion of saints, of which the Blessed Virgin Mary is the representative figure.

'It seems hard to believe that one can meditate on a theme while mentally repeating certain prayers even though these are so thoroughly known that little effort is required. As one becomes familiar with the Rosary the prayers gradually recede, to form a kind of 'background music', and the mystery is before the mind as though one is looking at a religious picture or icon. The balance frequently changes, and the prayers occupy the foreground of the mind for a time, and this may lead to a form of simple attention to God which is more like contemplation. If one finds one's mind being led into a stillness and concentration of this kind it is good to let it happen. It is just a fact of Christian history that the saints put their money on contemplation rather than meditation for producing their longing for God. And the longing for God, if it is not the treasure itself, is certainly the field in which it is hidden.

'This movement of the mind between meditation and contemplation and petition and praise is a feature of this way of praying that gives it great flexibility and may well explain in part why it appeals to so many people so different in religious make-up.

'The images of the themes for meditation, the mysteries, tend to haunt the mind out of prayer, at any time and any place drifting in and out of one's preoccupied consciousness, sometimes only momentarily, sometimes staying to give new significance to one's personal life, or simply bringing a breath from the world of God's action in Christ into the hurry and stress of the busy day.

'This thinking about the mysteries outside prayer profoundly enriches the use of the prayer. It seems to me to be essential to the whole exercise. It is not possible to meditate discursively while actually saying the Rosary. It is enough to have a single thought in connection with each mystery or simply to look at it in love and faith. But the saying is infinitely deepened in value if we at other times think about these great themes, penetrating as far

365

as we can into their meaning ... I am sure that one of the most hopeful means of realising Christian unity is for Christians of one tradition to seek to share another tradition's experience of the riches of Christ.'

The Joyful Mysteries[1]

I. The Annunciation

'Rejoice, so highly favoured! The Lord is with you' (Lk 1:28).

'I am the handmaid of the Lord; let what you have said be done to me' (Lk 1:38).

II. The Visitation

'Blessed is she who believed that the promise made her by the Lord would be fulfilled' (Lk 1:45).

'My soul proclaims the greatness of the Lord, for the Almighty has done great things for me' (Lk 1:46).

III. The Nativity

'Today in the town of David, a saviour has been born to you: he is Christ, the Lord' (Lk 2:11).

IV. The Presentation of Jesus in the Temple

'Now Master, you can let your servant go in peace just as you promised; because my eyes have seen the salvation which you have prepared for all the nations to see' (Lk 2:29).

V. The Finding of Jesus in the Temple

'Did you not know that I must be busy with my Father's affairs?'

'He then went down with them and came to Nazareth, and lived under their authority. His mother stored up all these things in her heart' (Lk 2:49–51).

The Sorrowful Mysteries

I. The Agony in the Garden

'Father, if you are willing, take this cup away from me. Nevertheless let your will be done, not mine' (Lk 22:42, 43).

---

[1] Scripture quotations in the Rosary section are from *The Jerusalem Bible*, © 1966, 1967 and 1968 by Darton, Longman & Todd Ltd and Doubleday & Co., Inc.

II. The Scourging at the Pillar

'So Pilate, anxious to placate the crowd, released Barabbas for them, and having ordered Jesus to be scourged, handed him over to be crucified' (Mk 15:15).

III. The Crowning with thorns

'The soldiers twisted some thorns into a crown and put it on his head, and dressed him in a purple robe. They kept coming up to him and saying, "Hail, king of the Jews," and they slapped him in the face' (Jn 19:1, 2).

IV. The Carrying of the Cross

'Then when they had finished making fun of him, they took off the cloak, and dressed him in his own clothes, and led him away to crucify him' (Mt 27:31).

V. The Crucifixion

'When they reached the place called The Skull they crucified him there and the two criminals also, one on the right and the other on the left . . . and Jesus cried out in a loud voice, "Father, into your hands I commend my spirit." With these words he breathed his last' (Lk 22:33, 46).

The Glorious Mysteries

I. The Resurrection

'Jesus, who was crucified, is not here, for he has risen as he said he would' (Mt 28:6, 7).

'Christ has in fact been raised from the dead, the first-fruits of all who have fallen asleep. Death came through one man and in the same way the resurrection of the dead has come through one man' (1 Cor 15:21).

II. The Ascension

'He was lifted up while they looked on, and a cloud took him from their sight. Two men in white said to them, "Jesus who has been taken up from you into heaven, this same Jesus will come back in the same way as you have seen him go there"' (Acts 1:8, 9).

III. Pentecost

'Suddenly they heard what sounded like a powerful wind

from heaven and something appeared to them that seemed like tongues of fire, and they were all filled with the Holy Spirit' (Acts 2:2, 4).

IV. *The Assumption of Mary*

'From eternity in the beginning he created me and for eternity I shall remain. I ministered before him in the holy temple and thus was I established in Jerusalem' (Eccl 24:9, 10).

V. *The Coronation of Mary as Queen of heaven*

'Now a great sign appeared in heaven, a woman adorned with the sun, standing on the moon with twelve stars on her head for a crown. The woman brought a male child into the world, the son who was to rule all nations with an iron sceptre' (Rev 12:1, 5).

THE ANGELUS

The angel of the Lord declared unto Mary,
and she conceived by the Holy Spirit.

Hail Mary, full of grace,
the Lord is with thee.
Blessed art thou among women,
and blessed is the fruit of thy womb, Jesus.
Holy Mary, Mother of God,
pray for us sinners, now, and at the hour of our death.
Amen.

Behold the handmaid of the Lord:
be it done unto me according to thy word. Hail Mary . . .

The Word was made flesh
and dwelt among us. Hail Mary . . .

Pray for us, O Holy Mother of God,
that we may be made worthy of the promises of Christ.
Let us pray:

Pour forth, we beseech thee, O Lord, thy grace into our hearts, that we to whom the Incarnation of Christ, thy Son, was made known by the message of an angel, may, by his Passion and Cross, be brought to the glory of his Resurrection, through the same Christ our Lord. Amen.

A Simple Prayer

Lord, make me an instrument of your peace;
Where there is hatred, let me sow love;
Where there is injury, pardon;
Where there is discord, union;
Where there is doubt, faith;
Where there is despair, hope:
Where there is darkness, light;
Where there is sadness, joy,
For thy mercy and truth's sake:
O Divine Master, grant that I may not so much seek
To be consoled as to console,
To be understood as to understand,
To be loved as to love,
   for
It is in giving that we receive
It is pardoning that we are pardoned
It is in dying that we are born to eternal life.

A Prayer of Saint Richard

Thanks be to thee, Lord Jesus Christ,
for all the benefits and blessings which thou hast given to
   me,
for all the pains and insults which thou hast borne for me.
O most merciful Friend, Brother, and Redeemer;
may I know thee more clearly,
love thee more dearly,
and follow thee more nearly.

Index of poems quoted

Anon.	I offer thee 293
	I sing of a maiden 328
	Lament not thy path of woe 198
	Listen for I mean to tell 230
	Now you have heard the tale 239
Auden, W H	Alone, alone, about a dreadful wood 47
Bridges, R	Come O Creator Spirit come 314
(trans.)	O gladsome light, O Grace 356
Berrigan, D	The tragic beauty of the face of Christ 137
Carpenter, E	Let your mind be quiet 353
Chesterton, G K	Great God, that bowest sky and star 146
Constable, H	Great God, within whose simple essence, we 319
Crashaw, R	Lord, when the sense of thy sweet grace 142
	Rise, heire of fresh eternity 266
Cynewulf	Hail, heavenly beam, brightest of angels thou 1
Dante	Maiden and mother 332
	Within the clear profound Light's aureole 323
de Chardin, T	It is done 310
Dickinson, E	This world is not Conclusion 29
Donne, J	Batter my heart 168
	Deigne at my hand this crown 21
	I am a little world made cunningly 185
	Since I am coming to that holy roome 349
Eliot, T S	A cold coming we had of it 75
	It is hard for those who have never known persecution 340
	O Light invisible, we praise thee 115
	Son of Man, behold with thine eyes 85
	The wounded surgeon plies the steel 203
	There are several attitudes towards Christmas 17
	We praise thee O God for thy glory 91
Herbert, G	Come, my Way, my Truth, my Life 4
	Lord, who hast form'd me out of mud 164
	Love bade me welcome 297
	Throw away the rod 172
Herrick, R	Is this a Fast 181
Hopkins, G M	Cloud puffballs, torn tufts 280
	Glory be to God for dappled things 111
	I caught this morning morning's minion 257
	O God, I love thee 155
	The world is charged with the glory of God 9

Jennings, E	Nothing will ease the pain to come	56
Jonson, B	Good and great God	43
Larkin, P	At one the wind rose	306
	Side by side, their faces blurred	262
Lawrence, D H	Are you willing to be sponged out	208
Maritain, R	God, my God, before you I stand	177
Marvell, A	See how the Irient dew	275
Milner-White, E	Let me love thee, O Christ	34
Milton, J	Blest pair of sirens	96
	These are thy glorious works	301
Moore, S	Those who go on dark ways	194
Muir, E	One foot in Eden, still I stand	212
	That was the day they killed the Son of God	226
Newman, J H	Iesu by that shuddering dread	345
	Lead, kindly Light	159
	Praise to the holiest	335
Oosterhuis, H	You wait for us	51
Patrick, St	I bind unto myself	101
Pope, A	O thou, whose all-creating hands sustain	271
Pound, E (trans)	Most high Lord	284
Raine, K	Let in the wind	37
	My soul and I last night	189
	Sorrow is true for everyone	244
Rilke, R M	Who was ever so wake	128
	You, neighbour God	124
Sitwell, E	In the plain of the world's dust	252
	The emeralds are singing on the grasses	25
Spenser, E	Most glorious Lord of Life	248
Southwell, R	Let folly praise	66
Stanbrook Abbey	The mighty Word of God	222
	When Jesus comes to be baptized	81
	Who is this who comes	289
Trad.	On Christmas night all Christians sing	61
Thompson, F	O world invisible	106
Traherne, T	These little Limmes	119
Underhill, E	Come, dear heart	217
Vaughan, H	I saw eternity the other night	12
	My soul, there is a country	150
Wanley, N	The off'rings of the Eastern Kings	71
Yeats, W B	That is no country for old men	132

Index of psalms and scriptural songs

1	336	90(91)	357
2	61	91(92)	17
3	245	92(93)	249
4	245	95(96)	62, 76, 103, 258
8	18, 111, 290	96(97)	77, 268
13(14)	169	97(98)	295
14(15)	298	98(99)	303
15(16)	120, 276	99(100)	139, 200
20(21)	258	101(102)	208
21(22)	204, 205, 233	107(108)	53, 210
22(23)	214, 350	109(110)	67, 97, 160, 253, 315
23(24)	1, 2, 286, 336	110(111)	341
24(25)	48, 49, 115, 116	111(112)	342
26(27)	124, 125, 298	112(113)	289, 324, 333
28(29)	311	113A(114)	98, 254, 316
29(30)	248	113B(115)	160
30(31)	186	114(116)	143
31(32)	156	115(116)	223
32(33)	57, 320	116(117)	147, 183
33(34)	218, 302	117(118)	271, 272
34(35)	194, 195, 227, 302	120(121)	34, 142, 354
36(37)	169	122(123)	35, 107
37(38)	164	123(124)	108
39(40)	5, 82, 277	124(125)	134
41(42)	307, 345, 346	125(126)	267, 354
44(45)	6, 328	129(130)	67, 147, 173, 351
45(46)	329	130(131)	242, 308
46(47)	286	131(132)	52
50(51)	138, 198, 199	132(133)	219
60(61)	134	135(136)	263, 264
61(62)	242	136(137)	22
62(63)	92	137(138)	22
64(65)	165	138(139)	177, 178
65(66)	281, 282	141(142)	213
66(67)	112	142(143)	81, 129, 182
71(72)	30, 31, 71, 72	143(144)	9, 10
72(73)	150, 151	144(145)	13, 14
79(80)	26, 27	145(146)	87, 121, 174
83(84)	102, 294	146(147)	88, 130
84(85)	44, 333	147	222, 325
85(86)	190, 191	149	45, 157
88(89)	39, 40	150	93, 312

OT songs
(chapters only given)

Ex	15	260
Wis	7	7
Is	11	84
	12	28
	24	41
	25	32
	35	3
	42	89
	49	188, 192
	50	196
	52	201
	53	206
	54	20
	55	59
	60	74, 79
	61	11
	63	291, 296
	64, 40	15, 296
Jer	11	184
	14	175
	30	158, 211
	31	158, 211
Lam 3		243
Bar 4		24
Ez 36		180, 313
Dan 3		95
Song of 3		167
Hos 6		288
Mic 5		50
Zeph 3		54

NT songs
(chapters only given)

Mt 11		113, 171
John	3	46, 122
	6	224
	15	220
Rom 8		140
1 Cor 13		105
1 Cor passim		278
2 Cor 4		283, 347
Eph 1		109, 321, 330
Phil 2		153, 215, 247, 250, 352
Col 1		69, 126
1 Tim 3, 4		131
1 Pet 1		265
1 Pet 2		162, 338
	3	300
Rev 4		117
	11, 12	135
	15	144
	19	100, 255, 317
	22	36
	passim	326, 338, 343
Simeon		358
Virgin Mary		99
Zechariah		94

Acknowledgements

The publishers gratefully acknowledge permission from the following for the use of copyright material:

George Allen and Unwin for Edward Carpenter, 'The Lake of Beauty', from *Towards Democracy*. BBC Publications for lines from *New Every Morning*. Rev. E. Colledge for translation of 'Dream of the Rood'.

Dodd, Mead and Co Inc, 'Hymn for a Church Militant,' from *The Collected Poems of G K Chesterton*, copyright 1932 by Dodd, Mead & Company Inc, copyright renewed 1959 by Oliver Chesterton. Doubleday and Company Inc, for lines from J Neville Ward, *Five for Sorrow, Ten for Joy*. Wm B Eerdmans Publishing Co, for lines from Caryl Micklem, *Contemporary Prayers for Public Worship*, and *More Contemporary Prayers for Public Worship*.

Faber & Faber Ltd, for Philip Larkin, 'Night Music' from *The Night Ship*.

ACKNOWLEDGEMENTS

Victor Gollanz Ltd for Cynewulf 'To Christ our Lord' from *God of a Hundred Names*.

Hamish Hamilton, for Kathleen Raine, 'Northumbrian Sequence IV', 'Sorrow' and 'Night Thought' from *Collected Poems of Kathleen Raine* © 1965 Kathleen Raine and *The Hollow Hill* © 1965 Kathleen Raine. Harcourt Brace Jovanovich Inc, for T S Eliot, *Journey of the Magi*. Choruses from *The Rock, VI and IX and X, East Coker IV*, all from *Collected Poems 1909–1962*, copyright 1936 by Harcourt Brace Jovanovich Inc; copyright © 1963, 1964, by T S Eliot; and Chorus from *Murder in the Cathedral*, copyright 1935 by Harcourt Brace Jovanovich Inc; copyright 1963, by T S Eliot. Harper & Row, Publishers, Inc, lines from Teilhard de Chardin, *Hymn of the Universe*. Harvard University Press for Emily Dickinson, 'This world is not conclusion' reprinted by permission of the publishers and the Trustees of Amherst College, from Thomas H Johnson, Editor, *The Poems of Emily Dickinson*, Cambridge, Mass., The Belknap Press of Harvard University Press, copyright, 1951, 1955, by the President and Fellows of Harvard College. David Higham Associates, for Elizabeth Jennings, 'The Annunciation', from *A Sense of the World* (Andre Deutsch); and for Edith Sitwell, 'How Many Heavens' (Duckworth), 'The Bee Keeper' and 'Still falls the rain' (Macmillan).

The Macmillan Company, New York, for lines from *The Face of Christ*, © Daniel Berrigan 1958, 1959, 1960, 1961, 1962; and for W B Yeats, 'Sailing to Byzantium', copyright 1928 by The Macmillan Company, renewed 1956 by Georgie Yeats.

Jacques Maritain and Stanbrook Abbey, for Raissa Maritain, 'God, my God, before you I stand'. Dom Sebastian Moore OSB for 'Psalm Ninety – New Style' from *The Experience of Prayer*.

New Directions Publishing Corp, for Ezra Pound, 'Cantico del Sole' from *Personae*, copyright 1926 by Ezra Pound; for Rainer Maria Rilke, 'You Neighbour God', from *Poems from the Book of Hours*, translated by Babette Deutsch, copyright 1941 by New Directions Publishing Corporation; and for Rainer Maria Rilke, 'Who was ever so wake' from Rainer Maria Rilke, *Selected Works II*, translated by J B Leishman, copyright © The Hogarth Press Ltd, 1960.

Oxford University Press for 'Come O Creator Spirit, Come' and 'O Gladsome Light, O Grace', both translated R S Bridges, from *The Yattendon Hymnal*, edited by Robert Bridges and H Ellis Woolridge.

Paulist Newman Press for lines from Huub Oosterhuis, *Your Word is Near*, copyright the Missionary Society of St Paul the Apostle in the State of New York.

Random House Inc, for W H Auden, Chorus III from 'For the Time Being' from *Collected Longer Poems*, by W H Auden; and for Philip Larkin, 'An Arundel Tomb' copyright 1962 by Philip Larkin, from *The Whitsun Weddings* by Philip Larkin. The Society of Authors and Mrs Nicolete Gray, for Laurence Binyon, translations from Dante. SPCK for Eric Milner-White 'Morning Prayer' from *My God, My Glory*. Stanbrook Abbey, for 'When Jesus comes to be baptised', 'The mighty Word of God came forth', 'Who is this who comes'.

The Viking Press Inc., for 'The Phoenix' from *The Complete Poems of D H Lawrence*, ed. by Vivian de Sola Pinto and F Warren Roberts, copyright © 1964, 1971, by Angelo Ravagli and C M Weekly, Executors of the Estate of Frieda Lawrence Ravagli. The World Publishing Company, lines from Rita Snowden, *Prayers for the Family*.